THE PERFECTION LEARNING
PARALLEL TEXT SERIES

British Literature 449–1798

In Classic and Modern English

Perfection Learnin
Logan, Iowa 5

Editorial Director: Julie A. Schumacher
Writer: Wim Coleman
Design: Kay Ewald

Cover Art: *The Accolade* by Edmund Blair Leighton (1853–1922), Christie's Images, London, UK/Bridgeman Art Library

Image Credits: ArtToday (www.ArtToday.com) pp. 16, 34, 52, 109, 137, 138, 149, 162, 172, 183, 186, 195, 203, 211, 214, 215, 216, 217, 218, 263, 288, 289, 291, 293, 359, 383, 390; *The Arming and Departure of the Knights*, tapestry designed by the artist and woven by Morris & Co., 1895–96 (textile) by Sir Edward Burne-Jones (1833–98), Birmingham Museums and Art Gallery/Bridgeman Art Library p. 8; Roy 18 D 11 f.148 *Lydgate and the Canterbury Pilgrims leaving Canterbury* from "Troy Book and the Siege of Thebes," 1412–22, John Lydgate Poetry, (15th century), British Library, London, UK/Bridgeman Art Library p. 50; *La Belle Dame Sans Merci*, 1893 (oil on canvas) by John William Waterhouse (1849–1917) Hessisches Landesmuseum, Darmstadt, Germany/Bridgeman Art Library p. 166; *Arthur in Avalon* 1881–98, (detail) by Sir Edward Burne-Jones (1833–98) Museo de Arte, Ponce, Puerto Rico, West Indies/Bridgeman Art Library p. 209, *Elizabeth I*, Armada portrait, c. 1588 (oil on panel) by English School (16th century) Private Collection/Bridgeman Art Library p. 210; *Fair Is My Love*, 1900 (oil on canvas) by Edwin Austin Abbey (1853–1911) Harris Museum and Art Gallery, Preston, Lancashire, UK/Bridgeman Art Library p. 221; *The Hireling Shepherd* by William Holman Hunt (1827–1910) The Makins Collection/Bridgeman Art Library p. 227; *Bristol Docks and Quay*, c. 1780s by Philip van Dijk (1680–1753) (attr. to) Bristol City Museum and Art Gallery, UK/Bridgeman Art Library p. 284; *On Strike*, c. 1891 by Sir Hubert von Herkomer (1849–1914) Royal Academy of Arts, London, UK/Bridgeman Art Library p. 357; Dover p. 309; The Granger Collection, New York pp. 15, 48; Library of Congress pp. 12, 56, 58, 60, 64, 68, 70, 74, 80, 84, 90, 96, 110; Mary Evans/Arthur Rackham Collection p. 197; North Wind Picture Archives pp. 324, 335, 415; PhotoDisc pp. 230, 232; The Pierpont Morgan Library/Art Resource, NY p. 150; Tate Gallery, London/Art Resource, NY p. 184; Werner Forman/Art Resource, NY pp. 24, 38

5 6 7 8 9 10 PP 08 07 06 05

Paperback ISBN 0-7891-5471-4
Cover Craft® ISBN 0-7569-0241-x

Using This Parallel Text

Languages change as years and centuries pass. Even the English you speak now is slightly different from what your parents learned to speak. And today's English will seem quaint and hard to understand sometime in the future.

Small wonder that readers often struggle with the language of Shakespeare, who wrote some 400 years ago. Works from still earlier times can be even more difficult to read.

This parallel text edition is designed to help. The original text or a translation of that text is found on the left-hand page. A modern English version is located on the right. Matching numbers help you keep track as you move back and forth between the two versions. The symbol of the quill pen in the upper left corner of the page will help you remember that the left pages contain the original text.

If you are having difficulty with the original text or translation, try reading a passage of the right-hand version first. Then read the same passage on the left-hand side. After a while, you may find that the original text becomes easier to understand.

In any case, remember that the modern paraphrase should never be used as a substitute for the original. The words of the writers you're about to meet make fascinating reading, partly because they shine a brilliant light on the past.

Viewed as a whole, British literature from 449 to 1798 tells a sweeping story—the story of a people and a language coming to be.

Table of Contents

Unit Three The Restoration and the Enlightenment (1660–1798)

Unit One

The Anglo-Saxon and Medieval Periods
(449–1485)

The Anglo-Saxons

During the 5th century A.D., Germanic peoples of three different tribes—Angles, Saxons, and Jutes—took over England. As these tribes blended into the population, the English people themselves came to be called Anglo-Saxons. It was with the Anglo-Saxons that British literature really began.

The Anglo-Saxons spoke what is now called Old English. It was very different from the English that we speak today. Here, for example, are the opening lines of the Anglo-Saxon epic *Beowulf* in the original:

Hwæt wē Gār-Dena   in geār-dagum

þēod-cyninga   þryum gefrūnon,

hū ôā æþelingas   ellen fremedon.

Don't worry if you can't make sense of these words! Scholars and specialists are really the only people who can do it. This unit uses Burton Raffel's translation of *Beowulf*. Here is a translation of these same three lines:

Hear me! We've heard of Danish heroes,

Ancient kings and the glory they cut

For themselves, swinging mighty swords!

The musical aspect of Old English poetry is harder for us to imagine today. The poems

The Arming and Departure of the Knights by Sir Edward Burne-Jones

were chanted by singer-poets called *scops*, who some-times made things up as they went along. These singers accompanied themselves with harps. At pauses or important words in the poem, the singer would pluck a harp string.

The Anglo-Saxons were originally pagans (non-Christians), but Christianity found its way to England during their rule. Christian missionaries began to arrive there in 597, and little by little, the Anglo-Saxons were converted to the new religion. *Beowulf* was written while this transition was still in process, so the poem reflects a strange mix of pagan and Christian beliefs.

Medieval England

In 1066, sweeping changes came to England. William the Conqueror, a leader from Normandy in France, invaded England. He declared himself King William I of England and put Norman-French nobles in charge of the country.

The Anglo-Saxons had been a warrior culture in which strength, bravery, and martial skill were the highest values. The arrival of the Normans brought the beginning of the medieval period in England—a time marked by feudalism and chivalry.

Feudalism was a political system in which kings and lords ruled over noble subjects called vassals. Vassals in turn ruled over landless peasants. *Chivalry* was a code of conduct under feudalism. Knights especially were expected to behave with great courtesy and a sense of honor.

For a time after the Norman Conquest, Old English and French were spoken separately in England. Old English was used by English subjects, French by their Norman-French rulers. But little by little, the two peoples and their languages began to merge. As Old English took on French and Latin characteristics, it became what we now call Middle English. Here, for example, are the first four lines of Chaucer's *The Canterbury Tales* in the Middle English original:

Whan that Aprille, with hise shoures soote,

The droghte of March hath perced to the roote

And bathed every veyne in swich licour,

Of which vertu engendred is the flour . . .

The words certainly seem strange today, but by no means as strange as Old English. With care, you can probably pick out some meaning in these lines. Nevertheless, many readers today prefer to read Middle English in translation. Here is a translation of the lines above:

When in April the sweet showers fall

And pierce the drought of March to the root, and all

The veins are bathed in liquor of such power

As brings about the engendering of the flower . . .

By the time Sir Thomas Malory's *Le Morte d'Arthur* was written in the late 15th century, English was recognizably the language we speak today. For today's readers, Malory's work requires editing but no real translation. *Le Morte d'Arthur* is a massive collection of stories concerning King Arthur and his followers. It is also a celebration of chivalric behavior.

Soon, England's medieval period would come to an end, and the Renaissance would arrive. British literature would reach amazing heights during the Elizabethan Renaissance. But great writers like William Shakespeare, Ben Jonson, and John Donne did not appear out of nowhere. Their way had been paved by authors of earlier times—authors like Malory, Chaucer, the Pearl Poet, and the composer of *Beowulf*.

Unit One Author Biographies

Beowulf's poet

No one knows who wrote the Old English poem *Beowulf*, but it was composed between 700 and 750 A.D. The text makes clear that the poet was a Christian, even though he was retelling stories from a pagan (non-Christian) tradition. No one even knows whether the *Beowulf* poet could read or write. Perhaps he was a singer who dictated his epic to someone else.

Geoffrey Chaucer (c. 1343–1400)

Geoffrey Chaucer lived a remarkable and active life. He was a soldier, diplomat, and public servant under three English kings. His work and travels brought him in contact with some of the most important ideas and people of his time.

Today, Chaucer is best remembered for his great contribution to literature. More than any other poet, he helped establish English as a true literary language. Before Chaucer's time, English poets were generally expected to write in French.

Chaucer's most famous work by far is *The Canterbury Tales*, which he did not live to complete. Chaucer's poetry is marked by rich language, exciting storytelling, earthy humor, and incredibly vivid characters.

English Ballads

Both "Lord Randal" and "Get Up and Bar the Door" are anonymous, popular English ballads. Because they were passed along orally, they exist in many versions. The story of "Lord Randal" has reappeared as several American folk songs, especially in Appalachia. These two ballads have even found their way into different languages around the world.

The ballad form is still used in popular songs and stories. In fact, medieval English ballads continue to influence songwriters in our own age. For example, clear echoes of "Lord Randal" can be heard in Bob Dylan's song "A Hard Rain's A-Gonna Fall."

The "Pearl Poet"

The unknown author of *Sir Gawain and the Green Knight* wrote during the second half of the 14th century. Three other poems are thought to have been written by him: "Purity," "Patience," and "The Pearl." Because of the last, he is commonly referred to as the "Pearl Poet." His power of language and characterization rivals even that of Chaucer, who lived at the same time.

Sir Thomas Malory

Sir Thomas Malory's actual identity remains something of a mystery. From a note in his manuscript, we know that he finished writing *Le Morte d'Arthur* in 1469 or 1470, and also that he was in prison at the time. *Le Morte d'Arthur* has influenced countless authors since Malory wrote it.

INTRODUCTION TO

Beowulf

Composed by an unknown poet between 700 and 750 A.D., *Beowulf* was written in Old English. This was the language spoken by the Anglo-Saxons during their long rule of England.

The poem has a strange history. It only survives in one badly damaged manuscript, written down by a scribe around 1000 A.D. *Beowulf* remained almost unknown for centuries, and many of the greatest English authors, including Chaucer, Shakespeare, and Milton, knew nothing about it. It finally appeared in print in 1815. Since then, it has usually been read in translation.

Although written in England, the story itself takes place in Scandanavia. The first section of the poem is set in Denmark, where the Danish people are troubled by a monster called Grendel. To their rescue comes the great warrior, Beowulf. The second part of the poem takes place in Beowulf's home country of Geatland, located in what is now southern Sweden. In this section, the elderly warrior battles a fire-breathing dragon.

Possibly the strangest thing about *Beowulf* is its combination of Christian and pagan (non-Christian) themes. That the poem was composed by a Christian is clear from many biblical references, especially to the Old Testament. The poet often praises the power of a kindly, loving God.

And yet, the poet drew his stories from pagan, Germanic sources. In its original Anglo-Saxon, *Beowulf* makes many references to *wyrd*, a word which translates best as "Fate." Sometimes, *wyrd* and God are treated as much the same thing. Other times, *wyrd* is a darker, crueler force. This is especially true toward the end of the poem, when Beowulf must fight the dragon even though *wyrd* is against him.

So there is a tension in the world of Beowulf between Germanic paganism and a newly arrived Christianity. When threatened by Grendel, the Danes sacrifice to "old stone gods" and make "heathen vows." Even so, the Danish king Hrothgar praises the Christian God for sending Beowulf as a protector.

Christianity and paganism blend most strikingly in the story's monsters, especially Grendel and his mother. These awful creatures are surely drawn from old pagan legends. And yet the poet has given them a Christian history. They are descendants of the biblical Cain, a son of Adam and Eve. In the Bible, Cain was the world's first murderer, having killed his brother, Abel. So slaying Grendel and his mother becomes, for Beowulf, a Christian mission.

The overall mood of *Beowulf* is grim and violent. After more than a thousand years, it still has a haunting power.

Helmet reconstruction from Sutton Hoo ship burial.

from **Beowulf**

translated by Burton Raffel

Grendel

A powerful monster, living down
In the darkness, growled in pain, impatient
As day after day the music rang
Loud in that hall, the harp's rejoicing
5   Call and the poet's clear songs, sung
Of the ancient beginnings of us all, recalling
The Almighty making the earth, shaping
These beautiful plains marked off by oceans,
Then proudly setting the sun and moon
10   To glow across the land and light it;
The corners of the earth were made lovely with trees
And leaves, made quick with life, with each
Of the nations who now move on its face. And then
As now warriors sang of their pleasure:
15   So Hrothgar's men lived happy in his hall
Till the monster stirred, that demon, that fiend,

from **Beowulf**

translated by Burton Raffel

Beowulf *begins as the monster Grendel approaches the mead*[1] *hall of Hrothgar, the Danish king. After an evening of drinking and celebration, Hrothgar's warriors fall into a heavy sleep, unaware of the danger that lurks outside.*

Grendel

A powerful monster lived down
in the darkness. He growled in pain impatiently
as day after day the music rang
loudly in that hall. The harp called joyfully,
5 and the poet's bright songs sung
of the early beginnings of us all.
The songs recalled how God made the earth,
shaping beautiful plains bordered by oceans.
Then he proudly made the sun and moon
10 to glow across the land and light it.
The corners of the earth were made lovely
as trees and leaves quickened to life,
and he made all the nations that now fill the earth.
Then, as now, warriors sang of their pleasure,
15 and Hrothgar's men lived happily in his hall
until the monster stirred—that demon, that devil.

1 **mead:** a fermented, alcoholic drink made from honey

Grendel, who haunted the moors, the wild
Marshes, and made his home in a hell
Not hell but earth. He was spawned in that slime,
20 Conceived by a pair of those monsters born
Of Cain, murderous creatures banished
By God, punished forever for the crime
Of Abel's death. The Almighty drove
Those demons out, and their exile was bitter,
25 Shut away from men; they split
Into a thousand forms of evil—spirits
And fiends, goblins, monsters, giants,
A brood forever opposing the Lord's
Will, and again and again defeated.

30   Then, when darkness had dropped, Grendel
Went up to Herot, wondering what the warriors
Would do in that hall when their drinking was done.
He found them sprawled in sleep, suspecting
Nothing, their dreams undisturbed. The monster's
35 Thoughts were as quick as his greed or his claws:
He slipped through the door and there in the silence
Snatched up thirty men, smashed them
Unknowing in their beds and ran out with their bodies,

The blood dripping behind him, back
40 To his lair, delighted with his night's slaughter.
     At daybreak, with the sun's first light, they saw
How well he had worked, and in that gray morning

Broke their long feast with tears and laments
For the dead. Hrothgar, their lord, sat joyless
45 In Herot, a mighty prince mourning
The fate of his lost friends and companions,
Knowing by its tracks that some demon had torn

Grendel haunted the moors[2] and the wild marshes,
and made his home a hell on earth.
He was created in that marsh slime,
20 the child of a pair of monsters born of Cain.
These murderous creatures were banished by God,
punished forever for the crime
of Abel's death. God drove
those demons out, and their exile was bitter,
25 shut away from men.
They split into a thousand forms of evil—
spirits, devils, goblins, monsters, giants.
This family forever opposed God's will,
and again and again they were defeated.

30 When darkness had come, Grendel
went up to Herot wondering what the warriors
would do in that hall when their drinking was done.
He found them sprawled in sleep, suspecting
nothing, their dreams undisturbed. The monster's
35 thoughts were as quick as his greed or his claws.
He slipped through the door, and in the silence
he snatched up thirty men. He smashed them
unknowingly in their beds and ran out with their
      bodies,
blood dripping behind him. He went back to his lair,
40 delighted with his night's slaughter.
      Daybreak came with the sun's first light,
and the men saw how well he had worked. In that
      gray morning,
their long feast ended with tears and cries of sorrow
for the dead. Hrothgar, their lord and mighty prince,
45 sat joylessly in Herot. He mourned
the fate of his lost friends and companions.
He knew by its tracks that some demon had torn

---

2 **moors:** stretches of desolate land

His followers apart. He wept, fearing
The beginning might not be the end. And that night

50 Grendel came again, so set
On murder that no crime could ever be enough,
No savage assault quench his lust
For evil. Then each warrior tried
To escape him, searched for rest in different
55 Beds, as far from Herot as they could find,
Seeing how Grendel hunted when they slept.
Distance was safety; the only survivors
Were those who fled him. Hate had triumphed.
So Grendel ruled, fought with the righteous,
60 One against many, and won; so Herot
Stood empty, and stayed deserted for years,
Twelve winters of grief for Hrothgar, king
Of the Danes, sorrow heaped at his door
By hell-forged hands. His misery leaped
65 The seas, was told and sung in all
Men's ears: how Grendel's hatred began,
How the monster relished his savage war
On the Danes, keeping the bloody feud
Alive, seeking no peace, offering
70 No truce, accepting no settlement, no price
In gold or land, and paying the living
For one crime only with another. No one
Waited for reparation from his plundering claws:
That shadow of death hunted in the darkness,
75 Stalked Hrothgar's warriors, old
And young, lying in waiting, hidden
In mist, invisibly following them from the edge
Of the marsh, always there, unseen.
So mankind's enemy continued his crimes,
80 Killing as often as he could, coming
Alone, bloodthirsty and horrible. Though he lived
In Herot, when the night hid him, he never

his followers apart. He wept,
fearing that his troubles were just beginning. And
that night
50   Grendel came again, so set
on murder that no crime could ever be enough.
No cruel attack could satisfy his desire for evil.
Then each warrior tried to escape him,
searching for rest in different beds.
55   They stayed as far from Herot as they could,
seeing how Grendel hunted when they slept.
Distance was safety. The only survivors
were those who fled him. Hate had triumphed.
     So Grendel ruled. He fought with the righteous,
60   one against many, and won.
So Herot was empty and stayed deserted for years.
Twelve winters of grief passed for Hrothgar,
King of the Danes. Sorrow was heaped at his door
by hellish hands. His misery was reported over the
65   seas, told and sung in all men's ears.
People heard how Grendel's hatred began,
how the monster enjoyed his cruel war on the Danes.
They heard how he kept the bloody feud alive,
seeking no peace, offering no truce.
70   He would accept no agreement,
no price in gold or land, and he committed
one crime after another against the living.
No one expected relief from his thieving claws.
That shadow of death hunted in the darkness,
75   stalking Hrothgar's warriors, old and young.
It lay in wait, hidden in mist,
invisibly following them from the edge
of the marsh, always there, unseen.
     So mankind's enemy continued his crimes,
80   killing as often as he could, coming alone,
bloodthirsty and horrible.
He lived in Herot when the night hid him,

Dared to touch king Hrothgar's glorious

Throne, protected by God—God,
85 Whose love Grendel could not know. But Hrothgar's
Heart was bent. The best and most noble
Of his council debated remedies, sat
In secret sessions, talking of terror
And wondering what the bravest of warriors could
      do.
90 And sometimes they sacrificed to the old stone gods,
Made heathen vows, hoping for Hell's
Support, the Devil's guidance in driving
Their affliction off. That was their way,
And the heathen's only hope, Hell
95 Always in their hearts, knowing neither God
Nor His passing as He walks through our world, the
      Lord
Of Heaven and earth; their ears could not hear
His praise nor know His glory. Let them
Beware, those who are thrust into danger,
100 Clutched at by trouble, yet can carry no solace

In their hearts, cannot hope to be better! Hail
To those who will rise to God, drop off
Their dead bodies and seek our Father's peace!

The Coming of Beowulf

*S*o the living sorrow of Healfdane's son
105 Simmered, bitter and fresh, and no wisdom
Or strength could break it: that agony hung
On king and people alike, harsh
And unending, violent and cruel, and evil.
      In his far-off home Beowulf, Higlac's

but he never dared touch King Hrothgar's glorious
    throne.
It was protected by God,

85   whose love Grendel could not know. But Hrothgar's
heart was sad. His best and noblest
advisors argued over solutions,
meeting secretly, talking of terror.
They wondered what the bravest of warriors could
    do.

90   And they sometimes sacrificed to the old stone gods
and made heathen[3] vows. They hoped for hell's
support, the Devil's guidance in driving
their troubles off. That was their way,
and the heathen's only hope.

95   Hell was always in their hearts,
for they knew not God, how he passes through our
    world,
the Lord of heaven and earth.
Their ears could not hear his praise nor glory.
Let those who are thrust into danger beware

100   when they are gripped by trouble, yet can find no
    comfort
in their hearts, cannot hope to be better.
Hail to those who rise to God, letting go of
their dead bodies, seeking our Father's peace!

The Coming of Beowulf

*S*o Hrothgar's living sorrow continued,

105   bitter and fresh, and no wisdom
or strength could end it.
Misery hung on the king and his people alike,
harsh, unending, violent, cruel, and evil.
    In his far-off home, Beowulf heard all this.

---

3 **heathen:** irreligious; not Christian

110 Follower and the strongest of the Geats—greater
And stronger than anyone anywhere in this world—

Heard how Grendel filled nights with horror
And quickly commanded a boat fitted out,
Proclaiming that he'd go to that famous king,
115 Would sail across the sea to Hrothgar,
Now when help was needed. None
Of the wise ones regretted his going, much
As he was loved by the Geats: the omens were good,

And they urged the adventure on. So Beowulf
120 Chose the mightiest men he could find,
The bravest and best of the Geats, fourteen
In all, and led them down to their boat;
He knew the sea, would point
    the prow
Straight to that distant
    Danish shore.

Carved dragon-
head post from
the ship burial at
Oserberg,
Norway. Viking
Ship Museum,
Bygdoy, Norway.

The Battle with Grendel

125 *O*ut from the marsh, from the foot of misty
Hills and bogs, bearing God's hatred,
Grendel came, hoping to kill

110 Higlac's[4] follower was the strongest of the Geats—
   greater and stronger than anyone anywhere in this
     world.
   He heard how Grendel filled nights with horror
   and quickly ordered a boat to be readied,
   saying he'd go to that famous king.
115 He'd sail across the sea to Hrothgar,
   now when help was needed.
   None of the wise men regretted his going,
   much as he was loved by the Geats. The signs were
     good,
   and they urged the adventure on.
120 So Beowulf chose the mightiest men he could find,
   the bravest and best of the Geats, 14 in all.
   He led them down to their boat.
   He knew the sea, and he set sail
   straight to that distant Danish shore.

> *Beowulf and 14 brave warriors set sail for Denmark to offer help to Hrothgar. Upon their arrival they are taken to Herot where they are served a welcoming banquet. After eating, Hrothgar and the Danes leave the hall, while Beowulf and his men remain to face Grendel. Beowulf states that he will fight without a sword and lies awake waiting for the monster.*

The Battle with Grendel

125 *G*rendel came out of the marsh,
   from the edge of misty hills and swamps.
   He carried God's hatred, hoping to kill

   4 **Higlac:** king of Geatland

Anyone he could trap on this trip to high Herot.
He moved quickly through the cloudy night,
130   Up from his swampland, sliding silently
Toward that gold-shining hall. He had visited
      Hrothgar's
Home before, knew the way—
But never, before nor after that night,
Found Herot defended so firmly, his reception
135   So harsh. He journeyed, forever joyless,
Straight to the door, then snapped it open,
Tore its iron fasteners with a touch
And rushed angrily over the threshold.
He strode quickly across the inlaid
140   Floor, snarling and fierce: his eyes
Gleamed in the darkness, burned with a gruesome
Light. Then he stopped, seeing the hall
Crowded with sleeping warriors, stuffed
With rows of young soldiers resting together.
145   And his heart laughed, he relished the sight,
Intended to tear the life from those bodies
By morning; the monster's mind was hot
With the thought of food and the feasting his belly
Would soon know. But fate, that night, intended
150   Grendel to gnaw the broken bones
Of his last human supper. Human
Eyes were watching his evil steps,
Waiting to see his swift hard claws.
Grendel snatched at the first Geat
155   He came to, ripped him apart, cut
His body to bits with powerful jaws,
Drank the blood from his veins and bolted
Him down, hands and feet; death
And Grendel's great teeth came together,
160   Snapping life shut. Then he stepped to another
Still body, clutched at Beowulf with his claws,

anyone he could trap on this trip to great Herot.
He moved quickly through the cloudy night,
130   up from his swampland, sliding silently
toward the golden hall.
He had visited Hrothgar's home before and knew the
    way.
But he never found Herot defended so well,
neither before nor after that night. His greeting
135   was harsh. He journeyed, forever joyless,
straight to the door. He snapped it open,
tore its iron fasteners with a touch,
then rushed angrily inside.
He strode quickly across the finely made floor,
140   snarling and fierce. His eyes gleamed
in the darkness and burned with a grim light.
Then he stopped, seeing the hall
crowded with sleeping warriors,
stuffed with rows of young soldiers resting together.
145   His heart laughed, enjoying the sight, for he meant
to tear the life from those bodies by morning.
The monster's mind was hot
with the thought of the feasting his belly
would soon know. But that night,
150   Grendel would gnaw the broken bones
of his last human supper. Fate had planned it so.
Human eyes were watching his evil steps,
waiting to see his swift hard claws.
Grendel snatched at the first Geat he came to,
155   ripped him apart,
cut his body to bits with powerful jaws.
He drank the blood from his veins
and gulped him down, hands and feet.
Death and Grendel's great teeth came together,
160   snapping life shut. Then he stepped to another
still body, clutched at Beowulf with his claws,

Grasped at a strong-hearted wakeful sleeper
—And was instantly seized himself, claws
Bent back as Beowulf leaned up on one arm.
165　　That shepherd of evil, guardian of crime,
Knew at once that nowhere on earth
Had he met a man whose hands were harder;
His mind was flooded with fear—but nothing
Could take his talons and himself from that tight

170　Hard grip. Grendel's one thought was to run
From Beowulf, flee back to his marsh and hide there:
This was a different Herot than the hall he had
　　　emptied.
But Higlac's follower remembered his final
Boast and, standing erect, stopped
175　The monster's flight, fastened those claws
In his fists till they cracked, clutched Grendel
Closer. The infamous killer fought
For his freedom, wanting no flesh but retreat,
Desiring nothing but escape; his claws
180　Had been caught, he was trapped. That trip to Herot
Was a miserable journey for the writhing monster!

　　　The high hall rang, its roof boards swayed,
And Danes shook with terror. Down
The aisles the battle swept, angry
185　And wild. Herot trembled, wonderfully
Built to withstand the blows, the struggling
Great bodies beating at its beautiful walls;

Shaped and fastened with iron, inside
And out, artfully worked, the building
190　Stood firm. Its benches rattled, fell
To the floor, gold-covered boards grating
As Grendel and Beowulf battled across them.
Hrothgar's wise men had fashioned Herot

grasped at the strong-hearted wakeful sleeper.
And he was instantly seized himself,
claws bent back as Beowulf leaned up on one arm.

165   That shepherd of evil, guardian of crime,
was frightened at once. Nowhere on earth
had he met a man with stronger hands.
His mind was flooded with fear,
but he couldn't pull his claws and himself from that
     tight, hard grip.

170 Grendel's one thought was to run from Beowulf,
flee back to his marsh and hide there.
This was a different Herot than the hall he had
     emptied.
But Higlac's follower remembered his final boast,
and standing straight, he stopped

175 the monster's flight. He gripped those claws
in his fists till they cracked, clutched Grendel closer.
The wicked killer fought for his freedom,
wanting retreat instead of flesh,
desiring nothing but to escape.

180 His claws had been caught, he was trapped.
That trip to Herot was miserable to the writhing
     monster!
     The great hall rang, its roof boards swayed,
and the Danes shook with terror.
The battle swept down the aisles,

185 angry and wild. Herot trembled,
wonderfully built to withstand the blows,
the struggling great bodies beating at its beautiful
     walls.
It was shaped and fastened with iron, inside and out,
and artfully built, so the building stood firm.

190 Its benches rattled and fell to the floor,
and gold-covered boards grated
as Grendel and Beowulf battled across them.
Hrothgar's wise men had built Herot

To stand forever; only fire,
195 They had planned, could shatter what such skill had
put
Together, swallow in hot flames such splendor
Of ivory and iron and wood. Suddenly
The sounds changed, the Danes started
In new terror, cowering in their beds as the terrible
200 Screams of the Almighty's enemy sang

In the darkness, the horrible shrieks of pain
And defeat, the tears torn out of Grendel's
Taut throat, hell's captive caught in the arms
Of him who of all the men on earth
205 Was the strongest.

           That mighty protector of men
Meant to hold the monster till its life
Leaped out, knowing the fiend was no use
To anyone in Denmark. All of Beowulf's
210 Band had jumped from their beds, ancestral
Swords raised and ready, determined
To protect their prince if they could. Their courage
Was great but all wasted: they could hack at Grendel

From every side, trying to open
215 A path for his evil soul, but their points
Could not hurt him, the sharpest and hardest iron
Could not scratch at his skin, for that sin-stained
demon
Had bewitched all men's weapons, laid spells
That blunted every mortal man's blade.

220 And yet his time had come, his days
Were over, his death near; down
To hell he would go, swept groaning and helpless

to stand forever. Only fire,
195 they had planned, could shatter what such skill had
    built.
Only hot flames could swallow such splendor
of ivory, iron, and wood.
Suddenly the sounds changed. The Danes started in
    new terror, cowering in their beds
200 as the terrible screams of God's enemy sang in the
    darkness,
horrible shrieks of pain and defeat.
Tears were torn out of Grendel's tense throat
as hell's captive was caught in the arms
of Beowulf, who was stronger
205 than any man on earth.

            That mighty protector of men
meant to hold the monster till its life was gone.
He knew that devil was no use
to anyone in Denmark. All of Beowulf's men
210 had jumped from their beds,
their age-old swords raised and ready,
determined to protect their prince if they could.
Their courage was great, but wasted. They hacked at
    Grendel
from every side, trying to open
215 a path for his evil soul. But their points
could not hurt him. The sharpest and hardest iron
Could not scratch his skin. That sin-stained demon

had bewitched all men's weapons,
had cast spells that blunted every mortal man's
    blade.
220 And yet his time had come,
his days were over, his death near.
Down to hell he would go, groaning and helpless

To the waiting hands of still worse fiends.
Now he discovered—once the afflictor

225   Of men, tormentor of their days—what it meant
To feud with Almighty God: Grendel
Saw that his strength was deserting him, his claws
Bound fast, Higlac's brave follower tearing at

His hands. The monster's hatred rose higher,
230   But his power had gone. He twisted in pain,
And the bleeding sinews deep in his shoulder
Snapped, muscle and bone split
And broke. The battle was over, Beowulf
Had been granted new glory: Grendel escaped,
235   But wounded as he was could flee to his den,
His miserable hole at the bottom of the marsh,
Only to die, to wait for the end
Of all his days. And after that bloody
Combat the Danes laughed with delight.
240   He who had come to them from across the sea,
Bold and strong-minded, had driven affliction
Off, purged Herot clean. He was happy,
Now, with that night's fierce work; the Danes
Had been served as he'd boasted he'd serve them;
     Beowulf,
245   A prince of the Geats, had killed Grendel,
Ended the grief, the sorrow, the suffering
Forced on Hrothgar's helpless people
By a bloodthirsty fiend. No Dane doubted
The victory, for the proof, hanging high
250   From the rafters where Beowulf had hung it, was the
     monster's
Arm, claw and shoulder and all.

And then, in the morning, crowds surrounded
Herot, warriors coming to that hall
From faraway lands, princes and leaders

into the waiting hands of still-worse demons.
Once he had been the tormentor of men and their
     days,
225   but now he discovered what it meant
to feud with Almighty God.
Grendel saw that his strength was leaving him.
His claws were bound, and Higlac's brave follower
     tore at his hands.
The monster's hatred rose higher,
230   but his power had gone. He twisted in pain,
the bleeding tendons deep in his shoulder snapped,
and muscle and bone split and broke.
The battle was over,
and Beowulf had won a new glory. Grendel escaped,
235   but was badly wounded. He could only flee to his den,
his miserable hole at the bottom of the marsh,
and die there. He could only wait for the end
of all his days. And after that bloody combat,
the Danes laughed with delight.
240   Beowulf had come to them from across the sea,
bold and strong-minded. He had driven evil off,
had made Herot clean. Now he was happy
with that night's fierce work.
He'd served the Danes as he'd boasted he would.

245   Beowulf, a prince of the Geats, had killed Grendel—
had ended the grief, sorrow, and suffering
forced on Hrothgar's helpless people
by a bloodthirsty demon. No Dane doubted the victory,
for Beowulf had hung the proof
250   high from the rafters. There hung the monster's
     arm—
claw, shoulder, and all.

    And then, in the morning, crowds surrounded
Herot. Warriors, princes, and leaders of men
came to that hall from faraway lands.

255 Of men hurrying to behold the monster's
Great staggering tracks. They gaped with no sense
Of sorrow, felt no regret for his suffering,
Went tracing his bloody footprints, his beaten
And lonely flight, to the edge of the lake
260 Where he'd dragged his corpselike way, doomed
And already weary of his vanishing life.
The water was bloody, steaming and boiling
In horrible pounding waves, heat

Sucked from his magic veins; but the swirling
265 Surf had covered his death, hidden
Deep in murky darkness his miserable
End, as hell opened to receive him.
    Then old and young rejoiced, turned back
From that happy pilgrimage, mounted their
        hard-hooved
270 Horses, high-spirited stallions, and rode them
Slowly toward Herot again, retelling
Beowulf's bravery as they jogged along.
And over and over they swore that nowhere
On earth or under the spreading sky

275 Or between the seas, neither south nor north,
Was there a warrior worthier to rule over men.
(But no one meant Beowulf's praise to belittle
Hrothgar, their kind and gracious king!)
        And sometimes, when the path ran straight and
            clear,
280 They would let their horses race, red
And brown and pale yellow backs streaming
Down the road. And sometimes a proud old soldier

Who had heard songs of the ancient heroes
And could sing them all through, story after story,
285 Would weave a net of words for Beowulf's
Victory, tying the knot of his verses

255 They hurried to behold the monster's
    great staggering tracks. They gaped with no sense
    of sorrow, felt no regret for his suffering.
    They traced his bloody footprints,
    his beaten and lonely flight, to the edge of the lake.
260 He'd dragged his corpselike way there,
    doomed and already weary of his vanishing life.
    The water was bloody, steaming and boiling
    in horrible pounding waves. The lake had sucked the
        heat
    from his magic veins, but the swirling surf
265 had covered his death. His miserable end
    was hidden deep in cloudy darkness
    as hell opened to receive him.
        Then old and young rejoiced and turned back
    from that happy trip. They mounted their
        hard-hoofed horses,
270 high-spirited stallions,
    and rode them slowly toward Herot again.
    They retold Beowulf's bravery as they jogged along.
    Over and over they swore that nowhere
    was there a warrior worthier to rule over men—
    nowhere on earth, under the spreading sky,
275 or between the seas to the south or north.
    (But no one meant Beowulf's praise to belittle
        Hrothgar,
    their kind and gracious king!)
        And sometimes, when the path ran straight and
        clear,
280 They would let their horses race.
    Red, brown, and pale yellow backs
    streamed down the road. And sometimes a proud old
        soldier
    would weave a net of words for Beowulf's victory.
    Such a soldier had heard songs of ancient heroes
285 and could sing them all through, story after story.
    So he tied the knot of his verses smoothly,

Smoothly, swiftly, into place with a poet's
Quick skill, singing his new song aloud
While he shaped it, and the old songs as well. . . .

Grendel's Mother

290   *S*o she reached Herot,
Where the Danes slept as though already dead;
Her visit ended their good fortune, reversed

The bright vane of their luck. No female, no matter
How fierce, could have come with a man's strength,
295   Fought with the power and courage men fight with,
Smashing their shining swords, their bloody,
Hammer-forged blades onto boar-headed helmets,
Slashing and stabbing with the sharpest of points.
The soldiers raised their shields and drew

300   Those gleaming swords, swung them above
The piled-up benches, leaving their mail shirts
And their helmets where they'd lain when the terror
       took hold of them.

swiftly into place with a poet's quick skill,
singing his new song aloud while he shaped it,
and the old songs as well. . . .

*Although Grendel is no longer a threat, his evil
mother still lives, and she is determined to
avenge the death of her son. Slowly she rises
from the depths of her dark, watery home and
moves toward Herot.*

Grendel's Mother

290   *S*o she reached Herot,
where the Danes slept as though already dead.
Her visit ended their good fortune, turned their luck
   around
like a weathervane. No female, no matter how fierce,
could have come with a man's strength.
295 No female can fight with the power and courage of men,
smashing their shining, bloody,
hammer-forged blades into boar-headed helmets,[5]
slashing and stabbing with the sharpest points.
The soldiers raised their shields and drew those
   gleaming swords,
300 swinging them above the piled-up benches.
They left their mail[6] shirts and helmets
where they'd lain when terror seized them.

---

5 **boar-headed:** sometimes medieval helmets featured
    images of animals

6 **mail:** a kind of armor made from tiny steel rings, woven
    together into a fabric

To save her life she moved still faster,
305   Took a single victim and fled from the hall,
Running to the moors, discovered, but her supper
Assured, sheltered in her dripping claws.
She'd taken Hrothgar's closest friend,
The man he most loved of all men on earth;
310   She'd killed a glorious soldier, cut
A noble life short. No Geat could have stopped her:
Beowulf and his band had been given better
Beds; sleep had come to them in a different
Hall. Then all Herot burst into shouts:
315   She had carried off Grendel's claw. Sorrow
Had returned to Denmark. They'd traded deaths,
Danes and monsters, and no one had won,
Both had lost!

Eagle harness mount from Gotland. The exaggerated beak and talons emphasize the ferocity of the eagles which were widely associated with the cult of Odin. Statens Historiska Museet, Stockholm, Sweden.

The Battle with Grendel's Mother

*H*e leaped into the lake, would not wait for anyone's
320   Answer; the heaving water covered him
Over. For hours he sank through the waves;
At last he saw the mud of the bottom.
And all at once the greedy she-wolf

To save her life she moved still faster,
305   took a single victim and fled from the hall.
She'd been seen, but her supper was assured,
held in her dripping claws as she ran to the moors.
She'd taken Hrothgar's closest friend,
the man he loved most on earth.
310   She'd killed a glorious soldier, cut
a noble life short. No Geat could have stopped her.
Beowulf and his men had been given better beds
and had slept in a different hall.
Then all Herot burst into shouts.
315   She had carried off Grendel's claw. Sorrow
had returned to Denmark. They'd traded deaths,
Danes and monsters, and no one had won.
Both had lost!

*Hrothgar sends for Beowulf and tells him what
has happened. Hrothgar then describes the lake
where Grendel's mother lives and offers Beowulf
a golden treasure if he will help the Danes once
more. Beowulf agrees and approaches the lake
eager to do battle with the monster.*

The Battle with Grendel's Mother

*H*e leaped into the lake without waiting for
anyone's answer.
320   The rolling water covered him over.
For hours he sank through the waves.
At last he saw the mud of the bottom.
And all at once the greedy she-wolf

Who'd ruled those waters for half a hundred
325 Years discovered him, saw that a creature
From above had come to explore the bottom
Of her wet world. She welcomed him in her claws,
Clutched at him savagely but could not harm him,
Tried to work her fingers through the tight
330 Ring-woven mail on his breast, but tore
And scratched in vain. Then she carried him, armor
And sword and all, to her home; he struggled
To free his weapon, and failed. The fight
Brought other monsters swimming to see
335 Her catch, a host of sea beasts who beat at
His mail shirt, stabbing with tusks and teeth
As they followed along. Then he realized, suddenly,
That she'd brought him into someone's battle-hall,
And there the water's heat could not hurt him,
340 Nor anything in the lake attack him through
The building's high-arching roof. A brilliant
Light burned all around him, the lake
Itself like a fiery flame.
            Then he saw
The mighty water witch, and swung his sword,
345 His ring-marked blade, straight at her head;
The iron sang its fierce song,
Sang Beowulf's strength. But her guest
Discovered that no sword could slice her evil
Skin, that Hrunting could not hurt her, was useless
350 Now when he needed it. They wrestled, she ripped
And tore and clawed at him, bit holes in his helmet,
And that too failed him; for the first time in years
Of being worn to war it would earn no glory;
It was the last time anyone would wear it. But
            Beowulf
355 Longed only for fame, leaped back
Into battle. He tossed his sword aside,
Angry; the steel-edged blade lay where

who'd ruled those waters for half a hundred years
325   discovered him. She saw that a creature
from above had come to explore the bottom
of her wet world. She welcomed him in her claws,
clutched at him cruelly but could not harm him.
She tried to work her fingers through the tight,
330   ring-woven mail on his breast,
but tore and scratched in vain. Then she carried him
to her home—armor, sword, and all. He struggled
but failed to free his weapon. The fight
brought other monsters swimming to see her catch.
335   A swarm of sea beasts beat at his mail shirt,
stabbing with tusks and teeth
as they followed along. Then he suddenly realized
that she'd brought him into someone's battle-hall.
There the water's heat could not hurt him,
340   nor could anything in the lake attack him through
the building's high-arching roof.
A brilliant light burned all around him,
and the lake itself was like a fiery flame.
            Then he saw
the mighty water witch. He swung his sword,
345   his decorated blade, straight at her head.
The iron sang its fierce song,
sang Beowulf's strength. But her guest
discovered that no sword could slice her evil skin.
Hrunting[7] could not hurt her, was useless
350   now when he needed it. They wrestled, and she ripped,
tore, and clawed at him, bit holes in his helmet,
and that, too, failed him. For the first time in years
of wear in war it would earn no glory.
It was the last time anyone would wear it.

355   But Beowulf longed only for fame, so he leaped
back into battle. He angrily tossed his sword aside,
and the steel-edged blade lay where he'd dropped it.

---

7 **Hrunting:** Beowulf's sword, lent to him by one of
   Hrothgar's followers

He'd dropped it. If weapons were useless he'd use
His hands, the strength in his fingers. So fame
360 Comes to the men who mean to win it
And care about nothing else! He raised
His arms and seized her by the shoulder; anger
Doubled his strength, he threw her to the floor.
She fell, Grendel's fierce mother, and the Geats'
365 Proud prince was ready to leap on her. But she rose
At once and repaid him with her clutching claws,
Wildly tearing at him. He was weary, that best
And strongest of soldiers; his feet stumbled
And in an instant she had him down, held helpless.
370 Squatting with her weight on his stomach, she drew
A dagger, brown with dried blood, and prepared
To avenge her only son. But he was stretched

On his back, and her stabbing blade was blunted
By the woven mail shirt he wore on his chest.
375 The hammered links held; the point
Could not touch him. He'd have traveled to the
bottom of the earth,
Edgetho's son, and died there, if that shining
Woven metal had not helped—and Holy
God, who sent him victory, gave judgment
380 For truth and right, Ruler of the Heavens,
Once Beowulf was back on his feet and fighting.
Then he saw, hanging on the wall, a heavy
Sword, hammered by giants, strong
And blessed with their magic, the best of all weapons

385 But so massive that no ordinary man could lift
Its carved and decorated length. He drew it
From its scabbard, broke the chain on its hilt,
And then, savage, now, angry
And desperate, lifted it high over his head
390 And struck with all the strength he had left,

If weapons were useless he'd use his hands,
the strength in his fingers.
360 So fame comes to men who mean to win it
and care about nothing else! He raised
his arms and seized her by the shoulder. Anger
doubled his strength, and he threw her to the floor.
Grendel's fierce mother fell, and the Geats'
365 proud prince was ready to leap on her. But she rose
at once and repaid him with her clutching claws,
wildly tearing at him. That best
and strongest of soldiers was weary. He stumbled,
and in an instant she had him down, held helpless.
370 She squatted with her weight on his stomach,
then drew a dagger, brown with dried blood,
and prepared to avenge her only son. But he was
      stretched
on his back, and her stabbing blade was blunted
by the woven mail shirt he wore on his chest.
375 The hammered links held. The point
could not touch him. He would have gone

to those depths and died there
if that shining woven metal had not helped.
And Holy God, Ruler of the Heavens,
380 sent him victory, gave judgment for truth and right.
So Beowulf was back on his feet and fighting.
      Then he saw something hanging on the wall.
It was a heavy sword, hammered by giants,
strong and blessed with their magic. It was the best
      of all weapons,
385 but so huge that no ordinary man could lift
its carved and decorated length. He drew it
from its scabbard and broke the chain on its hilt.
And then, wild, angry, and desperate,
he lifted it high over his head
390 and struck with all the strength he had left.

Caught her in the neck and cut it through,
Broke bones and all. Her body fell
To the floor, lifeless, the sword was wet
With her blood, and Beowulf rejoiced at the sight.
395   The brilliant light shone, suddenly,
As though burning in that hall, and as bright as Heaven's
Own candle, lit in the sky. He looked
At her home, then following along the wall
Went walking, his hands tight on the sword,
400 His heart still angry. He was hunting another
Dead monster, and took his weapon with him
For final revenge against Grendel's vicious
Attacks, his nighttime raids, over
And over, coming to Herot when Hrothgar's
405 Men slept, killing them in their beds,
Eating some on the spot, fifteen
Or more, and running to his loathsome moor
With another such sickening meal waiting
In his pouch. But Beowulf repaid him for those visits,
410 Found him lying dead in his corner,
Armless, exactly as that fierce fighter
Had sent him out from Herot, then struck off
His head with a single swift blow. The body
Jerked for the last time, then lay still.
415   The wise old warriors who surrounded Hrothgar,
Like him staring into the monsters' lake,
Saw the waves surging and blood
Spurting through. They spoke about Beowulf,
All the graybeards, whispered together
420 And said that hope was gone, that the hero
Had lost fame and his life at once, and would never
Return to the living, come back as triumphant
As he had left; almost all agreed that Grendel's
Mighty mother, the she-wolf, had killed him.
425 The sun slid over past noon, went further
Down. The Danes gave up, left

He caught her in the neck and cut it through,
broke bones and all. Her body fell
lifeless to the floor. The sword was wet with her
blood, and Beowulf rejoiced at the sight.

395   Suddenly, the brilliant light shone,
burning in the hall. It was as bright as the sun

as it lights the sky. He looked at her home,
then followed along the wall and went walking.
His hands were tight on the sword,

400 his heart still angry. He was hunting another
dead monster and took his weapon with him.
He wanted final revenge against Grendel's vicious
attacks, when he'd made his nighttime raids over
and over, coming to Herot when Hrothgar's

405 men slept. He'd killed them in their beds,
eating some on the spot, fifteen or more.
Then he'd run to his foul moor
with another sickening meal waiting in his pouch.
But Beowulf repaid him for those visits.

410 He found him lying dead in his corner,
armless, exactly as that fierce fighter
had sent him out from Herot. Then Beowulf struck
off his head with a single swift blow.
The body jerked for the last time, then lay still.

415   The wise old warriors surrounding Hrothgar
stared with him into the monster's lake.
They saw the waves surging and blood
spurting through. They spoke about Beowulf,
all the old men. They whispered together

420 and said that hope was gone, that the hero
had lost fame and his life at once.
He would never return to the living as triumphant
as he had left. Almost all agreed that Grendel's
mighty mother, the she-wolf, had killed him.

425 The sun slid over past noon
and went further down. The Danes gave up,

The lake and went home, Hrothgar with them.
The Geats stayed, sat sadly, watching,
Imagining they saw their lord but not believing
430 They would ever see him again.
                                    —Then the sword
Melted, blood-soaked, dripping down
Like water, disappearing like ice when the world's
Eternal Lord loosens invisible
Fetters and unwinds icicles and frost
435 As only He can, He who rules
Time and seasons, He who is truly
God. The monsters' hall was full of
Rich treasures, but all that Beowulf took
Was Grendel's head and the hilt of the giants'
440 Jeweled sword; the rest of that ring-marked
Blade had dissolved in Grendel's steaming
Blood, boiling even after his death.
And then the battle's only survivor
Swam up and away from those silent corpses;
445 The water was calm and clean, the whole
Huge lake peaceful once the demons who'd lived in it
Were dead.
                    Then that noble protector of all seamen
Swam to land, rejoicing in the heavy
Burdens he was bringing with him. He
450 And all his glorious band of Geats
Thanked God that their leader had come back
        unharmed;
They left the lake together. The Geats
Carried Beowulf's helmet, and his mail shirt.
Behind them the water slowly thickened
455 As the monsters' blood came seeping up.
They walked quickly, happily, across
Roads all of them remembered, left
The lake and the cliffs alongside it, brave men
Staggering under the weight of Grendel's skull,

left the lake and went home, Hrothgar with them.
The Geats stayed and sat sadly, watching.
They imagined they saw their lord, but did not believe
430   they would ever see him again.
                                    —Then
the blood-soaked sword melted, dripping down
like water. It disappeared like ice does
when God looses invisible chains
and unwinds icicles and frost.
435   Only he can do this—he who rules
time and seasons, he who is truly God.
The monster's hall was full of rich treasures,
but all that Beowulf took was Grendel's head
and the hilt of the giants' jeweled sword.
440   The rest of the decorated blade
had dissolved in Grendel's steaming blood,
which boiled even after his death.
And then the battle's only survivor
swam up and away from those silent corpses.
445   The water was calm and clean. The whole huge lake
was peaceful now that the demons who'd lived there
were dead.
                    Then that noble leader of sailors
swam to land, rejoicing in the heavy
burdens he brought with him.
450   He and all his glorious band of Geats
thanked God that he had come back unharmed.

They left the lake together. The Geats
carried Beowulf's helmet and his mail shirt.
Behind them the water slowly thickened
455   as the monster's blood came seeping up.
They walked quickly, happily
across roads all of them remembered,
left the lake and the cliffs alongside it.
Those brave men staggered under the weight of
    Grendel's skull,

460   Too heavy for fewer than four of them to handle—
        Two on each side of the spear jammed through it—
        Yet proud of their ugly load and determined
        That the Danes, seated in Herot, should see it.
        Soon, fourteen Geats arrived

465   At the hall, bold and warlike, and with Beowulf,
        Their lord and leader, they walked on the mead-hall
        Green. Then the Geats' brave prince entered
        Herot, covered with glory for the daring
        Battles he had fought . . .

Beowulf on the Funeral Pyre by Rockwell Kent

460   too heavy for fewer than four of them to handle.
    Two carried each side of the spear jammed through it.
    But they were proud of their ugly load, and wanted
    the Danes in Herot to see it.
    Soon, fourteen Geats arrived at the hall,
465   bold and warlike. With Beowulf,
    their lord and leader, they walked on the mead-hall
    green. Then the Geats' brave prince entered
    Herot, covered with glory for the daring
    battles he had fought . . .

> *Beowulf and his men are honored by the Danes and then return home to Geatland. Beowulf becomes king and rules for many years. When a dragon threatens his kingdom, Beowulf, 'tho old, prepares to kill the beast. The king is deserted by all his men except for one brave warrior named Wiglaf. Together they slay the dragon, but Beowulf is severely wounded. After leaving his treasure and kingdom to Wiglaf, he dies and his body is given a warrior's funeral.*

The Canterbury Tales

The 14th–century poet Chaucer was a remarkably learned and well-traveled man. His journeys brought him in contact with the most advanced ideas of his age and allowed him to observe people in all their richness and diversity.

Chaucer did a great deal to establish English as a literary language. England had been conquered by the French-speaking Normans back in 1066. Ever since then, French had been preferred to English as a language for poetry.

From the very start of his literary career, Chaucer wrote poetry in English even though his earliest works were heavily based on French styles and themes. For a time, Chaucer found it difficult to shake off his French influence and find a truly English voice.

Then, in the 1370s, Chaucer began to travel to Italy on diplomatic missions. There he became familiar with great Italian poets like Dante, Petrarch, and Boccaccio. Under the influence of these poets, Chaucer began to write English poetry in a new and exciting way.

In 1387, however, he began to

Miniature of John Lydgate and the Canterbury pilgrims leaving Canterbury, from a volume of Lydgate's poems (15th century).

write *The Canterbury Tales*—a story of travelers telling each other stories.

Chaucer's travelers are religious pilgrims—people on a religious journey. They are on their way to visit the shrine of St. Thomas á Becket, the Archbishop of Canterbury who was murdered in 1170. They begin at an actual inn called the Tabard in the town of Southwark, just south of London.

Giving his poem a contemporary English setting and true English characters was a stroke of genius. In doing so, Chaucer made *The Canterbury Tales* an authentic English poem. At the same time, the pilgrims' stories come from many different ages and cultures. They give the poem amazing range and universality.

Chaucer's beautiful but earthy Middle English often captured the everyday speech of people he knew. And his portrayals of his pilgrims are incredibly vivid and varied.

The Pardoner is an especially striking character. Through him, Chaucer expressed his outrage at corrupt religious practices. Professional pardoners sold indulgences, documents that supposedly saved people from going to hell for their sins.

The Pardoner doesn't pretend that "pardoning" is an honest practice. In fact, he brags about this and other misdeeds, including the selling of phony religious relics. The Pardoner then tells a story of three young men who want to kill Death, but die themselves because of their own selfishness.

Taken by itself, the story would make a powerful statement against greed. But because the man telling it is himself openly greedy, the story takes on a whole different edge. It completes Chaucer's portrait of the Pardoner, a man whose lies and falseness know no bounds.

Unfortunately, Chaucer didn't live to finish *The Canterbury Tales*. He planned to write 120 stories, but only completed 24 before he died in 1400.

from
The Canterbury Tales

Geoffrey Chaucer
translated by Nevill Coghill

The Prologue

*W*hen in April the sweet showers fall
And pierce the drought of March to the root, and all
The veins are bathed in liquor of such power
As brings about the engendering of the flower,
5   When also Zephyrus with his sweet breath
Exhales an air in every grove and heath
Upon the tender shoots, and the young sun
His half-course in the sign of the *Ram* has run,
And the small fowl are making melody
10   That sleep away the night with open eye
(So nature pricks them and their heart engages)
Then people long to go on pilgrimages
And palmers long to seek the stranger strands
Of far-off saints, hallowed in sundry lands,
15   And specially, from every shire's end
Of England, down to Canterbury they wend
To seek the holy blissful martyr, quick
To give his help to them when they were sick.

❊ ❊ ❊

from
The Canterbury Tales

Geoffrey Chaucer
translated by Nevill Coghill

The Prologue

*I*t was in April, when sweet showers fall,
piercing the dryness of March down to the root,
bathing each vein with a liquid
that gives birth to the flowers.
5   The sweet breath of the west wind
swept down through every grove and field
upon the tender shoots. The sun
had passed through the constellation Aries,
and all the little birds
10   that sleep at night with open eyes
(as nature urges them to do) were making melody.
It is then that people long to go on pilgrimages,
and travelers seek the strange and faraway homes
of saints well-known in many lands.
15   From every county throughout England,
they come especially to Canterbury
to seek the holy blissful martyr,
hoping for his help when they are sick.

It happened in that season that one day
20 In Southwark, at *The Tabard*, as I lay
Ready to go on pilgrimage and start
For Canterbury, most devout at heart,
At night there came into that hostelry
Some nine and twenty in a company
25 Of sundry folk happening then to fall
In fellowship, and they were pilgrims all
That towards Canterbury meant to ride.
The rooms and stables of the inn were wide;
They made us easy, all was of the best.
30 And, briefly, when the sun had gone to rest,
I'd spoken to them all upon the trip
And was soon one with them in fellowship,
Pledged to rise early and to take the way
To Canterbury, as you heard me say.

35 But none the less, while I have time and space,
Before my story takes a further pace,
It seems a reasonable thing to say
What their condition was, the full array
Of each of them, as it appeared to me,
40 According to profession and degree,
And what apparel they were riding in;
And at a Knight I therefore will begin.
There was a *Knight*, a most
        distinguished man,
Who from the day on which he first began
45 To ride abroad had followed chivalry,
Truth, honor, generousness and courtesy.

He had done nobly in his sovereign's war
And ridden into battle, no man more,
As well in Christian as in heathen places,
50 And ever honored for his noble graces.

It all began in that season, when one day
20 I was staying in Southwark at the Tabard Inn,
ready to go on my pilgrimage
to Canterbury, feeling full of devout spirit.
That night, some 29 people
arrived at that inn—
25 various kinds of folk who happened to fall
in with one another. They, too, were all pilgrims
who planned to ride towards Canterbury.
The rooms and stables at the inn were large,
so we were comfortable, and all was of the best.
30 To put it briefly, when the sun went down,
I spoke to them all about the trip
and soon felt quite comfortable among them.
So we promised each other to rise early and start on
our way
to Canterbury, as you heard me say before.

35 But nonetheless, while I have time and space
before my story goes much further,
it seems reasonable for me to say
something about these people.
I'll tell all about them as I saw them—
40 their appearances, professions, and social ranks,
and the clothes they wore for riding.
I'll begin with a knight—
a most distinguished man,

who began following the ways of chivalry
45 the very day he first began to ride,
devoting himself to truth, honor, generosity, and
courtesy.
He'd served nobly in a war for his king—
none had served better. And he had ridden into battle
in both Christian and non-Christian lands,
50 and was always honored for his noble ways.

* * *

When we took Alexandria, he was there.
He often sat at table in the chair

Of honor, above all nations, when in Prussia.
In Lithuania he had ridden, and Russia,
55 No Christian man so often, of his rank.
When, in Granada, Algeciras sank
Under assault, he had been there, and in
North Africa, raiding Benamarin;
In Anatolia he had been as well
60 And fought when Ayas and Attalia fell,
For all along the Mediterranean coast
He had embarked with many a noble host.
In fifteen mortal battles he had been
And jousted for our faith at Tramissene
65 Thrice in the lists, and always killed his man.
This same distinguished knight had led the van
Once with the Bey of Balat, doing work
For him against another heathen Turk;
He was of sovereign value in all eyes.
70 And though so much distinguished, he was wise
And in his bearing modest as a maid.
He never yet a boorish thing had said
In all his life to any, come what might;
He was a true, a perfect gentle-knight.

* * *

75   Speaking of his equipment, he
            possessed
Fine horses, but he was not gaily
    dressed.
He wore a fustian tunic stained and
    dark
With smudges where his armor had
    left mark;

The Knight

The Prologue from *The Canterbury Tales*

When we took Alexandria,[1] he was there.
And in Prussia, he often sat at a table in the chair of
    honor
above the knights of all other nations.
No Christian man of his rank rode so often
55   in Lithuania and Russia.
In Granada, when Algeciras lost his battle,
he had been there—and also in
North Africa, raiding Benamarin.
He had been in Anatolia, too,
60   and fought when Ayas and Attalia fell,
for all along the Mediterranean coast
he sailed with many noble armies.
He'd been in fifteen deadly battles,
and at Tramissene he jousted for his faith
65   three times, and always killed his man.
This same worthy knight also joined
once with the Bey of Balat, aiding him
against another non-Christian Turk.
Everyone held him in the highest respect,
70   and although he was so famous, he was wise,
and as modest as a maid.
He never said a single rude thing
in all his life to anyone, no matter what.
He was a true, perfect, gentle knight.

* * *

75   Regarding his equipment, he had
fine horses, but he was not gaily dressed.
He wore a stained, dark jacket of heavy cloth,
smudged where his armor had marked it.

---

1 **Alexandria:** The Egyptian city of Alexandria was
   captured by Christians from Muslims in Chaucer's time.
   The following lines refer to other episodes of fighting
   between Christians and non-Christians.

Just home from service, he had joined our ranks
80 To do his pilgrimage and render thanks.

❋ ❋ ❋

He had his son with him, a fine young *Squire*,
A lover and cadet, a lad of fire
With locks as curly as if they had been pressed.

He was some twenty years of age, I guessed.
85 In stature he was of a moderate length,
With wonderful agility and strength.
He'd seen some service with the cavalry
In Flanders and Artois and Picardy
And had done valiantly in little space
90 Of time, in hope to win his lady's grace.
He was embroidered like a meadow bright
And full of freshest flowers, red and white.
Singing he was, or fluting all the day;
He was as fresh as is the month of May.

The Squire

95 Short was his gown, the sleeves were long and wide;
He knew the way to sit a horse and ride.
He could make songs and poems and recite,
Knew how to joust and dance, to draw and write.
He loved so hotly that till dawn grew pale
100 He slept as little as a nightingale.
Courteous he was, lowly and serviceable,
And carved to serve his father at the table.

❋ ❋ ❋

There was a *Yeoman* with him at his side,
No other servant; so he chose to ride.
105 This Yeoman wore a coat and hood of green,
And peacock-feathered arrows, bright and keen
And neatly sheathed, hung at his belt the while

He had just come home from service, and he joined us
80   to go on the pilgrimage and offer thanks.

His son was with him, a fine young squire[2]—
A fiery lover and soldier in training,
with hair so curly, it looked as though it had been
     pressed.
I guessed he was about 20 years old.
85   He was of moderate height,
with great strength and agility.
He'd seen some cavalry service
in parts of northern Europe,
and had fought bravely in little time,
90   hoping to win his lady's favor.
His clothes were stitched as brightly as a meadow
with the freshest red and white flowers.
All day long, he sang or played the flute,
and was as youthful as the month of May.
95   His gown was short, his sleeves long and wide,
and he knew how to sit and ride on a horse.
He could make up and recite songs and poems,
and knew how to joust and dance, to draw and write.
He hotly loved all night long
100   and slept as little as a nightingale.
He was courteous, humble, and eager to serve,
and carved meat for his father at his table.

The knight had a yeoman,[3]
the only servant he chose to ride with.
105   This yeoman wore a green coat and hood,
and a sheath hung at his belt
full of bright, sharp, peacock-feathered arrows—

2 **squire:** a knight's attendant
3 **yeoman:** a small landholder

—For he could dress his gear in yeoman style,
His arrows never drooped their feathers low—
110 And in his hand he bore a mighty bow.
His head was like a nut, his face was brown.
He knew the whole of woodcraft up and down.
A saucy brace was on his arm to ward
It from the bow-string, and a shield and sword
115 Hung at one side, and at the other slipped

A jaunty dirk, spear-sharp and well-equipped.
A medal of St. Christopher he wore
Of shining silver on his breast, and bore
A hunting-horn, well slung and burnished clean,
120 That dangled from a baldrick of bright green.
He was a proper forester, I guess.

✳ ✳ ✳

There also was a *Nun*, a Prioress,
Her way of smiling very simple and coy.
Her greatest oath was only "by St. Loy!"
125 And she was known as Madam Eglantyne.
And well she sang a service, with a fine
Intoning through her nose, as was most seemly,
And she spoke daintily in French, extremely,
After the school of Stratford-atte-Bowe;

130 French in the Paris style she did not know.
At meat her manners were well taught withal;
No morsel from her lips did she let fall,
Nor dipped her fingers in the sauce too deep;
But she could carry a morsel up and keep
135 The smallest drop from falling on her breast.
For courtliness she had a special zest,

The Nun

and because he took good care of his gear,
the feathers on those arrows never drooped.
110 And he carried a mighty bow in his hand.
His head was like a nut, and his face was brown.
He knew the craft of carpentry inside and out.
He wore a tough leather strap on his arm
to guard it from the bowstring. On one side
115 he carried a shield and sword, and at the other he
     wore
a fine dagger, sharp as a spear and well-kept.
He wore a shining silver medal
of St. Christopher[4] on his breast, and carried
a brilliantly polished hunting horn
120 that dangled from a bright, green shoulder harness.
I thought him a proper forester.

There also was a nun, a prioress,[5]
with a very simple, modest smile.
She scarcely ever uttered even the mildest oath,
125 and she was known as Madam Eglantyne.
And she sang her prayers and hymns with a fine
tone through her nose, in a lovely way,
and she spoke the most charming French—
the kind they teach in the nunnery at Stratford [in
     England],
130 not the kind spoken in Paris.
When eating, she had marvellous manners.
She never let a crumb fall from her lips
or dipped her fingers too deep in the sauce.
She hung on to every tiny morsel,
135 and not even the smallest drop fell to her breast.
She had a special zest for fine conduct,

4 **St. Christopher:** patron saint of travelers
5 **Prioress:** a high-ranking nun

And she would wipe her upper lip so clean
That not a trace of grease was to be seen
Upon the cup when she had drunk; to eat,
140   She reached a hand sedately for the meat.
She certainly was very entertaining,
Pleasant and friendly in her ways, and straining

To counterfeit a courtly kind of grace,
A stately bearing fitting to her place,
145   And to seem dignified in all her dealings.
As for her sympathies and tender feelings,
She was so charitably solicitous
She used to weep if she but saw a mouse
Caught in a trap, if it were dead or bleeding.
150   And she had little dogs she would be feeding
With roasted flesh, or milk, or fine white bread.
And bitterly she wept if one were dead
Or someone took a stick and made it smart;
She was all sentiment and tender heart.
155   Her veil was gathered in a seemly way,
Her nose was elegant, her eyes glass-grey;
Her mouth was very small, but soft and red,
Her forehead, certainly, was fair of spread,
Almost a span across the brows, I own;
160   She was indeed by no means undergrown.
Her cloak, I noticed, had a graceful charm.
She wore a coral trinket on her arm,
A set of beads, the gaudies tricked in green,
Whence hung a golden brooch of brightest sheen
165   On which there first was graven a crowned A,
And lower, *Amor vincit omnia*.

Another *Nun*, the secretary at her cell,
Was riding with her, and *three Priests* as well.

and she would wipe her upper lip so clean
that you couldn't find a trace of grease
on a cup after she drank from it. When eating,
140 she reached for the meat with a steady hand.
She was certainly very entertaining,
pleasant and friendly in her ways, and tried very
 hard
to imitate the ways of a royal court.
She had a proper manner that fit her rank well,
145 and she seemed most dignified in all she did.
As for her sympathies and tender feelings,
she was so kind and charitable
that she would weep at the mere sight of a mouse
caught in a trap, if it were dead or bleeding.
150 And she was always feeding little dogs
on roasted meat, milk, or fine white bread.
And she wept bitterly if one died,
or if anybody hurt one with a stick.
She had a tender, sentimental heart.
155 She gathered her veil in a proper way;
her nose was elegant, and her eyes gray like glass.
Her mouth was very small, but soft and red;
her forehead was certainly fine and wide—
almost nine inches across, I think.
160 Indeed, she wasn't by any means small.
I noticed that her cloak was charming and graceful.
She wore a coral trinket on her arm
and a set of beads, the larger ones colored green.
From these hung a bright, shining, golden brooch
165 on which was carved an A with a crown on it—
and below that, "Love conquers all things."

Another nun, her secretary in her room,
rode with her, and three priests as well.

✳ ✳ ✳

A *Monk* there was, one of the finest sort
170 Who rode the country; hunting was his sport.

A manly man, to be an Abbot able;

Many a dainty horse he had in stable.
His bridle, when he rode, a man might hear
Jingling in a whistling wind as clear,
175 Aye, and as loud as does the chapel bell
Where my lord Monk was Prior of the cell.
The Rule of good St. Benet or St. Maur

As old and strict he tended to ignore;
He let go by the things of yesterday
180 And took the modern world's more spacious way.
He did not rate that text at a plucked hen
Which says that hunters are not holy men
And that a monk uncloistered is a mere
Fish out of water, flapping on the pier,
185 That is to say a monk out of his cloister.
That was a text he held not worth an oyster;
And I agreed and said his views were sound;
Was he to study till his head went round
Poring over books in cloisters? Must he toil

190 As Austin bade and till the very soil?
Was he to leave the world upon the shelf?
Let Austin have his labor to himself.

✳ ✳ ✳   The Monk

This Monk was therefore a good man to horse;
Greyhounds he had, as swift as birds, to course.
195 Hunting a hare or riding at a fence
Was all his fun, he spared for no expense.

There was also a monk, one of the finest
170 to be found riding through the country; his sport was
          hunting.
He was a manly man, quite worthy to serve as an
          abbot,
and he had many charming horses in his stable.
When he rode, you might hear his bridle
jingle in the whistling wind—
175 yes, ring as loudly as the bell in the chapel
where this monk oversaw other monks.
All the old, strict rules that monks were supposed to
          live by
he tended to ignore.
He wasn't bothered by old-fashioned ideas
180 and took to more modern, freer ways.
He had no use at all for the old notion
that hunters are not holy men,
and that a monk outside his monastery is just
a fish out of water, flopping about on the pier.
185 No, he didn't believe that at all,
didn't think that notion worth an oyster,
and I agreed with his views completely.
Was he supposed to study till his head spun,
poring over books in monasteries? Must he work the
          soil
190 as St. Augustine instructed in his writings?
Was he to forget all about the world?
Augustine could work the soil for himself.

This monk was an excellent horseback rider,
and for hunting, he had greyhounds as swift as birds.
195 He had great fun hunting a hare or leaping a fence,
and spared no cost in doing so.

I saw his sleeves were garnished at the hand
With fine grey fur, the finest in the land,
And on his hood, to fasten it at his chin
200 He had a wrought-gold cunningly fashioned pin;
Into a lover's knot it seemed to pass.
His head was bald and shone like looking-glass;
So did his face, as if it had been greased.
He was a fat and personable priest;
205 His prominent eyeballs never seemed to settle.
They glittered like the flames beneath a kettle;
Supple his boots, his horse in fine condition.
He was a prelate fit for exhibition,
He was not pale like a tormented soul.
210 He liked a fat swan best, and roasted whole.

His palfrey was as brown as is a berry.

There was a *Friar*, a wanton one and merry,
A Limiter, a very festive fellow.
In all Four Orders there was none so mellow,
215 So glib with gallant phrase and well-turned speech.
He'd fixed up many a marriage, giving each
Of his young women what he could afford her.
He was a noble pillar to his Order.
Highly beloved and intimate was he
220 With County folk within his boundary,
And city dames of honor and possessions;
For he was qualified to hear confessions,
Or so he said, with more than priestly scope;
He had a special license from the Pope.
225 Sweetly he heard his penitents at shrift
With pleasant absolution, for a gift.
He was an easy man in penance-giving
Where he could hope to make a decent living;
It's a sure sign whenever gifts are given

I noticed that the cuffs of his sleeves were sewn
with fine gray fur, the best in the land.
And fastened on his hood at his chin
200 was a finely made pin of gold,
which looked like a lover's knot.
His head was bald and shone like a mirror,
and so did his face, as if it were smeared with grease.
What a fat and friendly priest he was!
205 His bulging eyeballs were always moving
and glittered like flames beneath a kettle.
His boots were soft, his horse in fine condition.
He was a fine preacher, indeed—
not pale like a tortured soul.
210 He liked a fat swan roasted whole more than
anything,
and his riding horse was as brown as a berry.

And then there was a wild and merry friar
with a license to beg—a very happy man.
He was the cheeriest friar to be found in any order,
215 so quick with a bold or well-turned phrase.
He'd arranged the marriages of many young women,
and at his own cost, too.
He was a noble supporter of his order,
and was loved and known
220 by all the people in his county,
and also by honorable city ladies.
For he was more qualified to hear confessions
than even a priest—or so he said—
because he was licensed by the pope himself.
225 He listened sweetly to sinners at confession
and repaid them with kindly forgiveness.
He forgave sins easily
when he could hope to gain a little money by it.
He was always glad to forgive a man

230 To a poor Order that a man's well shriven,
     And should he give enough he knew in verity
     The penitent repented in sincerity.
     For many a fellow is so hard of heart
     He cannot weep, for all his inward smart.

235 Therefore instead of weeping and of prayer
     One should give silver for a poor Friar's care.
     He kept his tippet stuffed with pins for curls,
     And pocket-knives, to give to pretty girls.
     And certainly his voice was gay and sturdy,
240 For he sang well and played the hurdy-gurdy.
     At sing-songs he was champion of the hour.
     His neck was whiter than a lily-flower
     But strong enough to butt a bruiser down.

     He knew the taverns well in every town
245 And every innkeeper and barmaid too
     Better than lepers, beggars and that crew,

     For in so eminent a man as he
     It was not fitting with the dignity
     Of his position, dealing with a scum
250 Of wretched lepers; nothing good can come
     Of commerce with such slum-and-gutter dwellers,
     But only with the rich and victual-sellers.
     But anywhere a profit might accrue
     Courteous he was and lowly of service too.
255 Natural gifts like his were hard to match.
     He was the finest beggar of his batch,
     And, for his begging-district, paid a rent;
     His brethren did no poaching where he went.
     For though a widow mightn't have a shoe,
260 So pleasant was his holy how-d'ye-do
     He got his farthing from her just the same
     Before he left, and so his income came
     To more than he laid out. And how he romped,

The Friar

230   who was willing to make a gift to the poor order—
        and if he gave enough, the friar knew
        that the sinner was sincerely sorry.
        For there are many fellows so hard-hearted
        that they cannot weep, no matter how they hurt
            inside.
235   So instead of weeping and prayer,
        they should give silver to a poor Friar.
        He kept his pocket stuffed with hairpins
        and pocketknives to give to pretty girls.
        And his voice was certainly gay and strong,
240   for he sang well and played stringed instruments.
        At singing songs, no one could match him.
        His throat was whiter than a lily,
        but he was strong enough to knock a tough man
            down.
        In towns, he knew all the taverns,
245   and all the innkeepers and barmaids too—
        knew them better than lepers, beggars, and their
            kind.
        For he was a truly worthy man
        who thought it beneath the dignity
        of his position to deal with filthy lepers.
250   Nothing good could come
        of hanging around those who live in slums and gutters.
        It was better to know rich folks and food-sellers.
        But wherever he had a chance to make some money,
        he was always courteous and willing to serve.
255   Natural gifts like his were hard to match.
        He was the finest beggar around,
        and paid good rent for his begging district,
        so no other friars begged where he did.
        For though a widow might not have a shoe,
260   his holy talk was so pleasant
        that he always managed to get some money from her
        before he left. And so he always managed to take in
        more money than he laid out. And how he romped,

Just like a puppy! He was ever prompt
265   To arbitrate disputes on settling days
(For a small fee) in many helpful ways,
Not then appearing as your cloistered scholar
With threadbare habit hardly worth a dollar,
But much more like a Doctor or a Pope.
270   Of double-worsted was the semi-cope
Upon his shoulders, and the swelling fold
About him, like a bell about its mold

When it is casting, rounded out his dress.
He lisped a little out of wantonness
275   To make his English sweet upon his tongue.
When he had played his harp, or having sung,
His eyes would twinkle in his head as bright
As any star upon a frosty night.
This worthy's name was Hubert, it appeared.

❋ ❋ ❋

280   There was a *Merchant* with a forking beard
And motley dress; high on his horse he sat,
Upon his head a Flemish beaver hat
And on his feet daintily buckled boots.
He told of his opinions and pursuits
285   In solemn tones, he harped on his increase
Of capital; there should be sea-police
(He thought) upon the Harwich-Holland ranges;

He was expert at dabbling in exchanges.
This estimable Merchant so had set
290   His wits to work, none knew he was in debt,
He was so stately in administration,
In loans and bargains and negotiation.
He was an excellent fellow all the same;
To tell the truth I do not know his name.

The Merchant

just like a puppy! He was always quick
265 to referee on days when disputes were settled,
and was most helpful—for a small fee.
He wouldn't show up then as a monkish scholar
in worthless, threadbare clothes,
but much more like a doctor or a pope.
270 The short cloak on his shoulders
was made of expensive cloth,
and this completed his outfit well,
surrounding him like a bell when it is being cast on
its mold.
He lisped a little,
275 trying to make his English sound sweeter.
When he sang or played his harp,
his eyes would twinkle as brightly
as any star on a frosty night.
I believe this worthy man's name was Hubert.

280 There was also a merchant with a forked beard
and multicolored clothes. He sat high on his horse
and wore a Flemish beaver hat on his head
and charming buckled boots on his feet.
He told of his opinions and activities
285 in serious tones, carrying on about how rich
he was getting. There should be sea police
(he thought) patrolling between Holland and
England.
He was good at turning a profit
by exchanging money from different countries.
290 No one knew he was in debt, he seemed so shrewd
and skillful at managing things,
especially loans, bargains, and other kinds of business.
All the same, he was an excellent fellow—
but to tell the truth, I do not know his name.

❈ ❈ ❈

295   An *Oxford Cleric*, still a student though,

One who had taken logic long ago,
Was there; his horse was thinner than a rake,
And he was not too fat, I undertake,
But had a hollow look, a sober stare;
300 The thread upon his overcoat was bare.
He had found no preferment in the church
And he was too unworldly to make search
For secular employment. By his bed
He preferred having twenty books in red

305 And black, of Aristotle's philosophy,
Than costly clothes, fiddle or psaltery.
Though a philosopher, as I have told,
He had not found the stone for making gold.
Whatever money from his friends he took
310 He spent on learning or another book
And prayed for them most earnestly, returning
Thanks to them thus for paying for his learning.
His only care was study, and indeed
He never spoke a word more than was need,
315 Formal at that, respectful in the extreme,
Short, to the point, and lofty in his theme.
A tone of moral virtue filled his speech
And gladly would he learn, and gladly teach.

❈ ❈ ❈

    A *Sergeant at the Law* who paid his calls,
320 Wary and wise, for clients at St. Paul's
There also was, of noted excellence.
Discreet he was, a man to reverence,
Or so he seemed, his sayings were so wise.
He often had been Justice of Assize

* * *

| 295 | And an Oxford clergyman—though still a |
| | student— |

was also there. He had studied logic long ago.
His horse was thinner than a rake,
and I must say he was not too fat, himself.
He had a hollow look, a sober stare,
300 and he wore a threadbare overcoat.
He had not risen up through the ranks of the church
and was too unworldly to seek
worldly employment. He liked
having twenty books printed in red and black by his
bed—
305 especially Aristotle. He preferred this
to having costly clothes, fiddle, or harp.
Though a philosopher, he had clearly not succeeded
in the alchemist's quest for making gold.[6]
Whenever he took money from his friends,
310 he spent it on books and learning
then prayed for his friends most earnestly,
thus thanking them for paying for his studies.
Indeed, he cared for nothing but study,
and he never said a word more than he had to.
315 When he did, he was extremely respectful,
brief, to the point, and spoke of serious things.
His speech always had a highly moral tone,
and he was always glad to learn and teach.

* * *

And there was also a high-ranking lawyer
320 with many clients at St. Paul's [in London]—
a wary and wise man, noted for his excellence.
He was wise and worthy of respect,
or so he seemed, because he said so many fine things.
He often traveled to hear cases,

6 **alchemist's quest for making gold:** Alchemists, often
referred to as philosophers, sought the secret of making
gold from ordinary metals.

325 By letters patent, and in full commission.
His fame and learning and his high position
Had won him many a robe and many a fee.
There was no such conveyancer as he;

All was fee-simple to his strong digestion,
330 Not one conveyance could be called in question.
Though there was nowhere one so busy as he,
He was less busy than he seemed to be.
He knew of every judgement, case and crime
Ever recorded since King William's time.
335 He could dictate defenses or draft deeds;
No one could pinch a comma from his screeds
And he knew every statute off by rote.
He wore a homely parti-colored coat,
Girt with a silken belt of pin-stripe stuff;
340 Of his appearance I have said enough.

There was a *Franklin* with him, it appeared;
White as a daisy-petal was his beard.
A sanguine man, high-colored and benign,
He loved a morning sop of cake in wine.

345 He lived for pleasure and had always done,
For he was Epicurus' very son,

In whose opinion sensual delight
Was the one true felicity in sight.
As noted as St. Julian was for bounty
350 He made his household free to all the County.
His bread, his ale were finest of the fine
And no one had a better stock of wine.
His house was never short of
    bake-meat pies,

The Franklin

325 commissioned by the king.
His fame, learning, and high position
had gotten him many robes and high fees.
There was no lawyer like him for dealing with
    property disputes.
He treated all lands as freely owned property,
330 so no one could question his decisions.
Though he was the busiest of men,
he wasn't as busy as he seemed to be.
He knew of every judgment, case, and crime
recorded since the time of King William.[7]
335 He could lay out defenses or draft deeds
so perfectly that no one could fault a comma,
and he knew every law in the books by heart.
He wore a simple, multicolored coat
tied with a pinstriped silk belt.
340 But I've said enough of his appearance.

A franklin[8] was with this lawyer,
and he had a beard as white as a daisy petal.
He was a cheerful man, rosy-cheeked and kindly,
who loved to have a piece of cake soaked in wine for
    breakfast.
345 He had always lived for pleasure,
for he was a true follower of [the philosopher]
    Epicurus,
who said that sensual delight
was the only true happiness.
He was as noted as St. Julian for generosity,
350 and opened up his house to all the county.
His bread and ale were of the very finest,
and no one kept better wine.
His house was never short of bake-meat pies,

---

7 **King William:** William the Conqueror, who invaded
   England in 1066
8 **franklin:** a wealthy landholder

Of fish and flesh, and these in such supplies
355 It positively snowed with meat and drink
And all the dainties that a man could think.
According to the seasons of the year
Changes of dish were ordered to appear.
He kept fat partridges in coops, beyond,
360 Many a bream and pike were in his pond.
Woe to the cook unless the sauce was hot
And sharp, or if he wasn't on the spot!
And in his hall a table stood arrayed
And ready all day long, with places laid.
365 As Justice at the Sessions none stood higher;
He often had been Member for the Shire.
A dagger and a little purse of silk
Hung at his girdle, white as morning milk.
As Sheriff he checked audit, every entry.
370 He was a model among landed gentry.

※ ※ ※

A *Haberdasher*, a *Dyer*, a *Carpenter*,
A *Weaver* and a *Carpet-maker* were
Among our ranks, all in the livery
Of one impressive guild-fraternity.
375 They were so trim and fresh their gear would pass
For new. Their knives were not tricked out with brass

But wrought with purest silver, which avouches
A like display on girdles and on pouches.
Each seemed a worthy burgess, fit to grace
380 A guild-hall with a seat upon the dais.
Their wisdom would have justified a plan
To make each one of them an alderman;
They had the capital and revenue,
Besides their wives declared it was their due.

fish, and meat—and he had so much of these
355 that it positively snowed meat, drink,
and all other tasty things.
He ordered changes of the menu
according to the seasons of the year.
He kept fat partridges in coops
360 and filled his pond with fish.
Woe to the cook if the sauce wasn't hot
and sharp, or if he was too slow!
And in his hall, a table was spread
and ready all day long, with places laid.
365 He ranked highest at local court sessions,
for he had often served in Parliament.[9]
A dagger and a little silk purse
hung on his belt, which was as white as milk.
As Sheriff, he collected taxes tirelessly.
370 He was a model among wealthy landowners.

A tailor, a dyer, a carpenter,
a weaver, and a carpet maker were also
with us. They wore the uniform
of their impressive guild.[10]
375 They were so neat and fresh that their outfits
looked new. Their knives weren't decorated with
        brass,
but with pure silver,
and their belts and purses were just as fine.
Each seemed a worthy citizen, fit to sit
380 in a seat upon the platform in a guild hall.
They were all wise enough
to have been made town councilors.
They certainly had the wealth for it—
and besides, their wives thought they deserved it.

9 **Parliament:** the governmental body that makes laws in
England
10 **guild:** a medieval organization of people involved in
similar trades

385 And if they did not think so, then they ought;
To be called *"Madam"* is a glorious thought,
And so is going to church and being seen
Having your mantle carried, like a queen.

❋ ❋ ❋

They had a *Cook* with them who stood alone
390 For boiling chicken with a marrow-bone,
Sharp flavoring-powder and a spice for savor.
He could distinguish London ale by flavor,
And he could roast and seethe and broil and fry,
Make good thick soup and bake a tasty pie.
395 But what a pity—so it seemed to me,
That he should have an ulcer on his knee.
As for blancmange, he made it with the best.

❋ ❋ ❋

There was a *Skipper* hailing from far west;
He came from Dartmouth, so I understood.

400 He rode a farmer's horse as best he could,
In a woolen gown that reached his knee.
A dagger on a lanyard falling free
Hung from his neck under his arm and down.
The summer heat had tanned his color brown,
405 And certainly he was an excellent fellow.
Many a draft of vintage, red and yellow,
He'd drawn at Bordeaux, while the trader snored.

The nicer rules of conscience he ignored.
If, when he fought, the enemy vessel sank,
410 He sent his prisoners home; they walked the plank.

As for his skill in reckoning his tides,
Currents and many another risk besides,
Moons, harbors, pilots, he had such dispatch

385 And after all, why wouldn't they think so?
To be called "Madam" is a glorious thought,
and so is going to church and having
your cloak carried, like a queen.

* * *

They had a cook with them who was unmatched
390 at boiling chicken with a marrow bone,
adding spice and powder for flavor.
He could tell London ales apart by taste,
and could roast, broil, fry, and boil,
and make good, thick soup and bake a tasty pie.
395 But it seemed a pity to me
that he had an ulcer on his knee.
As for chicken stew with almonds, no one made better.

* * *

There was a skipper who came from western
parts—
way over in Dartmouth, I believe.
400 He rode a farmer's horse as well as he could
in a woolen gown that reached his knee.
A dagger on a cord hung freely
from his neck, down around his arms.
The summer heat had tanned him brown,
405 and he certainly was an excellent fellow.
In Bordeaux, he'd drunk many glasses
of red and white wine while the man who sold it
dozed.
He wasn't a stickler for rules of conscience.
If he sank an enemy vessel in a fight,
410 he sent his prisoners home by water; they walked the
plank.
As for his skill in reckoning tides,
currents, moons, harbors, pilots,
and many kinds of risks, he was so sharp

That none from Hull to Carthage was his match.
415 Hardy he was, prudent in undertaking;
His beard in many a tempest had its shaking,
And he knew all the havens as they were
From Gottland to the Cape of Finisterre,

And every creek in Brittany and Spain;
420 The barge he owned was called *The Maudelayne*.

※　※　※

A *Doctor* too emerged as we proceeded;
No one alive could talk as well as he did
On points of medicine and of surgery,
For, being grounded in astronomy,
425 He watched his patient closely for the hours
When, by his horoscope, he knew the powers
Of favorable planets, then ascendent,
Worked on the images for his dependant.
The cause of every malady you'd got
430 He knew, and whether dry, cold, moist or hot;
He knew their seat, their humor and condition.
He was a perfect practicing physician.
These causes being known for what they were,
He gave the man his medicine then and there.
435 All his apothecaries in a tribe
Were ready with the drugs he would prescribe
And each made money from the other's guile;
They had been friendly for a goodish while.
He was well-versed in Aesculapius too
440 And what Hippocrates and Rufus knew
And Dioscorides, now dead and gone,
Galen and Rhazes, Hali, Serapion,
Averroes, Avicenna, Constantine,

The Doctor

that he had no match in England or in Europe.
415 He was a hardy man, and sensible, too.
His beard had been shaken in many storms,
and he knew all the ports
from Gottland [in the Baltic Sea] to Cape Finisterre
[in France],
and every creek in French Bretagne and in Spain.
420 The ship he owned was called the *Maudelayne*.

❅ ❅ ❅

A doctor joined us too, as we went along.
No man alive could talk as well as he could
about medicine and surgery,
for he knew his astrology well.
425 He watched his patient closely,
and used his horoscope
to determine when the planets were favorable
and what spells and charms to use.
He knew what caused every sickness you could get,
430 whether dry, cold, moist, or hot,[11]
and also where and how they affected the body.
He was really a perfect doctor.
Once he knew the cause of an illness,
he'd give the patient his medicine then and there.
435 All his druggists together
were ready with whatever he'd prescribe,
and each made money from the other's shrewdness,
for they'd been friends for quite a while.
He was well versed in the teachings of Aesculapius,
440 Hippocrates, Rufus,
Dioscorides, Galen,
Rhazes, Hali, Serapion,
Averroes, Avicenna, Constantine,

11 **dry, cold, moist or hot:** In Chaucer's time, sickness
and health were thought to depend upon the four so-
called elements—earth, air, fire, and water. Good health
required a proper balance of these elements.

Scotch Bernard, John of Gaddesden, Gilbertine.
445 In his own diet he observed some measure;
There were no superfluities for pleasure,
Only digestives, nutritives and such.
He did not read the Bible very much.
In blood-red garments, slashed with bluish grey
450 And lined with taffeta, he rode his way;
Yet he was rather close as to expenses
And kept the gold he won in pestilences.
Gold stimulates the heart, or so we're told.
He therefore had a special love of gold.

455 A worthy *woman* from beside *Bath* city
Was with us, somewhat deaf, which was a pity.
In making cloth she showed so great a bent
She bettered those of Ypres and of Ghent.
In all the parish not a dame dared stir
460 Towards the altar steps in front of her,
And if indeed they did, so wrath was she
As to be quite put out of charity.
Her kerchiefs were of finely woven ground;
I dared have sworn they weighed a good ten pound,

465 The ones she wore on Sunday, on her head.
Her hose were of the finest scarlet red
And gartered tight; her shoes were soft and new.

Bold was her face, handsome, and red in hue.
A worthy woman all her life, what's more
470 She'd had five husbands, all at the church door,
Apart from other company in youth;
No need just now to speak of that, forsooth.
And she had thrice been to Jerusalem,
Seen many strange rivers and passed over them;

Scotch Bernard, John of Gaddesen, and Gilbertine.[12]
445   He was careful in his own diet,
and never ate too much for pleasure—
only what was good for digestion and nutrition.
He did not read the Bible very much.
He went riding in blood-red clothes
450   with bluish-gray slashes, lined with smooth cloth.
All in all, he was rather tight-fisted
and kept all the gold he earned during plague times.
We've all heard that gold gladdens the heart,
so he had a special love for gold.

❋   ❋   ❋

455   A worthy wife from near the city of Bath
was with us—somewhat deaf, which was a pity.
She made even better cloth
than the fabric makers in the great Flemish cities.
No woman of her neighborhood dared step
460   in front of her toward the church altar—
and if they did, she became so angry
that she could be quite cruel.
Her shawls were finely woven,
and I'm sure the ones she wore on her head on
        Sundays
465   weighed a good ten pounds altogether.
Her hose were a fine, scarlet red
and tightly-gartered, and her shoes were soft and
        new.
Her face was bold, handsome, and reddish-colored.
She'd always been a worthy woman and had
470   married five husbands in proper church weddings—
apart from other lovers when she was young,
but we needn't speak of that right now.
She'd been to Jerusalem three times
and had seen and crossed many foreign rivers.

12 **Aesculapius . . . Gilbertine:** All these names are
connected with the practice of medicine; Aesculapius is a
mythical figure.

475 She'd been to Rome and also to Boulogne,
St. James of Compostella and Cologne,
And she was skilled in wandering by the way.
She had gap-teeth, set widely, truth to say.

Easily on an ambling horse she sat
480 Well wimpled up, and on her head a hat
As broad as is a buckler or a shield;
She had a flowing mantle that concealed
Large hips, her heels spurred sharply under that.

In company she liked to laugh and chat
485 And knew the remedies for love's mischances,
An art in which she knew the oldest dances.

    A holy-minded man of good renown
There was, and poor, the *Parson* to a town,
Yet he was rich in holy thought and work.
490 He also was a learned man, a clerk,
Who truly knew Christ's gospel and would preach it
Devoutly to parishioners, and teach it.
Benign and wonderfully diligent,
And patient when adversity was sent
495 (For so he proved in much adversity)
He hated cursing to extort a fee,

Nay rather he preferred beyond a doubt
Giving to poor parishioners round about
Both from church offerings and his property;
500 He could in little find sufficiency.
Wide was his parish, with houses far asunder,
Yet he neglected not in rain or thunder,

The Parson

475 She'd been to Rome and Boulogne [in Italy,
and on other pilgrimages in Spain and Germany],
and was a well-seasoned traveler.
To tell the truth, she had a widely set gap between
    her teeth.
She sat easily on a jogging horse,
480 her head and neck well-covered, and wore a hat
as broad as a shield.
Her flowing cloak covered
her large hips, and she wore sharp spurs on her
    heels.
She liked to laugh and chat with people,
485 and knew how to cure love's sicknesses—
for she knew that old, old dance by heart.

    There was also a well-known, holy-minded man—
the parson of a town. He was very poor,
but rich in pious thoughts and deeds.
490 He was learned and scholarly,
and knew Christ's gospel and would preach it
sincerely to his parishioners.
He was kind, extremely devoted,
and patient whenever there was trouble—
495 and he found plenty of trouble, indeed.
He hated using excommunication[13] to force people to
    make offerings.
Far from it, he preferred
giving church offerings and his own belongings
to poor parishioners,
500 so he often found it hard to get by.
His parish was large, with houses far and near,
but he was never neglectful even in thunder and
    rain.

13 **excommunication:** depriving a person of church
    membership

In sickness or in grief, to pay a call

On the remotest, whether great or small,
505   Upon his feet, and in his hand a stave.
This noble example to his sheep he gave
That first he wrought, and afterwards he taught;
And it was from the Gospel he had caught
Those words, and he would add this figure too,
510   That if gold rust, what then will iron do?
For if a priest be foul in whom we trust
No wonder that a common man should rust;
And shame it is to see—let priests take stock—
A shitten shepherd and a snowy flock.
515   The true example that a priest should give
Is one of cleanness, how the sheep should live.
He did not set his benefice to hire

And leave his sheep encumbered in the mire
Or run to London to earn easy bread
520   By singing masses for the wealthy dead,
Or find some Brotherhood and get enrolled.
He stayed at home and watched over his fold
So that no wolf should make the sheep miscarry.
He was a shepherd and no mercenary.
525   Holy and virtuous he was, but then
Never contemptuous of sinful men,
Never disdainful, never too proud or fine,
But was discreet in teaching and benign.
His business was to show a fair behavior
530   And draw men thus to Heaven and their Savior,
Unless indeed a man were obstinate;
And such, whether of high or low estate,
He put to sharp rebuke, to say the least.
I think there never was a better priest.
535   He sought no pomp or glory in his dealings,
No scrupulosity had spiced his feelings.

When folks were sick or grieving, he'd pay them a
        call,
no matter how far away they were, or rich or poor,
505   and always on foot with a staff in his hand.
In this way, he first *showed* his flock a noble example,
then taught it afterwards.
He learned all this from the Gospel,
and he liked to add, in his own words,
510   "If gold rusts, what will iron do?"
For if a priest we trust proves to be wicked,
it's no wonder that a common man should rust.
And it's a shame to see (let priests take note)
a filthy shepherd with a snow-white flock.
515   A priest should give an example
of true cleanliness, showing how the sheep should live.
This parson did not hire someone to perform his own
        parish duties,
leaving his sheep trapped in filth.
Nor did he hurry to London to earn easy money
520   singing masses for the wealthy dead,
or join some rich religious brotherhood.
He stayed at home and watched over his flock,
making sure no wolf carried off any sheep.
He was a shepherd, not a money seeker.
525   But as holy and virtuous as he was,
he never looked down his nose at sinful folks—
was never proud or snobbish.
Instead, he was a prudent, kindly teacher.
His business was to show a good example,
530   and in that way, draw men to heavenly salvation—
unless a man happened to be stubborn.
If so, he would scold him sharply,
to say the least, whether he was high-born or low.
I don't think there was ever a better priest.
535   He never sought pomp or glory,
nor did he quibble about what he believed.

Christ and His Twelve Apostles and their lore

He taught, but followed it himself before.

There was a *Plowman* with him there, his
    brother;
540 Many a load of dung one time or other
He must have carted through the morning dew.
He was an honest worker, good and true,
Living in peace and perfect charity,
And, as the gospel bade him, so did he,
545 Loving God best with all his heart and mind
And then his neighbor as himself, repined
At no misfortune, slacked for no content,

For steadily about his work he went
To thrash his corn, to dig or to manure
550 Or make a ditch; and he would help the poor
For love of Christ and never take a penny
If he could help it, and, as prompt as any,
He paid his tithes in full when they were due
On what he owned, and on his earnings too.
555 He wore a tabard smock and rode a mare.

There was a *Reeve*, also a *Miller*, there,
A College *Manciple* from the Inns of Court,
A papal *Pardoner* and, in close consort,
A Church-Court *Summoner*, riding at a trot,
560 And finally myself—that was the lot.

He taught the same lessons as Christ and His
    Twelve Apostles,
but followed those lessons himself first.

His brother, a plowman, came along with him.

540 He must have carted many a load of manure
through the morning dew at one time or other.
He was a good, true, honest worker,
and lived a peaceful, kindly existence,
always doing as the Gospel said.
545 He loved God best with all his heart and mind,
and then his neighbor as himself.
He never complained over misfortune, and never
    slacked off
in his work, just steadily
thrashed his corn, dug, fertilized,
550 or made a ditch. And he helped the poor
for love of Christ, never asking a penny
for it. And he was always prompt
to fully pay his tithes[14] when they were due—
not just on what he owned, but also on his earnings.
555 He wore a heavy jacket and rode a mare.

There were also a reeve, a miller,
a manciple from the Inns of Court,
and a pardoner. Along with the pardoner
rode a church-court summoner at a trot.[15]
560 Finally, there was myself—and that was everybody.

14 **tithes:** fees required for church membership

15 **reeve:** manager of an estate
manciple: servant who buys food
Inns of Court: London law schools
summoner: one who summons people to a church court

* * *

    The *Miller* was a chap of sixteen stone,
A great stout fellow big in brawn and bone.
He did well out of them, for he could go
And win the ram at any wrestling show.
565 Broad, knotty and short-shouldered, he would boast
He could heave any door off hinge and post,
Or take a run and break it with his head.
His beard, like any sow or fox, was red
And broad as well, as though it were a spade;
570 And, at its very tip, his nose displayed
A wart on which there stood a tuft of hair
Red as the bristles in an old sow's ear.
His nostrils were as black as they were wide.
He had a sword and buckler at his side,
575 His mighty mouth was like a furnace door.
A wrangler and buffoon, he had a store
Of tavern stories, filthy in the main.
His was a master-hand at stealing grain.
He felt it with his thumb and thus he knew
580 Its quality and took three times his due—
A thumb of gold, by God, to gauge an oat!
He wore a hood of blue and a white coat.
He liked to play his bagpipes up and down
And that was how he brought us out of town.

The Miller

* * *

585   The *Manciple* came from the Inner Temple;
All caterers might follow his example
In buying victuals; he was never rash
Whether he bought on credit or paid cash.
He used to watch the market most precisely
590 And got in first, and so he did quite nicely.
Now isn't it a marvel of God's grace

* * *

     The miller weighed some 220 pounds or so—
a big, bony, muscular fellow.
His strength served him well, for he could
win a ram at any wrestling contest.
565   Broad, knotty, and big-shouldered, he claimed
he could rip any door off its hinges
or break it open by running at it with his head.
His beard was as red as any sow or fox,
and was as broad as a shovel.
570   On the very tip of his nose
was a wart with a tuft of hair
as red as the bristles in an old sow's ear,
and his nostrils were wide and black.
He carried a sword and shield,
575   and his mighty mouth was like a furnace door.
A fighter and a fool, he had many
tavern stories, most of them filthy.
He was an expert at stealing grain.
By feeling it with his thumb, he could tell
580   its quality, then took three times what he'd paid for.
By God, he had a gold thumb for judging oats!
He wore a blue hood and a white coat.
He liked to play his bagpipes everywhere,
and did so as we rode out of town.

585   The manciple came from one of the Inns of Court.
All caterers might learn a thing or two from him
about buying food. He never rushed it,
whether buying on credit or with cash.
He used to watch the market carefully,
590   and got better deals than anybody.
Now isn't it a marvel of God's favor

That an illiterate fellow can outpace
The wisdom of a heap of learned men?
His masters—he had more than thirty then—
595 All versed in the abstrusest legal knowledge,
Could have produced a dozen from their College
Fit to be stewards in land and rents and game
To any Peer in England you could name,
And show him how to live on what he had
600 Debt-free (unless of course the Peer were mad)
Or be as frugal as he might desire,
And make them fit to help about the Shire
In any legal case there was to try;
And yet this Manciple could wipe their eye.

❋ ❋ ❋

605   The *Reeve* was old and choleric and thin;
His beard was shaven closely to the skin,
His shorn hair came abruptly to a stop
Above his ears, and he was docked on top
Just like a priest in front; his legs were lean,
610 Like sticks they were, no calf was to be seen.
        He kept his bins and garners very trim;

No auditor could gain a point on him.
And he could judge by watching drought and rain
The yield he might expect from seed and grain.
615 His master's sheep, his animals and hens,
Pigs, horses, dairies, stores and cattle-pens
Were wholly trusted to his government.
He had been under contract to present
The accounts, right from his master's earliest years.
620 No one had ever caught him in arrears.
No bailiff, serf or herdsman dared to kick,

He knew their dodges, knew their every trick;

that an illiterate fellow can outdo
the wisdom of many learned men?
For he had more than 30 masters
595   versed in the most difficult legal knowledge,
who could produce a dozen students
fit to manage land, rents, and game
for any nobleman in England. And those students
could show a nobleman how to live without debt
600   (unless, of course, the nobleman was mad),
and live as thriftily as he liked.
And these students could also serve the county
in any legal case to be tried.
And yet, this manciple was shrewder than them all.

✳ ✳ ✳

605   The reeve was old, thin, and irritable.
His beard was shaved close to the skin,
his hair was cut
above his ears, and he was shaved bald on top
just like a priest. His legs were as lean
610   as sticks, and he had no calf to speak of.
He managed his barrels and storage buildings so
      well
that no inspector could find anything against him.
And he could judge from dryness or rain
the amount of seed and grain he might need.
615   His master's sheep, hens,
pigs, horses, dairies, storage places, and cattle pens
were completely trusted to his care.
He'd been in charge of all accounts
since his master's earliest years.
620   No one had ever caught him with unpaid debts.
No manager, laborer, or herdsman dared pull
      anything on him,
for he knew all their tricks and dodges.

Feared like the plague he was, by those beneath.

He had a lovely dwelling on a heath,
625   Shadowed in green by trees above the sward.
A better hand at bargains than his lord,
He had grown rich and had a store of treasure
Well tucked away, yet out it came to pleasure
His lord with subtle loans or gifts of goods,
630   To earn his thanks and even coats and hoods.

When young he'd learnt a useful trade and still
He was a carpenter of first-rate skill.
The stallion-cob he rode at a slow trot
Was dapple-grey and bore the name of Scot.
635   He wore an overcoat of bluish shade
And rather long; he had a rusty blade
Slung at his side. He came, as I heard tell,
From Norfolk, near a place called Baldeswell.

His coat was tucked under his belt and splayed.
640   He rode the hindmost of our cavalcade.

There was a *Summoner* with us at that Inn,
His face on fire, like a cherubin,
For he had carbuncles. His eyes were narrow,
He was as hot and lecherous as a sparrow.
645   Black scabby brows he had, and a thin beard.
Children were afraid when he appeared.
No quicksilver, lead ointment, tartar creams,
No brimstone, no boracic, so it seems,
Could make a salve that had the power to bite,
650   Clean up or cure his whelks of knobby white
Or purge the pimples sitting on his cheeks.
Garlic he loved, and onions too, and leeks,
And drinking strong red wine till all was hazy.

He was feared like the plague by those who worked
    under him.
He had a lovely house out in the fields,
625   shaded by green, leafy trees.
He had a better way with bargains than his lord,
so he had grown rich and had a store of treasure
tucked away. Yet he used some of it to please
his lord with loans or gifts,
630   for which he received thanks, and even coats and
    hoods.
When young, he'd learned a useful trade,
and he was still a first-rate carpenter.
He rode at a slow trot on a thickset,
dapple-gray stallion named Scot.
635   He wore a rather long, bluish overcoat,
and had a rusty blade
slung at his side. I heard that he came
from Norfolk [in eastern England], near a place
    called Baldeswell.
His coat was tucked into his belt,
640   and he rode last in our group.

A summoner was with us at the inn
with a fiery, red face, like an angel's,
for he had huge pimples. He had narrow eyes,
and he was as hot and lewd as a sparrow.
645   He had black, scabby brows and a thin beard,
and he frightened children when he came along.
No mercury, lead ointment, tartar creams,
sulfur, or borax
worked as a cure
650   for his knobby, white swellings
or got rid of those pimples of his.
He loved garlic, onions, and leeks,
and drank too much strong, red wine.

Then he would shout and jabber as if crazy,
655   And wouldn't speak a word except in Latin
When he was drunk, such tags as he was pat in;
He only had a few, say two or three,
That he had mugged up out of some decree;
No wonder, for he heard them every day.

660   And, as you know, a man can teach a jay
To call out "Walter" better than the Pope.
But had you tried to test his wits and grope
For more, you'd have found nothing in the bag.
Then "*Questio quid juris*" was his tag.

665   He was a noble varlet and a kind one,
You'd meet none better if you went to find one.
Why, he'd allow—just for a quart of wine—
Any good lad to keep a concubine
A twelvemonth and dispense him altogether!
670   And he had finches of his own to feather:

And if he found some rascal with a maid
He would instruct him not to be afraid
In such a case of the Archdeacon's curse
(Unless the rascal's soul were in his purse)

675   For in his purse the punishment should be.
"Purse is the good Archdeacon's Hell," said he.   The Summoner
But well I know he lied in what he said;
A curse should put a guilty man in dread,

For curses kill, as shriving brings, salvation.

680   We should beware of excommunication.
Thus, as he pleased, the man could bring duress
On any young fellow in the diocese.
He knew their secrets, they did what he said.
He wore a garland set upon his head

When drunk, he would shout and jabber as if crazy
655 and only spoke in Latin,
using brief quotes he'd happened to learn.
He only knew two or three phrases
that he'd picked up out of some decree—
which was no surprise, for he heard decrees every
        day.
660 As you know, a man can teach a bird
to say "Walter" better than the pope could say it.
But if you tested that bird's wits,
you'd find it knew nothing more than mere words.
He liked to say the Latin phrase for "how does the
        law apply?"
665 He was as kind and noble a rascal
as you could ever hope to find.
Why, for just a quart of wine, he'd allow
any good lad to keep a prostitute
a full year without paying!
670 He did have ways getting money out of people,
        though.
If he caught some rascal with a girl,
he'd teach him not to be afraid
of excommunication by the Archdeacon—
although he'd tell that lad to fear the Archdeacon's
        purse,
675 which was where the real punishment was.
"His purse is the good Archdeacon's Hell," he'd say.
But I know well that he lied in saying so.
Excommunication should fill a guilty man with
        dread,
for it destroys salvation as surely as confession
        brings it.
680 We should beware of excommunication.
Anyway, the man could put pressure
on any young fellow in the church district.
He knew their secrets, and they did what he said.
Upon his head he wore a garland

685 Large as the holly-bush upon a stake
Outside an ale-house, and he had a cake,
A round one, which it was his joke to wield
As if it were intended for a shield.

❋ ❋ ❋

He and a gentle *Pardoner* rode together,
690 A bird from Charing Cross of the same feather,

Just back from visiting the Court of Rome.
He loudly sang, *"Come hither, love, come home!"*

The Summoner sang deep seconds to this song,
No trumpet ever sounded half so strong.
695 This Pardoner had hair as yellow as wax,
Hanging down smoothly like a hank of flax.
In driblets fell his locks behind his head
Down to his shoulders which they overspread;
Thinly they fell, like rat-tails, one by one.
700 He wore no hood upon his head, for fun;
The hood inside his wallet had been stowed,
He aimed at riding in the latest mode;
But for a little cap his head was bare
And he had bulging eye-balls, like a hare.
705 He'd sewed a holy relic on his cap;
His wallet lay before him on his lap,
Brimful of pardons come from Rome, all hot.
He had the same small voice a goat has got.
His chin no beard had harbored, nor would harbor,

710 Smoother than ever chin was left by barber.
I judge he was a gelding, or a mare.
As to his trade, from Berwick down to Ware
There was no pardoner of equal grace,
For in his trunk he had a pillow-case
715 Which he asserted was Our Lady's veil.

685 as large as the holly wreaths
you find on tavern signs, and he had a round cake
which he'd jokingly wave
as if it were a shield.

✻ ✻ ✻

He rode together with a gentle pardoner—
690 the same type of fellow, from Charing Cross [in
London],
just back from visiting the court of Rome.
He'd loudly sing that song, "Come Hither, Love, Come
Home!"
The summoner would sing right along,
sounding twice as strong as any trumpet.
695 The pardoner had bright yellow hair,
which hung down smoothly like yellow fabric.
His locks fell in wisps behind his head
and spread over his shoulders,
falling thinly, one by one, like rat tails.
700 To please himself, he wore no hood on his head.
He kept it inside his satchel,
for he wanted to ride in the latest style.
So his head was bare except for a little cap,
and he had bulging eyeballs like a hare.
705 He'd sewn upon his cap a holy relic,
and his satchel lay before him on his lap,
all full of pardons from Rome, fresh and hot.
His small voice sounded like a goat's,
and his chin had always been beardless, and always
would be—
710 smoother than a barber ever left a chin.
I suspect he wasn't quite altogether a man.
As for his trade, there was no pardoner in England,
north or south, to match him,
for in his trunk he had a pillowcase,
715 which he claimed to be the Virgin Mary's veil.

He said he had a gobbet of the sail
Saint Peter had the time when he made bold
To walk the waves, till Jesu Christ took hold.
He had a cross of metal set with stones
720 And, in a glass, a rubble of pigs' bones.
And with these relics, any time he found
Some poor up-country parson to astound,
In one short day, in money down, he drew
More than the parson in a month or two,
725 And by his flatteries and prevarication
Made monkeys of the priest and congregation.
But still to do him justice first and last
In church he was a noble ecclesiast.
How well he read a lesson or told a story!
730 But best of all he sang an Offertory,

For well he knew that when that song was sung
He'd have to preach and tune his honey-tongue

And (well he could) win silver from the crowd.

That's why he sang so merrily and loud.

735   Now I have told you shortly, in a clause,
The rank, the array, the number and the cause

Of our assembly in this company
In Southwark, at that high-class hostelry
Known as *The Tabard*, close beside *The Bell*.
740 And now the time has come for me to tell
How we behaved that evening; I'll begin
After we had alighted at the Inn,
Then I'll report our journey, stage by stage,
All the remainder of our pilgrimage.
745 But first I beg of you, in courtesy,

He said he had a piece of the sail of St. Peter's boat,
from when Peter tried to walk the waves
and was rescued by Jesus.
He had a metal cross with stones set in it
720 and a bottle of pigs' bones.
He'd get out these relics any time he found
some easily-impressed, poor country parson,
and in a single day, he'd make more money
than the parson did in a month or two.
725 And with flatteries and lies,
he'd make monkeys of the priest and his flock.
But to be completely fair to him,
he really was a fine preacher in church.
How well he read a lesson or told a story!
730 He was at his best chanting when bread and wine
were offered.
For he knew that when that song was over,
he'd have to tune his honey tongue and preach his
best
to win silver from the crowd—and then he'd do just
that.
That's why he sang so loudly and merrily.

❋ ❋ ❋

735 So now I've briefly told you
all about these people—their ranks, appearances, and
number,
and also why they had gathered
in Southwark, in that high-class inn
called the Tabard, not far from the Bell.
740 And now it's time for me to say
what we did that evening. I'll start
after we'd all arrived at the Inn.
Then I'll describe our journey, little by little,
and everything else about our pilgrimage.
745 But first, I must ask you for a favor.

Not to condemn me as unmannerly
If I speak plainly and with no concealings
And give account of all their words and dealings,
Using their very phrases as they fell.
750 For certainly, as you all know so well,
He who repeats a tale after a man
Is bound to say, as nearly as he can,
Each single word, if he remembers it,
However rudely spoken or unfit,
755 Or else the tale he tells will be untrue,
The things pretended and the phrases new.
He may not flinch although it were his brother,
He may as well say one word as another.
And Christ Himself spoke broad in Holy Writ,
760 Yet there is no scurrility in it,
And Plato says, for those with power to read,
"The word should be as cousin to the deed."
Further I beg you to forgive it me
If I neglect the order and degree
765 And what is due to rank in what I've planned.
I'm short of wit as you will understand.

Our *Host* gave us great welcome; everyone
Was given a place and supper was begun.
He served the finest victuals you could think,
770 The wine was strong and we were glad to drink.
A very striking man our Host withal,
And fit to be a marshal in a hall.
His eyes were bright, his girth a little wide;
There is no finer burgess in Cheapside.

775 Bold in his speech, yet wise and full of tact,
There was no manly attribute he lacked,
What's more he was a merry-hearted man.
After our meal he jokingly began

Please don't think me vulgar
if I speak plainly and frankly
as I tell of all these people's words and deeds,
using the very phrases that they used.

750 For you know very well
that anyone who repeats a tale
is obliged to say, as nearly as he can,
every single word exactly as he remembers it,
no matter how rude or improper.

755 Otherwise, the tale he tells will be untrue,
with made-up events and language.
Even if he's repeating his own brother's words,
he must say them accurately.
For Christ himself spoke bluntly in the Bible,

760 and yet there's no coarseness in what he said.
And Plato, if you have read him,
says, "The word should fit the deed."
Also, I beg you to forgive me
if I sometimes fail to take proper account

765 of the ranks and classes of the characters I speak of.
I'm not too bright, as you will learn.

Our host welcomed us warmly. Everyone
found a place at the table, and supper started.
He served the finest food you could imagine,

770 with strong wine that we were glad to drink.
Moreover, our Host was a very striking man,
fit to take charge of a nobleman's banquet.
His eyes were bright, and he was somewhat stocky.
You couldn't find a better citizen in Cheapside [in
London].

775 His speech was bold, but he was wise and tactful,
and he lacked no manly quality—
and what's more, he was a merry-hearted man.
After our meal, he began jokingly

To talk of sport, and, among other things
780 After we'd settled up our reckonings,
He said as follows: "Truly, gentlemen,
You're very welcome and I can't think when
—Upon my word I'm telling you no lie—
I've seen a gathering here that looked so spry,
785 No, not this year, as in this tavern now.
I'd think you up some fun if I knew how.
And, as it happens, a thought has just occurred
To please you, costing nothing, on my word.
You're off to Canterbury—well, God speed!

790 Blessed St. Thomas answer to your need!
And I don't doubt, before the journey's done
You mean to while the time in tales and fun.
Indeed, there's little pleasure for your bones
Riding along and all as dumb as stones.
795 So let me then propose for your enjoyment,
Just as I said, a suitable employment.
And if my notion suits and you agree
And promise to submit yourselves to me
Playing your parts exactly as I say
800 Tomorrow as you ride along the way,
Then by my father's soul (and he is dead)
If you don't like it you can have my head!
Hold up your hands, and not another word."

❋ ❋ ❋

Well, our opinion was not long deferred,
805 It seemed not worth a serious debate;
We all agreed to it at any rate
And bade him issue what commands he would.
"My lords," he said, "now listen for your good,
And please don't treat my notion with disdain.
810 This is the point. I'll make it short and plain.

to talk of fun. After we'd settled
780   up our bills, he said this,
       among other things: "Gentlemen,
       you're truly welcome. Upon my word,
       I'm telling you no lie—I can't remember when
       I've seen a gathering here that looked so lively.
785   No, not this year, not in this tavern.
       I wish I could think up some fun for you.
       And as it happens, a thought just dawned on me
       to please you—and will cost nothing, I promise.
       You're off to Canterbury—well, God give you good
           luck!
790   And may blessed St. Thomas answer all your wishes!
       And before the journey's over, I'm sure
       you'll pass the time with stories and fun.
       Indeed, it would give your bones little pleasure
       to ride along and say nothing at all.
795   So let me suggest a suitable activity
       for your enjoyment, just as I said.
       And if you like this idea, then promise
       to do as I tell you,
       playing your parts exactly as I say
800   tomorrow as you ride along.
       And then, by the soul of my dead father,
       if you don't like it, you can have my head!
       Hold up your hands if you want to hear what I've got
           in mind."

                        ❋ ❋ ❋

       Well, it didn't take long for us to decide,
805   nor did it seem worth a serious debate.
       We all agreed at once
       and asked him to give his instructions.
       "My lords," he said, "listen for your own good,
       and please don't sneer at my idea.
810   Here it is, I'll make it short and plain.

Each one of you shall help to make things slip
By telling two stories on the outward trip
To Canterbury, that's what I intend,
And, on the homeward way to journey's end
815 Another two, tales from the days of old;
And then the man whose story is best told,
That is to say who gives the fullest measure
Of good morality and general pleasure,
He shall be given a supper, paid by all,
820 Here in this tavern, in this very hall,
When we come back again from Canterbury.
And in the hope to keep you bright and merry
I'll go along with you myself and ride
All at my own expense and serve as guide.
825 I'll be the judge, and those who won't obey
Shall pay for what we spend upon the way.
Now if you all agree to what you've heard
Tell me at once without another word,
And I will make arrangements early for it."

830 Of course we all agreed, in fact we swore it
Delightedly, and made entreaty too
That he should act as he proposed to do,
Become our Governor in short, and be
Judge of our tales and general referee,
835 And set the supper at a certain price.
We promised to be ruled by his advice
Come high, come low; unanimously thus
We set him up in judgement over us.
More wine was fetched, the business being done;
840 We drank it off and up went everyone
to bed without a moment of delay.

To help the time pass, each of you
shall tell two stories on the outward trip
to Canterbury—that's what I have in mind.
Then, on the journey back home,

815 you'll tell another two stories from olden days.
We'll see which man tells the finest story—
that is, whose story has the best
moral message and is also the most pleasant.
He shall have his supper, paid by all of us,

820 right here in this tavern
when we come back again from Canterbury.
And to keep everyone happy and cheerful,
I'll ride along with you myself
at my own expense, serving as your guide.

825 I'll be the judge, and anyone who doesn't obey me
shall pay for what we spend along the way.
Now if you all agree to what you've heard,
tell me right away,
and I'll start arranging everything."

830 Of course, we all agreed. In fact, we swore to it
with joy. And we begged him
to do just as he proposed to do—
in short, to take charge of us,
judge and referee our tales,

835 then serve a supper at a certain price.
We promised to do just as he said,
no matter what. And so, with total agreement,
we made him judge over us all.
Business was then done, and more wine was served.

840 We drank it, and then everyone
went to bed without a moment's delay.

Early next morning at the spring of day
Up rose our Host and roused us like a cock,
Gathering us together in a flock,
845 And off we rode at slightly faster pace
Than walking to St. Thomas' watering-place;
And there our Host drew up, began to ease
His horse, and said, "Now, listen if you please,
My lords! Remember what you promised me.
850 If evensong and matins will agree

Let's see who shall be first to tell a tale.
And as I hope to drink good wine and ale
I'll be your judge. The rebel who disobeys,
However much the journey costs, he pays.
855 Now draw for cut and then we can depart;
The man who draws the shortest cut shall start."

Early next morning, right at daybreak,
our host got up and roused us like a rooster,
gathering us together in a flock.
845 Then we rode off at a pace slightly faster than a walk
until we got to St. Thomas' watering place.
There our host slowed down his horse
and said, "Now, please listen,
my lords! Remember what you promised me.
850 If you feel the same way this morning as you did last
night,
let's see who tells a tale first.
And as I hope to keep on drinking good wine and ale,
I'll be your judge. The rebel who disobeys
will pay for the journey, no matter how much it costs.
855 Now let's draw straws before we leave.
The man who draws the shortest straw shall start."

from

The Pardoner's Tale

The Prologue

"*M*y lords," he said, "in churches where I preach
I cultivate a haughty kind of speech
And ring it out as roundly as a bell;
I've got it all by heart, the tale I tell.
5   I have a text, it always is the same
And always has been, since I learnt the game,
Old as the hills and fresher than the grass,
Radix malorum est cupiditas.

❊   ❊   ❊

I preach, as you have heard me say before,
10   And tell a hundred lying mockeries more.
I take great pains, and stretching out my neck
To east and west I crane about and peck
Just like a pigeon sitting on a barn.
My hands and tongue together spin the yarn
15   And all my antics are a joy to see.
The curse of avarice and cupidity
Is all my sermon, for it frees the pelf.

The Pardoner

Out come the pence, and specially for myself,
For my exclusive purpose is to win
20   And not at all to castigate their sin.
Once dead what matter how their souls may fare?

from
The Pardoner's Tale

The Prologue

"*M*y lords," he said, "when I preach in churches,
I speak in a lofty style,
and my voice rings out as loudly as a bell.
I know what I'm going to say by heart,
5   and I use a saying which I've never changed
since I first learned this game.
It is as old as the hills, yet fresher than the grass:
'The love of money is the root of all evil.'

As I said before, I tell
10   a hundred false tales whenever I preach.
I really go all out, stretching my neck
to the east and west, and pecking
just like a pigeon sitting in a barn.
I spin my yarn, using hands and tongue together,
15   and my tricks are a joy to see.
My sermon is all about the curse
of greed and selfishness, for that loosens the purse
    strings.
Then out comes money, just for me.
For my real purpose is to get richer,
20   not at all to criticize sin.
Once they're dead, who cares what happens to their
    souls?

They can go blackberrying, for all I care!

* * *

And thus I preach against the very vice
I make my living out of—avarice.
25 And yet however guilty of that sin
Myself, with others I have power to win
Them from it, I can bring them to repent;
But that is not my principal intent.
Covetousness is both the root and stuff
30 Of all I preach. That ought to be enough.

* * *

"Well, then I give examples thick and fast
From bygone times, old stories from the past.
A yokel mind loves stories from of old,
Being the kind it can repeat and hold.
35 What! Do you think, as long as I can preach
And get their silver for the things I teach,
That I will live in poverty, from choice?
That's not the counsel of my inner voice!
No! Let me preach and beg from kirk to kirk
40 And never do an honest job of work,
No, nor make baskets, like St. Paul, to gain
A livelihood. I do not preach in vain.
There's no apostle I would counterfeit;
I mean to have money, wool and cheese and wheat
45 Though it were given me by the poorest lad

Or poorest village widow, though she had
A string of starving children, all agape.

No, let me drink the liquor of the grape
And keep a jolly wench in every town!

They can go gathering blackberries for all I care!

* * *

And so I preach against the very vice
I make my living out of—greed.
25　But although I'm guilty of that sin
myself, I have the power to save
others from it and bring them to repent.
Even so, that's not what I'm really trying to do.
Envy is both the message and the cause
30　of all my preaching. That ought to be enough.

* * *

"Well, I keep stories coming thick and fast
—old stories from bygone times.
A simpleton loves stories from long ago,
because they're easier to repeat and remember.
35　What! Do you think I'll willingly live in poverty
as long as I can preach
and get people's silver by it?
My conscience doesn't tell me to do that!
No! Let me preach and beg from church to church
40　and never take an honest job.
I'll not make baskets to earn a living
like St. Paul did. I do not preach for nothing.
There's no apostle I want to imitate.
I mean to have money, wool, cheese, and wheat.
45　I don't care if it's given to me by the poorest lad in
　　　the village—
or by the poorest widow, either, even if she has
a bunch of starving children with their mouths
　　　hanging open.
No, let me drink wine
and keep a jolly girl in every town!

* * *

50   "But listen, gentlemen; to bring things down
     To a conclusion, would you like a tale?
     Now as I've drunk a draft of corn-ripe ale,
     By God it stands to reason I can strike
     On some good story that you all will like.
55   For though I am a wholly vicious man
     Don't think I can't tell moral tales. I can!
     Here's one I often preach when out for winning. . . ."

from The Pardoner's Tale

*I*t's of three rioters I have to tell
     Who, long before the morning service bell,
60   Were sitting in a tavern for a drink.
     And as they sat, they heard the hand-bell clink

     Before a coffin going to the grave;
     One of them called the little tavern-knave
     And said "Go and find out at once—look spry!—
65   Whose corpse is in that coffin passing by;

     And see you get the name correctly too."
     "Sir," said the boy, "no need, I promise you;
     Two hours before you came here I was told.
     He was a friend of yours in days of old,
70   And suddenly, last night, the man was slain,
     Upon his bench, face up, dead drunk again.
     There came a privy thief, they call him Death,
     Who kills us all round here, and in a breath

     He speared him through the heart, he never stirred.

75   And then Death went his way without a word.

50   "But listen, gentlemen. To get right
      to the point, do you want a story?
      Now that I've drunk a glass of tasty ale,
      by God, you can be sure I'll tell
      some good story that you all will like.
55   For even though I'm completely vicious,
      don't think I can't tell moral tales. I can!
      Here's one I often preach when I'm really out for
            money. . . ."

from **The Pardoner's Tale**

"*I*'m going to tell a tale of three rioters.[16]
Long before the morning church bells rang,
60   they were sitting in a tavern, drinking.
      As they sat, they heard the clink of a little funeral
            bell
      going in front of a coffin headed for the grave.
      One of them called the little serving boy
      and said, "Go out there at once—look lively!
65   And find out whose corpse is in that coffin passing
            by.
      And be sure to get the name right, too."
      "Sir," said the boy, "I promise you, there is no need.
      I was told two hours before you showed up here.
      He used to be a friend of yours,
70   and suddenly, last night, he was killed,
      lying face up on his bench, dead drunk as usual.
      A cunning thief named Death,
      who kills us all around here, killed him. Death
            speared your friend
      through the heart with a breath, and he never
            stirred again.
75   Then Death went away without a word.

16 **rioters:** revelers; partiers

He's killed a thousand in the present plague,
And, sir, it doesn't do to be too vague
If you should meet him; you had best be wary.
Be on your guard with such an adversary,
80 Be primed to meet him everywhere you go,

That's what my mother said. It's all I know."

✳ ✳ ✳

The publican joined in with, "By St. Mary,

What the child says is right; you'd best be wary,
This very year he killed, in a large village
85 A mile away, man, woman, serf at tillage,
Page in the household, children—all there were.
Yes, I imagine that he lives round there.
It's well to be prepared in these alarms,
He might do you dishonor." "Huh, God's arms!"
90 The rioter said, "Is he so fierce to meet?
I'll search for him, by Jesus, street by street.
God's blessed bones! I'll register a vow!
Here, chaps! The three of us together now,
Hold up your hands, like me, and we'll be brothers
95 In this affair, and each defend the others,
And we will kill this traitor Death, I say!
Away with him as he has made away
With all our friends. God's dignity! Tonight!"

✳ ✳ ✳

They made their bargain, swore with appetite,
100 These three, to live and die for one another
As brother-born might swear to his born brother.
And up they started in their drunken rage
And made towards this village which the page

He's killed a thousand in the plague lately,
and sir, you'd better take care
if you should meet him. Be cautious
and on your guard against an enemy like that,
80   and always be prepared to meet him everywhere you
        go.
That's what my mother said, and that's enough for
        me."

❋ ❋ ❋

The innkeeper joined right in, and said, "By
        St. Mary,
the boy is right, you'd better watch out.
This very year, Death killed off an entire village
85   a mile from here. Men, women, farmers,
servants, children—he killed them all.
Yes, I imagine that he lives around there.
So be warned, and stay on guard,
or he might do you harm." "Huh, by God's arms!"
90   the rioter said. "Is he really so fierce?
I'll search for him, by Jesus, street by street.
God's blessed bones! I promise it right now.
Here, chaps! Let's all three of us
raise our hands together, and we'll be brothers
95   in this business. We'll defend each other
and kill this traitor Death, I swear!
We'll do away with him, just as he has done away
with all our friends. By God, we'll do it tonight!"

❋ ❋ ❋

All three of them agreed, and they swore eagerly
100   to live and die for one another,
just as born brothers might do.
And they got up in their drunken rage
and made toward the village that the servant

And publican had spoken of before.
105 Many and grisly were the oaths they swore,
Tearing Christ's blessed body to a shred;
"If we can only catch him, Death is dead!"

❋ ❋ ❋

When they had gone not fully half a mile,
Just as they were about to cross a stile,
110 They came upon a very poor old man
Who humbly greeted them and thus began,
"God look to you, my lords, and give you quiet!"
To which the proudest of these men of riot
Gave back the answer, "What, old fool? Give place!
115 Why are you all wrapped up except your face?
Why live so long? Isn't it time to die?"

❋ ❋ ❋

The old, old fellow looked him in the eye
And said, "Because I never yet have found,
Though I have walked to India, searching round
120 Village and city on my pilgrimage,

One who would change his youth to have my age.
And so my age is mine and must be still
Upon me, for such time as God may will.

❋ ❋ ❋

"Not even Death, alas, will take my life;
125 So, like a wretched prisoner at strife
Within himself, I walk alone and wait
About the earth, which is my mother's gate,
Knock-knocking with my staff from night to noon
And crying, 'Mother, open to me soon!

and innkeeper had spoken of before.
105 They swore many grim oaths,
tearing Christ's blessed body to shreds with words,
saying, "If we can only catch him, Death is dead!"

❋ ❋ ❋

They hadn't gone a full half a mile
when they reached some steps leading over a wall.
110 There they met a very poor old man,
who humbly greeted them with these words:
"God bless you, my lords, and give you peace!"
To which the proudest of these rioters
replied, "What, old fool? Get out of the way!
115 Why are you all wrapped up except for your face?
Why do you live so long? Isn't it about time you were
dead?"

❋ ❋ ❋

The old, old fellow looked him in the eye
and said, "I'm here because I've walked
all the way to India, searching
120 in villages and cities everywhere, but I've never
found
anyone who would give up his youth to take my age.
And so I have my age and always shall,
until God decides to take it from me.

❋ ❋ ❋

"Alas, not even Death will take my life.
125 So like a prisoner struggling
inside himself, I walk alone, waiting
upon the earth, which is like a mother's gate.
I knock on the ground with my staff night and day,
crying, 'Mother, open to me soon!

130   Look at me, mother, won't you let me in?
      See how I wither, flesh and blood and skin!
      Alas! When will these bones be laid to rest?
      Mother, I would exchange—for that were best—
      The wardrobe in my chamber, standing there
135   So long, for yours! Aye, for a shirt of hair
      To wrap me in!' She has refused her grace,

      Whence comes the pallor of my withered face.

❋   ❋   ❋

      "But it dishonored you when you began
      To speak so roughly, sir, to an old man,
140   Unless he had injured you in word or deed.
      It says in holy writ, as you may read,
      'Thou shalt rise up before the hoary head
      And honor it.' And therefore be it said
      'Do no more harm to an old man than you,
145   Being now young, would have another do
      When you are old'—if you should live till then.
      And so may God be with you, gentlemen,
      For I must go whither I have to go."

❋   ❋   ❋

      "By God," the gambler said, "you shan't do so,
150   You don't get off so easy, by St. John!
      I heard you mention, just a moment gone,
      A certain traitor Death who singles out
      And kills the fine young fellows hereabout.
      And you're his spy, by God! You wait a bit.
155   Say where he is or you shall pay for it,

      By God and by the Holy Sacrament!
      I say you've joined together by consent
      To kill us younger folk, you thieving swine!"

130 Look at me, mother, won't you let me in?
See how my flesh, blood, and skin all wither!
Alas! When will my bones be laid to rest?
Mother, I know it would be best to exchange
the chest which has long stood in my room
135 for yours! Oh, for a rough shirt
to wrap around myself!' But she has refused her
favor,
and that is why my withered face is pale.

✷ ✷ ✷

"But it was shameful of you
to speak so roughly to an old man, sir—
140 unless he had injured you in word or deed.
You may well read in the Bible where it says,
'You shall stand up before a white-haired man
and honor him.' And so let it be said,
'Do not harm an old man any more than you,
145 now young, would wish another to do
when you are old'—if you live that long.
And so may God be with you, gentlemen,
for I must go where I must go."

✷ ✷ ✷

"By God," the gambler said, "you won't go yet.
150 By St. John, you don't get off that easy!
Just a moment ago, I heard you mention
a certain traitor Death who chooses
and kills fine young people in these parts.
And you're his spy, by God! You wait a bit.
155 Tell where he is, or by God and the Holy
Sacrament,[17]
you'll pay for it!
I say you two have agreed to work together
to kill us younger folk, you thieving swine!"

17 **Holy Sacrament:** the taking of communion, in which
bread and wine represent the body of Christ

＊ ＊ ＊

"Well, sirs," he said, "if it be your design
160 To find out Death, turn up this crooked way
Towards that grove, I left him there today
Under a tree, and there you'll find him waiting.
He isn't one to hide for all your prating.
You see that oak? He won't be far to find.
165 And God protect you that redeemed mankind,
Aye, and amend you!" Thus that ancient man.

＊ ＊ ＊

At once the three young rioters began
To run, and reached the tree, and there they found
A pile of golden florins on the ground,
170 New-coined, eight bushels of them as they thought.
No longer was it Death those fellows sought,
For they were all so thrilled to see the sight,
The florins were so beautiful and bright,
That down they sat beside the precious pile.
175 The wickedest spoke first after a while.
"Brothers," he said, "you listen to what I say.
I'm pretty sharp although I joke away.
It's clear that Fortune has bestowed this treasure
To let us live in jollity and pleasure.
180 Light come, light go! We'll spend it as we ought.
God's precious dignity! Who would have thought
This morning was to be our lucky day?

＊ ＊ ＊

"If one could only get the gold away,
Back to my house, or else to yours, perhaps—
185 For as you know, the gold is ours, chaps—
We'd all be at the top of fortune, hey?
But certainly it can't be done by day.

❋ ❋ ❋

"Well, sirs," the old man said, "if it's your plan
160 to find Death, go up this crooked path
toward the grove. I left him there today
under a tree, and you'll find him waiting there.
He isn't likely to hide, despite all your talk.
You see that oak? He won't be far away.
165 And may God, who saved mankind, protect you—
yes, and improve you, too!" So said that old, old man.

❋ ❋ ❋

The three young rioters ran at once
and reached the tree, where they found
a pile of golden coins, newly minted, on the ground.
170 It looked as if there were eight bushels of them.
Those young fellows no longer sought Death,
so thrilled were they at what they saw.
The coins were so beautiful and bright
that they sat down beside the precious pile.
175 After a while, the wickedest spoke first.
"Brothers," he said, "listen to what I say.
I'm pretty sharp, for all my joking.
It's clear that Fortune has given us this treasure.
so that we can live jolly, pleasant lives.
180 Easy come, easy go! We'll spend it as we please.
God's precious dignity! Who would have guessed
this morning would be our lucky day?

❋ ❋ ❋

"If only we could get this gold away,
back to my house or to yours—
185 for as you know, the gold is ours, boys.
Then we'd be riding high, eh?
But it certainly can't be done by day.

People would call us robbers—a strong gang,
So our own property would make us hang.
190 No, we must bring this treasure back by night
Some prudent way, and keep it out of sight.

And so as a solution I propose
We draw for lots and see the way it goes;
The one who draws the longest, lucky man,
195 Shall run to town as quickly as he can
To fetch us bread and wine—but keep things dark—
While two remain in hiding here to mark
Our heap of treasure. If there's no delay,
When night comes down we'll carry it away,
200 All three of us, wherever we have planned."

He gathered lots and hid them in his hand
Bidding them draw for where the luck should fall.
It fell upon the youngest of them all,
And off he ran at once towards the town.

205 As soon as he had gone the first sat down
And thus began a parley with the other:
"You know that you can trust me as a brother;
Now let me tell you where your profit lies;
You know our friend has gone to get supplies
210 And here's a lot of gold that is to be
Divided equally amongst us three.
Nevertheless, if I could shape things thus
So that we shared it out—the two of us—
Wouldn't you take it as a friendly act?"

215 "But how?" the other said. "He knows the fact

People would call us a gang of robbers,
and so we'd hang because of our own property.
190 No, we must find some careful way
to bring this treasure back by night and keep it
    hidden.
So I propose this solution:
Let's draw straws.
The lucky one who draws the longest
195 shall run to town as quickly as he can
to get us bread and wine, saying nothing to anyone.
The other two will stay hiding here, watching over
our heap of treasure. If all goes right,
we'll carry it away when night comes
200 to someplace we've agreed upon."

He gathered straws and hid them in his hand,
telling the others to draw for them.
The youngest picked the longest,
and he ran away at once toward the town.

205 As soon as he had gone, the first sat down
with the other and began to talk to him:
"You know that you can trust me as a brother,
so let me tell you what's best for you.
Our friend has gone to get supplies,
210 and here's a lot of gold that's supposed to be
divided equally among the three of us.
But if I could work things out
so that only we two shared it—
wouldn't you think that friendly of me?"

215 "But how?" the other said. "He knows

That all the gold was left with me and you;
What can we tell him? What are we to do?"

* * *

"Is it a bargain," said the first, "or no?
For I can tell you in a word or so
220   What's to be done to bring the thing about."
"Trust me," the other said, "you needn't doubt
My word. I won't betray you, I'll be true."

* * *

"Well," said his friend, "you see that we are two,

And two are twice as powerful as one.
225   Now look; when he comes back, get up in fun

To have a wrestle; then, as you attack,
I'll up and put my dagger through his back
While you and he are struggling, as in game;
Then draw your dagger too and do the same.
230   Then all this money will be ours to spend,
Divided equally of course, dear friend.
Then we can gratify our lusts and fill
The day with dicing at our own sweet will."
Thus these two miscreants agreed to slay
235   The third and youngest, as you heard me say.

* * *

The youngest, as he ran towards the town,
Kept turning over, rolling up and down
Within his heart the beauty of those bright
New florins, saying, "Lord, to think I might
240   Have all that treasure to myself alone!
Could there be anyone beneath the throne

that all the gold is here with you and me.
What can we tell him? What can we do?"

✳ ✳ ✳

"Is it a deal or not?" replied the first.
"For I can tell you very quickly
220   what we can do to make it happen."
"Trust me," the other said. "You needn't doubt
my word. I won't betray you. I'll be true."

✳ ✳ ✳

"Well," said his friend, "you see that there are two
    of us,
and two are twice as powerful as one.
225   Now look—when he comes back, get up and wrestle
    him,
as if in fun. Then, as you attack,
I'll stab him in the back with my dagger
while you and he are struggling.
Draw your dagger, too, and do the same.
230   Then all his money will be ours—
divided equally, of course, dear friend.
Then we can satisfy our lusts and spend
our days playing dice as much as we want."
And so these two villains agreed to kill
235   the third and youngest, as you've heard me say.

✳ ✳ ✳

As the youngest ran toward the town,
he kept remembering in his heart again and again
the beauty of those bright new coins.
He said, "Lord, to think I might
240   have all that treasure, just for myself!
Could anyone beneath God's throne

Of God so happy as I then should be?"

❄ ❄ ❄

    And so the Fiend, our common enemy,
Was given power to put it in his thought
245   That there was always poison to be bought,
And that with poison he could kill his friends.
To men in such a state the Devil sends
Thoughts of this kind, and has a full permission
To lure them on to sorrow and perdition;
250   For this young man was utterly content
To kill them both and never to repent.

❄ ❄ ❄

    And on he ran, he had no thought to tarry,
Came to the town, found an apothecary
And said, "Sell me some poison if you will,
255   I have a lot of rats I want to kill
And there's a polecat too about my yard
That takes my chickens and it hits me hard;
But I'll get even, as is only right,
With vermin that destroy a man by night."

❄ ❄ ❄

260   The chemist answered, "I've a preparation
Which you shall have, and by my soul's salvation
If any living creature eat or drink
A mouthful, ere he has the time to think,
Though he took less then makes a grain of wheat,
265   You'll see him fall down dying at your feet;
Yes, die he must, and in so short a while
You'd hardly have the time to walk a mile,
The poison is so strong, you understand."

be as happy as I would be then?"

✻ ✻ ✻

And so the Devil, everyone's enemy,
put this idea into his head:
245   There is always poison that can be bought,
and with poison, he could kill his friends.
The Devil often sends thoughts of this kind
to men in such a state, and he has full permission
to lure them on to sorrow and damnation.
250   For this young man was completely happy
to kill them both and never repent.

✻ ✻ ✻

And on he ran, not stopping to think further.
He came to the town, where he found a druggist,
and said, "Please, sell me some poison.
255   I have a lot of rats I want to kill,
and there's also a polecat[18] about my yard
that takes my chickens, and it costs me a lot.
It's only right that I get even
with animals that trouble me by night."

✻ ✻ ✻

260   The druggist answered, "I've just the poison
for you. And by my soul's salvation,
I promise you this: If any creature eats or drinks
a mouthful, he'll fall down dying at your feet
before he has time to think—
265   even if he took only the tiniest amount.
Yes, he must die, and so quickly
that you'll hardly have time to walk a mile.
That's how strong the poison is, you see."

18 **polecat:** a weasel-like animal

＊ ＊ ＊

This cursed fellow grabbed into his hand
270 The box of poison and away he ran
Into a neighboring street, and found a man
Who lent him three large bottles. He withdrew
And deftly poured the poison into two.
He kept the third one clean, as well he might,
275 For his own drink, meaning to work all night
Stacking the gold and carrying it away.
And when this rioter, this devil's clay,
Had filled his bottles up with wine, all three,
Back to rejoin his comrades sauntered he.

＊ ＊ ＊

280 Why make a sermon of it? Why waste breath?
Exactly in the way they'd planned his death
They fell on him and slew him, two to one.
Then said the first of them when this was done,
"Now for a drink. Sit down and let's be merry,
285 For later on there'll be the corpse to bury."
And, as it happened, reaching for a sup,
He took a bottle full of poison up
And drank; and his companion, nothing loth,
Drank from it also, and they perished both.

＊ ＊ ＊

290 There is, in Avicenna's long relation
Concerning poison and his operation,
Trust me, no ghastlier section to transcend
What these two wretches suffered at their end.
Thus these two murderers received their due,

295 So did the treacherous young poisoner too.

This cursed fellow grabbed
270   the box of poison and ran
to a neighboring street, where he found a man
who lent him three large bottles.
Then he carefully poured the poison into two.
As you might guess, he kept the third one clean
275   to drink from himself. He planned to work all night,
stacking the gold and carrying it away.
And when this rioter, this devilish creature,
had filled all three of his bottles up with wine,
he strolled back to rejoin his friends.

280   Why make a sermon of it? Why waste breath?
They fell on him and killed him, two to one,
just as they'd planned all along.
When this was done, the first one said,
"Now for a drink. Sit down, let's be merry,
285   for we'll have to bury this corpse shortly."
And as things turned out, he reached for a bottle,
taking one that was full of poison,
and drank. And his companion, all too willingly,
drank from it also, and they both died.

※ ※ ※

290   Now, [an Arabic doctor] once wrote at length
about how poisons work.
But trust me, he wrote nothing to surpass
how those two wretches suffered as they died.
And so those two murderers got what they
      deserved—
295   and so did the treacherous young poisoner, too.

O cursed sin! O blackguardly excess!
O treacherous homicide! O wickedness!
O gluttony that lusted on and diced!

Dearly beloved, God forgive your sin
300 And keep you from the vice of avarice!
My holy pardon frees you all of this,
Provided that you make the right approaches,
That is with sterling, rings, or silver brooches.
Bow down your heads under this holy bull!
305 Come on, you women, offer up your wool!
I'll write your name into my ledger; so!
Into the bliss of Heaven you shall go.
For I'll absolve you by my holy power,
You that make offering, clean as at the hour
310 When you were born. . . . That, sirs, is how I preach.
And Jesu Christ, soul's healer, aye, the leech
Of every soul, grant pardon and relieve you
Of sin, for that is best, I won't deceive you.

One thing I should have mentioned in my tale,
315 Dear people. I've some relics in my bale
And pardons too, as full and fine, I hope,
As any in England, given me by the Pope.

If there be one among you that is willing
To have my absolution for a shilling
320 Devoutly given, come! and do not harden
Your hearts but kneel in humbleness for pardon;
Or else, receive my pardon as we go.
You can renew it every town or so

※ ※ ※

Oh, cursed sin! Oh, villainous waste!
Oh, treacherous murder! Oh, wickedness!
Oh, gluttony, lust, and dice-playing!

※ ※ ※

Dearly beloved, God forgive your vices
300   and keep you from the sin of greed!
My holy pardon will free you from this,
provided you pay me properly—
that is, with silver rings or brooches.
Humble yourself with this holy paper!
305   Come on, women, offer me some wool!
I'll write your name into my records, just so!
And then you'll go to Heaven in bliss.
For if you make an offering, I'll forgive you
by my holy power, making you as clean as the hour
310   when you were born. . . . And that is how I preach, sirs.
May Jesus Christ, soul's healer—indeed, the doctor
of every soul—pardon you and forgive your sins.
For that is best, I won't lie to you.

※ ※ ※

One thing I should have mentioned in my tale,
315   dear people. I've got some relics in my satchel—
and some pardons, too. I think they are as fine
as any pardons in England, since they were given me
      by the pope.
If there is anyone here who wants
a holy pardon for a shilling,[19]
320   then come! Do not harden
your hearts, but kneel humbly for forgiveness.
Or if you like, receive my pardon as we ride.
You can renew it at every town or so,

19 **shilling:** twelve English pence

Always provided that you still renew
325 Each time, and in good money, what is due.
It is an honor to you to have found
A pardoner with his credentials sound
Who can absolve you as you ply the spur
In any accident that may occur.
330 For instance—we are all at Fortune's beck—
Your horse may throw you down and break your
    neck.
What a security it is to all
To have me here among you and at call
With pardon for the lowly and the great
335 When soul leaves body for the future state!
And I advise our Host here to begin,
The most enveloped of you all in sin.
Come forward, Host, you shall be the first to pay,
And kiss my holy relics right away.
340 Only a groat. Come on, unbuckle your purse!"

❋ ❋ ❋

"No, no," said he, "not I, and may the curse
Of Christ descend upon me if I do! . . ."

❋ ❋ ❋

The Pardoner said nothing, not a word;
He was so angry that he couldn't speak.
345 "Well," said our Host, "if you're for showing pique,
I'll joke no more, not with an angry man."

❋ ❋ ❋

as long as you always pay
325   what you owe each time, with good money.
You are honored to have found
a pardoner in good standing,
who can forgive you as you spur your horse
if any accident should happen.
330   After all, you never know when bad luck could strike,
and your horse might throw you down and break
     your neck.
What a comfort it is to you all
to have me here, ready and waiting
with pardons for both low and high of rank,
335   whenever the soul should leave the body!
And I advise our host to start,
because he is the most sinful of you all.
Come forward, Host, and pay first,
and kiss my holy relics right away.
340   Just one little coin. Come on, open your purse!"

"No, no, not I," said the host.
"And may Christ curse me if I do! . . ."

The pardoner said nothing, not a word.
He was so angry that he couldn't speak.
345   "Well," said our host, "if you're so offended,
I won't joke anymore—not with an angry man."

The worthy Knight immediately began,
Seeing the fun was getting rather rough,
And said, "No more, we've all had quite enough.

350 Now, Master Pardoner, perk up, look cheerly!
And you, Sir Host, whom I esteem so dearly,
I beg of you to kiss the Pardoner.

"Come, Pardoner, draw nearer, my dear sir.
355 Let's laugh again and keep the ball in play."
They kissed, and we continued on our way.

The worthy Knight saw right away
that the fun was wearing rather thin,
and said, "No more of this, we've all had quite
    enough.
350   Now, Master Pardoner, perk up, be cheerful!
And you, Sir Host, whom I respect so much,
I beg of you to kiss the Pardoner.

❁ ❁ ❁

"Come nearer, Pardoner, my dear sir.
355   Let's laugh again and keep the stories coming."
They kissed, and we continued on our way.

Lord Randal

"***O*** where ha' you been, Lord Randal, my son?
And where ha' you been, my handsome young man?"
"I ha' been at the greenwood; mother, make my bed
    soon,
For I'm wearied wi' huntin', and fain wad lie down."

5   "And wha' met ye there, Lord Randal, my son?
And wha' met you there, my handsome
    young man?"
"O I met wi' my true-love; mother, make my
    bed soon,
For I'm wearied wi' huntin', and fain wad lie down."

"***O***, where have you been, Lord Randal, my son?
O, where have you been, my handsome young man?"
"I've been to the green woods. Mother, make my bed
    soon,
For I'm weary from hunting, and I'd like to lie down."

5   "And who did you meet there, Lord Randal, my son?
And who did you meet there, my handsome
    young man?"
"O, I met with my true love. Mother, make my
    bed soon,
For I'm weary from hunting, and I'd like to lie down."

"And wha' did she give you, Lord Randal, my son?
10   And wha' did she give you, my handsome young
      man?"
"Eels fried in a pan; mother, make my bed soon,
For I'm wearied wi' huntin', and fain wad lie down."

"And wha' gat your leavin's, Lord Randal, my son?
And wha' gat your leavin's, my handsome young man?"
15   "My hawks and my hounds; mother, make my bed
      soon,
For I'm wearied wi' huntin', and fain wad lie down."

"And wha' becam' of them, Lord Randal, my son?
And wha' becam' of them, my handsome
      young man?"
"They stretched their legs out and died; mother,
      make my bed soon,
20   For I'm wearied wi' huntin', and fain wad lie down."

"O I fear you are poisoned, Lord Randal, my son!
I fear you are poisoned, my handsome young man!"
"O yes, I am poisoned; mother, make my bed soon,
For I'm sick at the heart, and I fain wad lie down."

25   "What d' ye leave to your mother, Lord Randal, my
      son?
What d' ye leave to your mother, my handsome
      young man?"
"Four and twenty milk kye; mother, make my bed
      soon,
For I'm sick at the heart, and I fain wad lie down."

"And what did she give you, Lord Randal, my son?
And what did she give you, my handsome young
    man?"
"Eels fried in a pan. Mother, make my bed soon,
For I'm weary from hunting, and I'd like to lie down."

"And who ate the scraps, Lord Randal, my son?
And who ate the scraps, my handsome young man?"
"My hawks and my hounds. Mother, make my bed
    soon,
For I'm weary from hunting, and I'd like to lie down."

"And what happened to them, Lord Randal, my son?
And what happened to them, my handsome
    young man?"
"They stretched their legs out and died. Mother,
    make my bed soon.
For I'm weary from hunting, and I'd like to lie down."

"O, I fear you are poisoned, Lord Randal, my son!
I fear you are poisoned, my handsome young man!"
"O, yes, I am poisoned. Mother, make my bed soon,
For I'm sick at the heart, and I'd like to lie down."

"What do you leave to your mother, Lord Randal, my
    son?
What do you leave to your mother, my handsome
    young man?"
"Twenty-four milk cows. Mother, make my bed
    soon,
For I'm sick at the heart, and I'd like to lie down."

"What d' ye leave to your sister, Lord Randal, my
    son?
30 What d' ye leave to your sister, my handsome
    young man?"
"My gold and my silver; mother, make my bed soon,
For I'm sick at the heart, and I fain wad lie down."

"What d' ye leave to your brother, Lord Randal,
    my son?
What d' ye leave to your brother, my handsome
    young man?"
35 "My houses and my lands; mother, make my bed
    soon,
For I'm sick at the heart, and I fain wad lie down."

"What d' ye leave to your true-love, Lord Randal,
    my son?
What d' ye leave to your true-love, my handsome
    young man?"
"I leave her hell and fire; mother make my bed soon,
40 For I'm sick at the heart, and I fain wad lie down."

"What do you leave to your sister, Lord Randal, my
    son?
30   What do you leave to your sister, my handsome
    young man?"
My gold and my silver. Mother, make my bed soon,
For I'm sick at the heart, and I'd like to lie down."

"What do you leave to your brother, Lord Randal,
    my son?
What do you leave to your brother, my handsome
    young man?"
35   "My houses and lands. Mother, make my bed
    soon,
For I'm sick at the heart, and I'd like to lie down."

"What do you leave to your true love, Lord Randal,
    my son?
What do you leave to your true love, my handsome
    young man?"
"I leave her hell and fire. Mother, make my bed soon,
40   For I'm sick at the heart, and I'd like to lie down."

Get Up and
Bar the Door

*I*t fell about the Martinmas time,
    And a gay time it was then,
When our goodwife got puddings to make,
    And she's boild them in the pan.

5   The wind sae cauld blew south and north,
        And blew into the floor;
Quoth our goodman to our goodwife,
    "Gae out and bar the door."

"My hand is in my hussyfskap,
10   Goodman, as ye may see;
An it should nae be barrd this hundred year,
    It's no be barrd for me."

They made a paction tween them twa,
    They made it firm and sure,
15   That the first word whaeer should speak,
    Should rise and bar the door.

Then by there came two gentlemen,
    At twelve o clock at night,

Get Up and Bar the Door

*I*t happened around Martinmas,[1]
    And a gay time it was then.
Our goodwife[2] was making sausages
    And was boiling them in the pan.

5 The cold, cold wind blew south and north,
    And blew upon the floor.
Said our goodman[3] to our goodwife,
    "Go out and bar the door."

"I'm busy with my household work,
10   Goodman, as you can see.
If the door's not barred for a hundred years,
    It'll not be barred by me."

They made a pact between them then,
    They made it firm and sure,
15 That whichever of them did speak first,
    Must get up and bar the door.

Then two gentlemen came by
    At twelve o'clock at night.

1 **Martinmas:** the feast of St. Martin, celebrated on November 11
2 **goodwife:** Mrs.; woman of the house
3 **goodman:** Mr.; man of the house

And they could neither see house nor hall,
20   Nor coal nor candle-light.

"Now whether is this a rich man's house,
      Or whether it is a poor?"
But neer a word ane o them speak,
    For barring of the door.

25   And first they ate the white puddings,
      And then they ate the black;
Tho muckle thought the goodwife to hersel,
    Yet neer a word she spake.

Then said the one unto the other,
30   "Here, man, tak ye my knife;
Do ye tak aff the auld man's beard,
    And I'll kiss the goodwife."

"But there's nae water in the house,
      And what shall we do than?"
35   "What ails ye at the pudding-broo,
    That boils into the pan?"

O up then started our goodman,
      An angry man was he:
"Will ye kiss my wife before my een,
40   And scad me wi pudding-bree?"

Then up and started our goodwife,
      Gied three skips on the floor:
"Goodman, you've spoken the foremost word,
Get up and bar the door."

And they could see neither house nor hall,
20   Nor coal nor candlelight.

They asked, "Is this a rich man's house,
      Or is it instead poor?"
But neither wife nor husband spoke,
      For barring of the door.

25   The gentlemen ate the white sausages first,
      And then they ate the black.
Though the wife thought much of this,
      Not one word did she speak.

Then one gentleman said to the other,
30   "Here, man, take my knife.
Use it to shave the old man's beard,
      And I'll kiss the goodwife."

"But there's no water for shaving here,
      So what shall we do then?"
35   "What's wrong with using the sausage brew
      That boils up in the pan?"

Oh, then our goodman started up—
      An angry man it's true:
"Will you kiss my wife before my eyes,
40   And scald me with sausage brew?"

And then our goodwife started up,
      And skipped three times on the floor.
"Goodman, it's you who've spoken first.
      Get up and bar the door."

INTRODUCTION TO

Sir Gawain and the Green Knight

Sir Gawain and the Green Knight was written by an unknown author during the late 14th century. This author is commonly known as the "Pearl Poet" because of another poem he wrote entitled *The Pearl*.

Even when it was written, *Sir Gawain* was part of an old tradition of stories about Arthur, the legendary British king. Arthur and his wife Guinevere entertained the knights of the Round Table in the city of Camelot. Sir Gawain, one of these knights, was also Arthur's nephew.

In Medieval England, chivalry was valued very highly. Chivalry was a code of behavior to be followed by nobles, especially knights. As you read the following excerpts from *Sir Gawain*, notice how extremely well-mannered everyone is. For example, in order to simply approach the Green Knight, Sir Gawain must ask Arthur to request him to do so.

Knights were expected to obey countless rules of this sort. In addition to being skillful with arms, they had to be courteous, loyal, courageous, and generous. Above all else, a knight must be a man of his word.

Sir Gawain and the Green Knight can be read almost as a textbook in chivalrous behavior. In fact, the story tells how Sir Gawain's chivalry is tested by the Green Knight.

Gawain passes most of these tests very well. He is certainly a man of his word. He keeps a grim appointment with the Green Knight that seems to mean sure death.

Then, when he is a guest in the castle of a mysterious nobleman (really the Green Knight), Gawain shows great courtesy and loyalty. He does not surrender to the seductive charms of the nobleman's wife. He even shares the chaste kisses he receives from her with his host.

But Gawain falters slightly when it comes to

courage. He accepts the gift of a magical green sash from the nobleman's wife, hoping that it will protect him from injury. The nobleman has every right to kill Gawain for this lapse.

But the nobleman himself shows generosity in not taking Gawain's life. For it is also chivalrous to accept the frailties of virtuous men and women.

Medieval readers of *Sir Gawain* would have recognized another aspect of chivalry in the poem. This is called courtly love. A knight was typically in love with a beautiful lady. But because the lady was almost always married, the knight's love had to remain chaste.

Nevertheless, the knight would prove his devotion to the lady in all kinds of ways. For example, he would win tournaments and battles in her name. And he would always carry some gift he had received from her.

At the end of the poem, Sir Gawain vows to wear the green sash always as a reminder of his failure. But the sash really means more than that. In wearing it, Sir Gawain is keeping a promise to the lady who gave it to him. "I swear through fire and ice," Gawain tells her, "To be your humble knight."

Round table of King Arthur of Brittany, from a miniature of the fourteenth century.

Sir Gawain, from Le
Roman de Lancelot
du Lac (detail)
(c. 14th century)

from Sir Gawain
and the Green Knight

The "Pearl Poet"
translated by John Gardner

*S*plendid that knight errant stood in a splay of
green,
And green, too, was the mane of his mighty destrier;
Fair fanning tresses enveloped the fighting man's
shoulders,
And over his breast hung a beard as big as a bush;

5 The beard and the huge mane burgeoning forth from
his head
Were clipped off clean in a straight line over his
elbows,
And the upper half of each arm was hidden
underneath
As if covered by a king's chaperon, closed round the
neck.
The mane of the marvelous horse was much the
same,

10 Well crisped and combed and carefully pranked with
knots,

from Sir Gawain and the Green Knight

The "Pearl Poet"
translated by John Gardner

As King Arthur and his followers celebrate Christmas and the new year, they are interrupted by the arrival of a gigantic knight who is green from head to toe.

*T*hat wandering knight stood splendidly in a green space,
And the mane of his mighty horse was green too.
Light, thick hair covered the fighting man's
  shoulders
And a beard as big as a bush hung over his breast.
5 The beard and huge mane sprouting forth from
  his head
Were clipped off clean in a straight line over his
  elbows.
The upper half of each arm was hidden
  underneath
As if covered by a king's hood closed round the
  neck.
The mane of the marvelous horse was much the
  same,
10 Well cut and combed, and carefully tied with
  bows.

Threads of gold interwoven with the glorious green,
Now a thread of hair, now another thread of gold;
The tail of the horse and the forelock were tricked
    the same way,
And both were bound up with a band of brilliant
    green

15   Adorned with glittering jewels the length of the dock,
Then caught up tight with a thong in a criss-cross knot
Where many a bell tinkled brightly, all burnished gold.
So monstrous a mount, so mighty a man in the saddle
Was never once encountered on all this earth

20   till then;
            His eyes, like lightning, flashed,
            And it seemed to many a man,
            That any man who clashed
            With him would not long stand.

25   But the huge man came unarmed, without helmet or
    hauberk,
No breastplate or gorget or iron cleats on his arms;
He brought neither shield nor spearshaft to shove or
    to smite,
But instead he held in one hand a bough of the holly
That grows most green when all the groves are bare

30   And held in the other an ax, immense and
    unwieldy,
A pitiless battleblade terrible to tell of.

King Arthur stared down at the stranger before the
    high dais
And greeted him nobly, for nothing on earth
    frightened him.
And he said to him, "Sir, you are welcome in this
    place;

35   I am the head of this court. They call me Arthur.

Threads of gold were woven with the glorious green,
Here a thread of hair, there another thread of gold.
The horse's tail and the top of his mane were
    trimmed the same way,
And both were tied up with a band of brilliant green.

15   The tail had glittering jewels down its length,
Held tight with a strap in a criss-cross knot
Where many bells of glistening gold tinkled brightly.
So monstrous a horse, so mighty a man in the saddle
Was never once encountered on all this earth
20   till then.
               His eyes, like lightning, flashed.
               It seemed to many a man,
               That any man who clashed
               With him would not long stand.

25   But the huge man came unarmed, without helmet or
    armor—
No iron on his breast, throat, or arms.
He brought neither shield nor spear to shove or to
    strike.
Instead, he held in one hand a branch of the holly
That grows greenest when all the groves are bare.
30   And he held in the other hand an ax, huge and
    bulky—
A fierce battleblade terrible to tell of.

King Arthur stared down at the stranger before the
    high platform
And greeted him nobly, for nothing on earth
    frightened him.
He said to him, "Sir, you are welcome in this
    place.
35   I am the head of this court. They call me Arthur.

Get down from your horse, I beg you, and join us for
    dinner,
And then whatever you seek we will gladly see to."
But the stranger said, "No, so help me God on high,
My errand is hardly to sit at my ease in your castle!
40   But friend, since your praises are sung so far and
    wide,
Your castle the best ever built, people say, and your
    barons
The stoutest men in steel armor that ever rode
    steeds,
Most mighty and most worthy of all mortal men
And tough devils to toy with in tournament games,
45   And since courtesy is in flower in this court, they say,
All these tales, in truth, have drawn me to you at
    this time.
You may be assured by this holly branch I bear
That I come to you in peace, not spoiling for battle.
If I'd wanted to come in finery, fixed up for fighting,
50   I have back at home both a helmet and a hauberk,
A shield and a sharp spear that shines like fire,
And other weapons that I know pretty well how to
    use.
But since I don't come here for battle, my clothes are
    mere cloth.
Now if you are truly as bold as the people all say,
55   You will grant me gladly the little game that I ask
                    as my right."
               Arthur gave him answer
               And said, "Sir noble knight,
               If it's a duel you're after,
60   We'll furnish you your fight."

"Good heavens, I want no such thing! I assure you,
    Sire,
You've nothing but beardless babes about this bench!
If I were hasped in my armor and high on my horse,

Get down from your horse, I beg you, and join us for
    dinner.
Then whatever you seek we will gladly see to."
But the stranger said, "No, help me God on high,
My errand is hardly to sit at ease in your castle!
40   Friend, your praises are sung far and wide.

People say your castle is the best ever built, and your
    knights
Are the boldest men ever to ride horses in armor—

Most mighty and most worthy of all mortal men,
And tough devils to fight in tournament games.
45   And they say courtesy flowers in this court.
So all these tales have drawn me to you now.

Be assured by this holly branch I bear
That I come to you in peace, not eager for battle.
I could have come in finery, fixed up for fighting.
50   Back home I have both a helmet and armor,
A shield and a sharp spear that shines like fire,
And other weapons that I know pretty well how to
    use.
But since I don't come here for battle, my clothes are
    mere cloth.
Now if you are truly as bold as all people say,
55   You will grant me gladly the little game that I ask
              as my right."
          Arthur gave him answer.
          He said, "Sir noble knight,
          If it's a duel you're after,
60   We'll give you your fight."

"Good heavens, I want no such thing! I assure you,
    Sire,
You've nothing but beardless babes about this bench!
If I were clad in armor, high on my horse,

You haven't a man that could match me, your might
    is so feeble.
65   And so all I ask of this court is a Christmas game,
For the Yule is here, and New Year's, and here sit
    young men;
If any man holds himself, here in this house, so
    hardy,
So bold in his blood—and so brainless in his head—
That he dares to stoutly exchange one stroke for
    another,
70   I shall let him have as my present this lovely
    gisarme,
This ax, as heavy as he'll need, to handle as he likes,
And I will abide the first blow, bare-necked as I sit.
If anyone here has the daring to try what I've
    offered,
Leap to me lightly, lad; lift up this weapon;
75   I give you the thing forever—you may think it your
    own;
And I will stand still for your stroke, steady on the
    floor,
Provided you honor my right, when my inning comes,
                   to repay.
              But let the respite be
80   A twelvemonth and a day;
              Come now, my boys, let's see
              What any here can say."

If they were like stone before, they were stiller now,
Every last lord in the hall, both the high and the low;
85   The stranger on his destrier stirred in the saddle
And ferociously his red eyes rolled around;
He lowered his grisly eyebrows, glistening green,
And waved his beard and waited for someone to rise;
When no one answered, he coughed, as if embarrassed,
90   And drew himself up straight and spoke again:

You haven't a man that could match me, your might
　　is so feeble.

65　And so all I ask of this court is a Christmas game.
For Christmas is here, and New Year's, and here sit
　　young men.
Does any man in this house think himself so
　　hardy,
So bold in his blood and brainless in his head,
To bravely dare exchange one stroke for another?

70　If so, I'll let him have this lovely battle-ax for a
　　present,
As heavy as he'll need, to handle as he likes.
And I'll suffer the first blow, bare-necked as I sit.
If anyone here has the daring to try what I've
　　offered,
Leap to me lightly, lad. Lift up this weapon.

75　I give you the thing forever—you may think it your
　　own.
And I will stand still for your stroke, steady on the
　　floor,
As long as you honor my right, when my turn comes,
　　　　　　　　　　　　　　to repay.
　　　　　　　　But let the delay be
80　　　　　　　A year and a day.
　　　　　　　Come now, my boys, let's see
　　　　　　　What any here can say."

If they were like stone before, they were more still now,
Every last lord in the hall, both high and low.

85　The stranger on his horse stirred in the saddle
And rolled his red eyes fiercely.
He lowered his fearful, glistening green eyebrows,
And waved his beard and waited for someone to rise.
When no one answered, he coughed as if embarrassed,

90　And drew himself up straight and spoke again.

"What! Can this be King Arthur's court?" said the
      stranger,
"Whose renown runs through many a realm, flung
      far and wide?
What has become of your chivalry and your conquest,
Your greatness-of-heart and your grimness and
      grand words?
95   Behold the radiance and renown of the mighty
      Round Table
Overwhelmed by a word out of one man's mouth!
You shiver and blanch before a blow's been
      shown!"
And with that he laughed so loud that the lord was
      distressed;
In chagrin, his blood shot up in his face and limbs
100   so fair;
            More angry he was than the wind,
            And likewise each man there;
            And Arthur, bravest of men,
            Decided now to draw near.

105   And he said, "By heaven, sir, your request is strange;
But since you have come here for folly, you may as
      well find it.
I know no one here who's aghast of your great
      words.
Give me your gisarme, then, for the love of God,
And gladly I'll grant you the gift you have asked to
      be given."
110   Lightly the King leaped down and clutched it in his
      hand;
Then quickly that other lord alighted on his feet.
Arthur lay hold of the ax, he gripped it by the handle,
And he swung it up over him sternly, as if to strike.
The stranger stood before him, in stature higher
115   By a head or more than any man here in the house;
Sober and thoughtful he stood there and stroked his
      beard,

"What! Can this be King Arthur's court?" said the
        stranger,
"Whose fame runs through many a realm,
        far and wide?
What has become of your chivalry and conquests,
Your greatness-of-heart, your grimness and
        grand words?
95   Look, how the bright fame of the mighty
        Round Table
Is overwhelmed by a word out of one man's mouth!
You shiver and turn pale before a blow's been
        shown!"
And with that he laughed so hard that Arthur was
        disturbed.
In shame, his blood rose in his face and limbs
100   so fair.
                    He was more angry than the wind,
                    And so was each man there.
                    And Arthur, bravest of men,
                    Decided now to draw near.

105   And he said, "By heaven, sir, your request is strange.
But since you have come here for folly,
        you'll get it.
I know no one here who's frightened of your great
        words.
So give me your battle-ax, for the love of God,
And I'll gladly grant you the gift you've asked for."

110   Lightly the King leaped down and clutched it in his
        hand,
Then quickly that other lord lit on his feet.
Arthur lay hold of the ax, gripping it by the handle,
And sternly swung it up over him, as if to strike.
The stranger stood before him, taller
115   By a head or more than any man in the house.
Sober and thoughtful he stood there and stroked his
        beard,

And with patience like a priest's he pulled down his
    collar,
No more unmanned or dismayed by Arthur's
    might
Than he'd be if some baron on the bench had
    brought him a glass

120   of wine.
                Then Gawain, at Guinevere's side,
                Made to the King a sign:
                "I beseech you, Sire," he said,
                "Let this game be mine.

125 "Now if you, my worthy lord," said Gawain to the King,
    "Would command me to step from the dais and stand
        with you there,
    That I might without bad manners move down from
        my place
    (Though I couldn't, of course, if my liege lady
        disliked it)
    I'd be deeply honored to advise you before all the
        court;
130 For I think it unseemly, if I understand the
        matter,
    That challenges such as this churl has chosen to offer
    Be met by Your Majesty—much as it may
        amuse you—
    When so many bold-hearted barons sit about
        the bench:
    No men under Heaven, I am sure, are more hardy in
        will
135 Or better in body on the fields where battles are
        fought;
    I myself am the weakest, of course, and in wit the
        most feeble;
    My life would be least missed, if we let out the truth.
    Only as you are my uncle have I any honor,
    For excepting your blood, I bear in my body slight
        virtue.

And with patience like a priest's he pulled down his
    collar.
He was no more frightened or dismayed by Arthur's
    might
Than he'd be if some knight on the bench had
    brought him a glass

120   of wine.
                Then Gawain, at Guinevere's side,
                Made to the King a sign.
                "I beg you, Sire," he said,
                "Let this game be mine.

125 "Please, my worthy lord," said Gawain to the king,
    "Command me to step from the platform and stand
        with you there.
Then I might move down from my place without bad
    manners—
Though I couldn't, of course, if my queen
    disliked it.
I'd be deeply honored to advise you before all the
    court.
130 For this whole thing's wrong, if I understand the
    matter.
Challenges such as the one offered by this brute
Should not be met by Your Majesty, much as it may
    amuse you—
Not when so many bold-hearted knights sit around
    the bench.
I am sure no men under Heaven are more hardy in
    will
135 Or better in body on the fields where battles are
    fought.
Of course, I myself am the weakest, and the most
    feeble in wit.
To tell the truth, my life would be least missed.
My only honor is in having you as my uncle,
For except your blood, I bear little virtue in my body.

140 And since this affair that's befallen us here is so
foolish,
And since I have asked for it first, let it fall to me.
If I've reasoned incorrectly, let all the court say,
without blame."
       The nobles gather round
145   And all advise the same:
       "Let the King step down
       And give Sir Gawain the game!"

On the ground, the Green Knight got himself into
position,
His head bent forward a little, the bare flesh
showing,
150 His long and lovely locks laid over his crown
So that any man there might note the naked neck.
Sir Gawain laid hold of the ax and he hefted it high,
His pivot foot thrown forward before him on the floor,
And then, swiftly, he slashed at the naked neck;
155 The sharp of the battleblade shattered asunder the
bones
And sank through the shining fat and slit it in two,
And the bit of the bright steel buried itself in the
ground.
The fair head fell from the neck to the floor of the
hall
And the people all kicked it away as it came near
their feet.
160 The blood splashed up from the body and glistened
on the green,
But he never faltered or fell for all of that,

140 And since the business at hand is so foolish,

And since I have asked for it first, let it fall to me.
If I think wrongly, let all the court say so
                                    without blame."
                    The nobles gathered round,
145   And all advised the same:
                    "Let the King step down
                    And give Sir Gawain the game!"

*Gawain insists on taking King Arthur's place
and prepares to accept the Green Knight's
challenge.*

On the ground, the Green Knight got himself into
    position.
He bent his head forward a little so his bare flesh
    showed,
150 And his long and lovely hair spread over his head
So that any man there might note the naked neck.
Sir Gawain laid hold of the ax and raised it high,
With one foot braced before him on the floor,
Then swiftly slashed at the naked neck.
155 The edge of the battleblade shattered the
                bones apart
And sank through the shining fat and slit it in two,
And the bright steel buried itself in the
                ground.
The fair head fell from the neck to the floor of the
    hall,
And the people all kicked it away as it came near
    their feet.
160 The blood splashed from the body and glistened on
    the green,
But he never stumbled or fell even so.

But swiftly he started forth upon stout shanks
And rushed to reach out, where the King's retainers
　　　stood,
Caught hold of the lovely head, and lifted it up,
165　And leaped to his steed and snatched up the reins of
　　　the bridle,
Stepped into stirrups of steel and, striding aloft,
He held his head by the hair, high, in his hand;
And the stranger sat there as steadily in his saddle
As a man entirely unharmed, although he was
　　　headless
170　　　　　　　　　　　　　　　　on his steed.
　　　　　　　　He turned his trunk about,
　　　　　　　　That baleful body that bled,
　　　　　　　　And many were faint with fright
　　　　　　　　When all his say was said.

175　He held his head in his hand up high before him,
Addressing the face to the dearest of all on the dais;
And the eyelids lifted wide, and the eyes looked out,
And the mouth said just this much, as you may
　　　now hear:
"Look that you go, Sir Gawain, as good as your word,
180　And seek till you find me, as loyally, my friend,
As you've sworn in this hall to do, in the hearing of
　　　the knights.
Come to the Green Chapel, I charge you, and take
A stroke the same as you've given, for well you
　　　deserve
To be readily requited on New Year's morn.
185　Many men know me, the Knight of the Green Chapel;
Therefore if you seek to find me, you shall not fail.
Come or be counted a coward, as is fitting."
Then with a rough jerk he turned the reins
And haled away through the hall-door, his head in
　　　his hand,
190　And fire of the flint flew out from the hooves of the
　　　foal.

He swiftly started forth on sturdy legs
And rushed toward where the king's men
    stood.
He caught hold of the lovely head, lifted it up,
165   And leaped to his horse and snatched up the reins of
    the bridle.
He stepped into steel stirrups, and riding along,
He held his head high in his hand by the hair.
And the stranger sat there as steadily in his saddle
As a man entirely unharmed, although he was
    headless
170   on his horse.
          He turned his body about,
          That menacing body that bled.
          And many were faint with fright
          At what he then said.

175   He held his head in his hand high up before him,
Turning the face to the dearest of all on the platform.
And the eyelids lifted wide, and the eyes looked out,
And the mouth said just what you are about
    to hear:
"Sir Gawain, be sure to keep your word, and go
180   And seek till you find me. Do so loyally, my friend,
As you've sworn in this hall to do, in the hearing of
    the knights.
I command you to come to the Green Chapel, and take
A stroke the same as you've given. For you well
    deserve
To be readily repaid on New Year's morning.
185   Many men know me, the Knight of the Green Chapel.
So if you seek to find me, you shall not fail.
Come or be proved a coward, as is fitting."
Then with a rough jerk he turned the reins
And hurried away through the hall-door, his head in
    his hand.
190   And fire of the flint flew from the horse's hooves.

To what kingdom he was carried no man there knew,
No more than they knew what country it was he
    came from.

                What then?
        The King and Gawain there
195   Laugh at the thing and grin;
        And yet, it was an affair
        Most marvelous to men.

La Belle Dame Sans Merci by John William Waterhouse

She held toward him a ring of the yellowest gold
And, standing aloft on the band, a stone like a star
200 From which flew splendid beams like the light of the
    sun;
And mark you well, it was worth a rich king's ransom.
But right away he refused it, replying in haste,

To what kingdom he rode no man there knew,
No more than they knew what country he had come
    from.
                           What then?
                  The King and Gawain there

195   Laughed at the thing and grinned.
                  And yet, it was an affair
                  Most marvelous to men.

A year passes, and Sir Gawain sets out in search of the Green Chapel. After many dangerous adventures, he meets the lord of a magnificent castle. Gawain accepts the lord's offer of food and lodging and also agrees to an unusual proposal. The lord will go out to hunt each day while Gawain remains at the castle. At the end of each day, the men will exchange whatever they have received. For the first two days, the lady of the castle tries to seduce Gawain, but the honorable knight refuses her advances, accepting only a modest kiss. Gawain keeps his promise and passes each kiss on to the lord. On the third day, however, the lady not only gives Gawain a kiss, but also insists that he accept a magic green sash. Gawain passes on the kiss he receives but does not mention the sash.

She held toward him a ring of the most yellow gold.
Set in the band was a star-like stone
200   From which flew splendid beams like sunlight.

And you can be sure it was worth a rich king's ransom.
But right away he refused it, replying quickly,

"My lady gay, I can hardly take gifts at the moment;
Having nothing to give, I'd be wrong to take gifts in
    turn."

205 She implored him again, still more earnestly, but
    again
He refused it and swore on his knighthood that he
    could take nothing.
Grieved that he still would not take it, she told him
    then:
"If taking my ring would be wrong on account of its
    worth,
And being so much in my debt would be bothersome
    to you,

210 I'll give you merely this sash that's of slighter
    value."
She swiftly unfastened the sash that encircled her
    waist,
Tied around her fair tunic, inside her bright mantle:
It was made of green silk and was marked of
    gleaming gold
Embroidered along the edges, ingeniously stitched.

215 This too she held out to the knight, and she earnestly
    begged him
To take it, trifling as it was, to remember her by.
But again he said no, there was nothing at all he
    could take,
Neither treasure nor token, until such time as the Lord
Had granted him some end to his adventure.

220 "And therefore, I pray you, do not be displeased,
But give up, for I cannot grant it, however fair
                   or right.
        I know your worth and price,
        And my debt's by no means slight;

225   I swear through fire and ice
        To be your humble knight."

"Do you lay aside this silk," said the lady then,

"My lady gay, I can't take gifts at the moment.
I have nothing to give, so I'd be wrong to take gifts in
turn."

205 She begged him again, even more earnestly, but
again
He refused and swore on his knighthood that he
could take nothing.
Grieved that he still would not take it, she told him
then:
"Would taking my ring be wrong because of its
worth,
And would it be bothersome to you to be so much in
my debt?

210 Then I'll merely give you this sash that's of slighter
value."
She swiftly unfastened the sash around her
waist,
Tied around her pale blouse inside her bright cloak.
It was made of green silk and marked with
gleaming gold
Sewn along the edges, cleverly stitched.

215 This, too, she held out to the knight, and she
earnestly begged him
To take it, poor as it was, to remember her by.
But again he said no, there was nothing at all he
could take,
Neither treasure nor gift, until the Lord
Had granted some end of his adventure.

220 "And so I pray you, do not be displeased,
But give up, for I cannot grant it, however fair
or right.
I know your worth and price,
And my debt's by no means slight.

225 I swear through fire and ice
To be your humble knight."

"Do you refuse this silk," said the lady then,

"Because it seems unworthy—as well it may?
Listen. Little as it is, it seems less in value,
230 But he who knew what charms are woven within it
Might place a better price on it, perchance.
For the man who goes to battle in this green lace,
As long as he keeps it looped around him,
No man under Heaven can hurt him, whoever may
          try,
235 For nothing on earth, however uncanny, can kill him."
The knight cast about in distress, and it came to his
          heart
This might be a treasure indeed when the time came
          to take
The blow he had bargained to suffer beside the
          Green Chapel
If the gift meant remaining alive, it might well be
          worth it;
240 So he listened in silence and suffered the lady to
          speak,
And she pressed the sash upon him and begged him
          to take it,
And Gawain did, and she gave him the gift with
          great pleasure
And begged him, for her sake, to say not a word,
And to keep it hidden from her lord. And he said he
          would,
245 That except for themselves, this business would
          never be known
                          to a man.
                  He thanked her earnestly,
                  And boldly his heart now ran;
                  And now a third time she
250   Leaned down and kissed her man.

"Because it seems unworthy—as well it may?
Listen. Little as it is, it seems less in value.
230 But if you knew what charms are woven into it,
You might place a better price on it, perhaps.
For if a man goes into battle in this green lace
And keeps it looped around him,
No man under heaven can hurt him, whoever may try.
235 Nothing on earth, however amazing, can kill him."
The knight was distressed, and he wondered in his heart
If this might be treasure indeed when the time came to take
The blow he had agreed to suffer beside the Green Chapel.
If the gift meant remaining alive, it might well be worth it.
240 So he listened in silence and allowed the lady to speak,
And she pressed the sash upon him and begged him to take it.
And Gawain did, and she gave him the gift with great pleasure.
She begged him, for her sake, to say not a word,
And to keep it hidden from her lord. And he said he would.
245 Except for themselves, this business would never be known
                    to a man.
          He thanked her earnestly,
          And boldly his heart now ran.
          And now a third time she
250   Leaned down and kissed her knight.

*On New Year's Day, Gawain puts on the sash and
leaves the castle in search of the Green Chapel.
Instead, he encounters the Green Knight, who is*

Quickly then the man in
    the green made ready,
Grabbed up his keen-
    ground ax to strike Sir
    Gawain;

With all the might in his
    body he bore it aloft
And sharply brought it down as if to slay him;
255 Had he made it fall with the force he first intended
He would have stretched out the strongest man on
    earth.
But Sir Gawain cast a side glance at the ax
As it glided down to give him his Kingdom Come,
And his shoulders jerked away from the iron a little,
260 And the Green Knight caught the handle, holding it
    back,
And mocked the prince with many a proud reproof:
"*You* can't be Gawain," he said, "who's thought
    so good,
A man who's never been daunted on hill or dale!
For look how you flinch for fear before anything's
    felt!
265 I never heard tell that Sir Gawain was ever a coward!
I never moved a muscle when *you* came down;
In Arthur's hall I never so much as winced.
My head fell off at my feet, yet I never flickered;
But you! You tremble at heart before you're touched!
270 I'm bound to be called a better man than you, then,
                 my lord."
          Said Gawain, "I shied once:
          No more. You have my word.
          But if my head falls to the stones
275   It cannot be restored.

"But be brisk, man, by your faith, and come to the
    point!

carefully sharpening his ax. Frightened, but pre-
pared for an honorable death, Gawain bows his
head and waits for the blow.

Then the man in green quickly made ready
And grabbed up his keenly sharpened ax to strike
    Sir Gawain.
With all the might in his body he held it up
And sharply brought it down as if to slay him.
255 If he had made it fall with the force he first intended
He would have killed the strongest man
    on earth.
But Sir Gawain cast a side glance at the ax
As it glided down to send him to heaven,
And his shoulders jerked away from the iron a little.
260 The Green Knight caught the handle, holding
    it back,
And mocked and scolded the prince proudly.
He said, "*You* can't be Gawain, who's thought
    so good,
And who's never been frightened on hill or dale!
For look how you flinch for fear before anything's
    felt!
265 I never heard tell that Sir Gawain was ever a coward!
I never moved a muscle when *you* came down.
In Arthur's hall I never so much as winced.
My head fell off at my feet, yet I never moved.
But you! You tremble at heart before you're touched!
270 So I'm bound to be called a better man than you,
                 my lord."
           Said Gawain, "I shied once.
           No more. You have my word.
           But if *my* head falls to the stones
275   It cannot be restored.

"But be quick, man, by your word, and get to it!

Deal out my doom if you can, and do it at once,
For I'll stand for one good stroke, and I'll start
   no more
Until your ax has hit—and that I swear."
280 "Here goes, then," said the other, and heaves it aloft
And stands there waiting, scowling like a madman;
He swings down sharp, then suddenly stops again,
Holds back the ax with his hand before it
   can hurt,
And Gawain stands there stirring not even a nerve;
285 He stood there still as a stone or the stock of a tree
That's wedged in rocky ground by a hundred roots.
O, merrily then he spoke, the man in green:
"Good! You've got your heart back! Now I can hit you.
May all that glory the good King Arthur gave you
290 Prove efficacious now—if it ever can—
And save your neck." In rage Sir Gawain shouted,
"*Hit* me, hero! I'm right up to here with your threats!
Is it *you* that's the cringing coward after all?"
"Whoo!" said the man in green, "he's wrathful, too!
295 No pauses, then; I'll pay up my pledge at once,
                        I vow!"
          He takes his stride to strike
          And lifts his lip and brow;
          It's not a thing Gawain can like,
300   For nothing can save him now!

He raises that ax up lightly and flashes it down,
And that blinding bit bites in at the knight's
   bare neck—
But hard as he hammered it down, it hurt him no
   more
Than to nick the nape of his neck, so it split the skin;
305 The sharp blade slit to the flesh through the shiny
   hide,
And red blood shot to his shoulders and spattered
   the ground.

Deal out my doom if you can, and do it at once,
For I'll stand for one good stroke. I'll start
   no more
Until your ax has hit—and that I swear."
280 "Here goes, then," said the other, and he held it up
And stood there waiting, scowling like a madman.
He swung down sharp, then suddenly stopped again,
Holding back the ax with his hand before it
   could hurt.
And Gawain stood there, not even a nerve stirring.
285 He stood there still as a stone or the trunk of a tree
That's wedged in rocky ground by a hundred roots.
Oh, then he spoke merrily, the man in green:
"Good! You've got your heart back! Now I can hit you.
May all that glory the good King Arthur gave you
290 Prove useful now—if it ever can—
And save your neck." In rage Sir Gawain shouted,
"*Hit* me, hero! I'm right up to here with your threats!
Is it *you* that's the cringing coward after all?"
"Whoo!" said the man in green. "He's angry too!
295 No pauses, then. I'll keep my promise at once,
                I vow!"
         He took his stride to strike
         And lifted his lip and brow.
         It's not a thing Gawain could like,
300   For nothing could save him now!

He raised that ax up lightly and flashed it down,
And that blinding blade bit at the knight's
   bare neck.
But hard as he brought it down, it barely hurt him—

Just nicked the back of his neck so it split the skin.
305 The sharp blade slit to the flesh through the shiny
   hide,
And red blood shot to his shoulders and spattered
   the ground.

And when Gawain saw his blood where it blinked in
    the snow
He sprang from the man with a leap to the length of
    a spear;
He snatched up his helmet swiftly and slapped it on,
310 Shifted his shield into place with a jerk of his
    shoulders,
And snapped his sword out faster than sight;
    said boldly—
And, mortal born of his mother that he was,
There was never on earth a man so happy by half—
"No more strokes, my friend; you've had your swing!
315 I've stood one swipe of your ax without resistance;
If you offer me any more, I'll repay you at once
With all the force and fire I've got—as you
                      will see.
          I take one stroke, that's all,
320   For that was the compact we
          Arranged in Arthur's hall;
          But now, no more for me!"

The Green Knight remained where he stood, relaxing
    on his ax—
Settled the shaft on the rocks and leaned on the
    sharp end—
325 And studied the young man standing there,
    shoulders hunched,
And considered that staunch and doughty stance he
    took,
Undaunted yet, and in his heart he liked it;

And then he said merrily, with a mighty voice—
With a roar like rushing wind he reproved the
    knight—
330 "Here, don't be such an ogre on your ground!
Nobody here has behaved with bad manners toward
    you

And when Gawain saw his blood where it trickled in
the snow
He sprang from the man with a leap the length of a
spear.
He snatched up his helmet swiftly and slapped it on,
310   Shifted his shield into place with a jerk of his
shoulders,
And snapped his sword out faster than sight. Then
he spoke boldly,
For mortal born of his mother that he was,
There was never on earth a man half so happy—
"No more strokes, my friend. You've had your swing!
315   I've stood one swipe of your ax without struggle.
If you try it again, I'll repay you at once
With all the force and fire I've got—as you
will see.
I take one stroke, that's all.
320   For that's the agreement we
Came to in Arthur's hall.
But now, no more for me!"

The Green Knight remained where he stood, relaxing
on his ax,
Setting the handle on the rocks and leaning on the
sharp end.
325   His shoulders hunched, he studied the young man
standing there,
And considered that firm, brave stance he took,

Still unafraid. And in his heart the Green Knight
liked it.
And then he spoke merrily, with a mighty voice
And a roar like rushing wind, scolding the
knight—
330   "Here, don't be so beastly about it!
Nobody here has behaved with bad manners toward
you

Or done a thing except as the contract said.
I owed you a stroke, and I've struck; consider yourself
Well paid. And now I release you from all further
    duties.

335 If I'd cared to hustle, it may be, perchance, that I
    might
Have hit somewhat harder, and then you might well
    be cross!
The first time I lifted my ax it was lighthearted
    sport,
I merely feinted and made no mark, as was right,
For you kept our pact of the first night with honor

340 And abided by your word and held yourself
    true to me,
Giving me all you owed as a good man should.
I feinted a second time, friend, for the morning
You kissed my pretty wife twice and returned
    me the kisses;
And so for the first two days, mere feints, nothing
    more

345   severe.
            A man who's true to his word,
            There's nothing he needs to fear;
            You failed me, though, on the third
            Exchange, so I've tapped you here.

350 "That sash you wear by your scabbard belongs to me;
My own wife gave it to you, as I ought to know.
I know, too, of your kisses and all your words
And my wife's advances, for I myself arranged them.
It was I who sent her to test you. I'm convinced

355 You're the finest man that ever walked this earth.
As a pearl is of greater price than dry white peas,
So Gawain indeed stands out above all other knights.
But you lacked a little, sir; you were less than loyal;
But since it was not for the sash itself or for lust

360 But because you loved your life, I blame you less."

Or done a thing except as the contract said.
I owed you a stroke, and I've struck. Consider yourself
Well paid. And now I release you from all further
   duties.
335 If I'd put more into it, I might just

Have hit somewhat harder, and then you might well
   be cross!
The first time I lifted my ax it was lighthearted
   sport.
I merely bluffed and made no mark, as was right.
For you honorably kept our pact of the first night
340 And kept your word and held yourself
   true to me,
Giving me all you owed as a good man should.
I bluffed a second time, friend, for the morning
You kissed my pretty wife twice and returned
   me the kisses.
And so for the first two days, mere bluffs, nothing
   more
345   severe.
      A man who's true to his word
      Has nothing to fear.
      You failed me, though, on the third
      Exchange, so I've tapped you here.

350 "That sash you wear by your sheath belongs to me.
My own wife gave it to you, as I ought to know.
I also know of your kisses and all your words
And my wife's advances, for I myself arranged them.
It was I who sent her to test you. I'm convinced
355 You're the finest man that ever walked this earth.
Indeed, Gawain stands out above all other knights
As a pearl is more valuable than dry white peas.
But you lacked a little, sir. You were less than loyal.
But it was not for the sash itself or for lust,
360 But because you loved your life. So I blame you less."

Sir Gawain stood in a study a long, long while,
So miserable with disgrace that he wept within,
And all the blood of his chest went up to his face
And he shrank away in shame from the man's gentle
    words.
365 The first words Gawain could find to say were these:
"Cursed be cowardice and covetousness both,
Villainy and vice that destroys all virtue!"
He caught at the knots of the girdle and loosened
    them
And fiercely flung the sash at the Green Knight.
370 "There, there's my fault! The foul fiend vex it!
Foolish cowardice taught me, from fear of your
    stroke,
To bargain, covetous, and abandon my kind,
The selflessness and loyalty suitable in knights;
Here I stand, faulty and false, much as I've feared
    them,
375 Both of them, untruth and treachery; may they see
    sorrow

                     and care!
        I can't deny my guilt;
        My works shine none too fair!
        Give me your good will
380   And henceforth I'll beware."

At that, the Green Knight laughed, saying graciously,
"Whatever harm I've had, I hold it amended
Since now you're confessed so clean, acknowledging
    sins
And bearing the plain penance of my point;
385 I consider you polished as white and as perfectly
    clean
As if you had never fallen since first you were born.
And I give you, sir, this gold-embroidered girdle,
For the cloth is as green as my gown. Sir Gawain,
    think

Sir Gawain stood thinking a long, long while,
So miserable with disgrace that he wept within.
All the blood of his chest went up to his face
And he shrank away in shame from the man's gentle
      words.
365   The first words Gawain managed to say were these:
"Cursed be both cowardice and envy,
Villainy and vice that destroy all virtue!"
He tugged at the knots of the sash and loosened
      them,
Then fiercely flung the sash at the Green Knight.
370   "There, there's my fault! The devil take it!
I feared your stroke, and foolish cowardice
      taught me
To bargain and envy, and to betray my kind,
The selflessness and loyalty fit for knights.
Here I stand, faulty and false, much as I've
      feared
375   Untruth and treachery. May they see sorrow

                    and care!
          I can't deny my guilt.
          My deeds shine none too fair!
          Give me your good will
380   And from now on I'll beware."

At that, the Green Knight laughed and kindly said,
"Whatever harm I've had, I hold it righted
Since now you've confessed so clean, admitting
      sins
And bearing the plain punishment of my ax.
385   I see you polished as white and perfectly clean

As if you had never fallen since you were first born.
And I give you, sir, this gold-stitched sash,
For the cloth is as green as my gown. Sir Gawain,
      think

On this when you go forth among great princes;
390 Remember our struggle here; recall to your mind
This rich token. Remember the Green Chapel.
And now, come on, let's both go back to my castle
And finish the New Year's revels with feasting and
joy,

not strife,
395 I beg you," said the lord,
And said, "As for my wife,
She'll be your friend, no more
A threat against your life."

"No, sir," said the knight, and seized his helmet
400 And quickly removed it, thanking the Green Knight,
"I've reveled too well already; but fortune be with
you;
May He who gives all honors honor you well."

❋ ❋ ❋

And so they embraced and kissed and commended
each other
To the Prince of Paradise, and parted then
405 in the cold;
Sir Gawain turned again
To Camelot and his lord;
And as for the man in green,
He went wherever he would.

Of this when you go forth among great princes.
390 Remember our struggle here
And this rich gift. Remember the Green Chapel.
And now, come on, let's both go back to my castle
And finish the New Year's holiday with feasting and
        joy,

                            not trouble,
395   I beg you," said the lord.
                    Then he added, "As for my wife,
                    She'll be your friend, no more
                    A threat against your life."

"No, sir," said the knight, seizing his helmet
400 And quickly removing it, thanking the Green Knight.
"I've celebrated too much already. But luck be with
        you.
May he who gives all honors honor you well."

                    ✻ ✻ ✻

And so they embraced and kissed and entrusted each
        other
To Jesus, and parted then
405   in the cold.
                    Sir Gawain turned again
                    To Camelot and his lord.
                    As for the man in green,
                    He went wherever he would.

Le Morte d'Arthur

No one knows just when stories about King Arthur began to be told. There was a historical Arthur, a Welsh warrior who lived during the 6th century A.D. But it is possible that stories of a mythic British king of that name go back to even earlier times.

The stories, of course, varied greatly. But according to most traditions, Arthur was thought a perfectly

La Belle Iseult
(Queen
Guinevere) by
William Morris

ordinary boy until he pulled the magical sword, Excalibur, out of a stone. This feat, which no one else could do, made him king of England.

He was taught in his youth by a wise magician named Merlin. As a man, he built a wonderful city known as Camelot, where the greatest knights in the world came to join his court. They gathered around the famous Round Table, where they were all treated as equals. Arthur's queen was the beautiful Guinevere, and his favorite knight was Sir Lancelot.

The knights of the Round Table went forth on many amazing adventures. King Arthur's nephew Sir Gawain confronted a powerful Green Knight, a tale told earlier in this unit. Perhaps the knights' most famous exploit was the quest for the Holy Grail, a cup they believed was mysteriously connected with Jesus. Only Sir Galahad, the purest of all Arthur's knights, proved worthy to look upon this treasure.

Arthur wanted Camelot to be a perfect society, but his hopes were eventually dashed. His half-sister, the sorceress Morgan le Fay, caused him a great deal of trouble and even once stole Excalibur. And Arthur's illegitimate son Mordred proved a fatal enemy.

But the greatest threat to Camelot came from the two people Arthur loved most. Sir Lancelot and Queen Guinevere fell in love, and because of their relationship, Arthur's kingdom became hopelessly divided.

Seriously wounded in one-on-one combat with Sir Mordred, Arthur was magically transported to the island of Avalon. Did he die there? Or is he still in Avalon recovering from his wounds, waiting for the day when he will rule England again? No one can say.

The tone of Malory's book is elegiac—that is, it tells of bygone days and heroes. Himself a knight, Malory felt saddened over the decline of chivalry in England. That grand old code by which knights once lived was rapidly disappearing. *Le Morte d'Arthur* portrays a world in which chivalry is in full flower.

from **Le Morte d'Arthur**

Sir Thomas Malory

Illustration from Malory's *Le Morte d'Arthur,* 1529

1 *S*o upon Trinity Sunday at night King Arthur
dreamed a wonderful dream, and in his dream him
seemed that he saw upon a chafflet a chair, and the
chair was fast to a wheel, and thereupon sat King
Arthur in the richest cloth of gold that might be

2 made. And the King thought there was under him,
far from him, an hideous deep black water, and
therein was all manner of serpents, and worms, and
wild beasts, foul and horrible. And suddenly the King

from Le Morte d'Arthur

Sir Thomas Malory

King Arthur's dream of Camelot, a glorious kingdom ruled with honor and justice, is dealt a heavy blow when his favorite knight, Lancelot, falls in love with Queen Guinevere. Arthur travels to France in pursuit of Lancelot, but is forced to return to England when he learns that his illegitimate son Mordred has taken control of the kingdom. When the king arrives, Mordred attacks, and Arthur's nephew Gawain is killed. Before he dies, however, he manages to send a message to Lancelot telling him that Camelot is threatened and that Arthur needs help.

1   *S*o upon Trinity Sunday[1] at night, King Arthur had an amazing dream. And in his dream he thought he saw a chair upon a platform. And the chair was fastened to a wheel, and on it sat King Arthur in the richest gold cloth that could be made.

2   And the king thought that there was hideous, deep, black water far below him. And in it were all kinds of foul and horrible serpents, worms, and wild beasts. And suddenly, the king thought the wheel

---

1 **Trinity Sunday:** the eighth Sunday after Easter

thought that the wheel turned upside down, and he fell among the serpents, and every beast took him by a limb. And then the King cried as he lay in his bed, "Help, help!"

3   And then knights, squires, and yeomen awaked the King, and then he was so amazed that he wist not where he was. And then so he awaked until it was nigh day, and then he fell on slumbering again, not sleeping nor thoroughly waking. So the King

4   seemed verily that there came Sir Gawain unto him with a number of fair ladies with him. So when King Arthur saw him, he said, "Welcome, my sister's son. I weened ye had been dead. And now I see thee on-live, much am I beholden unto Almighty Jesu. Ah, fair nephew and my sister's son, what been these ladies that hither be come with you?"

5   "Sir," said Sir Gawain, "all these be ladies for whom I have foughten for when I was man living. And all these are those that I did battle for in right-eous quarrels, and God hath given them that grace, at their great prayer, because I did battle for them for their right, that they should bring me hither unto you. Thus much hath given me leave God, for to warn

6   you of your death. For and ye fight as tomorn with Sir Mordred, as ye both have assigned, doubt ye not ye must be slain, and the most party of your people on both parties. And for the great grace and goodness that Almighty Jesu hath unto you, and for pity of you and many more other good men there shall be slain, God hath sent me to you of his special grace to give you warning that in no wise ye do battle as tomorn, but that ye take a treaty for a month from today. And

7   proffer you largely you so that tomorn ye put in a delay. For within a month shall come Sir Lancelot with all his noble knights and rescue you worship-fully and slay Sir Mordred and all that ever will hold with him."

turned upside down, and he fell among the serpents, and every beast took him by a limb. And then the king cried, "Help, help!" as he lay in his bed.

3   And then knights, squires, and yeomen[2] woke up the king, who was so frightened that he didn't know where he was. He remained awake until it was nearly day, and then he fell slumbering again, neither sleeping nor fully waking.

4   And then it seemed to the king that Sir Gawain came to him with a number of fair ladies. So when King Arthur saw him, he said, "Welcome, my sister's son. I thought you had died. And now that I see you alive, I am much indebted to Almighty Jesus. Ah, fair nephew and my sister's son, who are these ladies who have come with you?"

5   "Sir," said Sir Gawain, "these are ladies whom I fought for when I was still alive. I did battle for them all in righteous quarrels. And because I fought on their behalf, they prayed greatly to God for the power to bring me here to you. So God has allowed me this much—to warn you of your death.

6   "For if you fight with Sir Mordred tomorrow, as you both have agreed, be sure that you will be killed along with most of the people on both sides. Almighty Jesus shows great goodness and pity to you and many other good men who might be slain there. So God has sent me out of special mercy to give you warning. By no means do battle tomorrow, but make a treaty to fight a month from today.

7   "Make generous offers tomorrow so you can agree to delay the fight. For within a month, Sir Lancelot will come with all his noble knights to rescue you. He will slay Sir Mordred and all who fight for him."

2 **squires:** knights' attendants
   yeomen: small landholders

8   Then Sir Gawain and all the ladies vanished. And anon the King called upon his knights, squires, and yeomen, and charged them wightly to fetch his noble lords and wise bishops unto him. And when they were come the King told them of his avision, that Sir Gawain had told him and warned him that, and he fought on the morn, he should be slain. Then the

9   King commanded Sir Lucan the Butler and his brother Sir Bedivere the Bold, with two bishops with them, and charged them in any wise to take a treaty for a month from today with Sir Mordred. "And spare not: proffer him lands and goods as much as ye think reasonable."

10   So then they departed and came to Sir Mordred where he had a grim host of an hundred thousand, and there they entreated Sir Mordred long time. And at the last Sir Mordred was agreed for to have Cornwall and Kent by King Arthur's days, and after that, all England, after the days of King Arthur.

11   Then were they condescended that King Arthur and Sir Mordred should meet betwixt both their hosts, and each of them should bring fourteen persons. And so they came with this word unto Arthur. Then said he, "I am glad that this is done," and so he went into the field.

12   And when King Arthur should depart, he warned all his host that, and they see any sword drawn, "Look ye come on fiercely and slay that traitor Sir Mordred, for I in no wise trust him." In like wise Sir Mordred warned his host that "And ye see any manner of sword drawn, look that ye come on fiercely, an so slay all that ever before you standeth, for in no wise I will not trust for this treaty." And in the same wise said Sir Mordred unto his host, "For I know well my father will be avenged upon me."

8   Then Sir Gawain and all the ladies vanished. And
soon, the king called upon his knights, squires, and
yeomen. He ordered them to quickly bring his noble
lords and wise bishops to him. And when they had
come, the king told them of his vision, how Sir
Gawain had warned him that he would be slain if he
fought in the morning.

9   Then he gave orders to Sir Lucan the Butler and
his brother Sir Bedivere the Bold, and also two
bishops. He commanded them to do whatever was
necessary to make a treaty with Sir Mordred, delay-
ing the fighting for a month from that day. "And
spare nothing," said the king. "Offer him as many
lands and goods as you think reasonable."

10   So they departed and went to Sir Mordred, who
had a grim army of a hundred thousand. They
pleaded with Sir Mordred a long time. And at last,
Sir Mordred agreed to accept Cornwall and Kent[3]
during King Arthur's days, and all England after the
death of King Arthur.

11   Then they agreed that King Arthur and Sir
Mordred should meet between their armies, and each
of them should bring fourteen people. And they
brought word of this back to Arthur. Then he said, "I
am glad this is done." And so he went into the field.

12   And King Arthur told his army what to do if they
saw any sword drawn once he left: "See to it that you
come and fiercely slay that traitor Sir Mordred. For I
don't trust him by any means." In the same way, Sir
Mordred warned his army: "If you see any sword
drawn, see to it that you fiercely slay all that stand
before you. For I will not trust this treaty by any
means." And then Sir Mordred added to his army, "I
know well that my father will be avenged on me."

---

3 **Cornwall and Kent:** counties in England

13   And so they met as their pointment was and were agreed and accorded thoroughly. And wine was fetched and they drank together. Right so came an adder out of a little heathbush, and it stung a knight in the foot. And so when the knight felt him so stung, he looked down and saw the adder. And anon he drew his sword to slay the adder, and thought none

14   other harm. And when the host on both parties saw that sword drawn, then they blew beams, trumpets, horns, and shouted grimly. And so both hosts dressed them together. And King Arthur took his horse and said, "Alas, this unhappy day!" and so rode to his party, and Sir Mordred in like wise.

15   And never since was there never seen a more dolefuller battle in no Christian land, for there was but rushing and riding, lunging and striking; and many a grim word was there spoken of either to other, and

16   many a deadly stroke. But ever King Arthur rode throughout the battle of Sir Mordred many times and did full nobly, as a noble king should do, and at all times he fainted never. And Sir Mordred did his devoir that day and put himself in great peril.

17   And thus they fought all the long day, and never stinted till the noble knights were laid to the cold earth. And ever they fought still till it was near night, and by then was there an hundred thousand laid dead upon the down. Then was King Arthur

18   wood-wroth out of measure when he saw his people so slain from him. And so he looked about him and could see no more of all his host, and good knights left no more on-live, but two knights: the t'one was Sir Lucan the Butler and the other his brother Sir Bedivere. And yet they were full sore wounded.

19   "Jesu, mercy," said the King, "where are all my noble knights become? Alas that ever I should see this doleful day! For now," said King Arthur, "I am come to mine end. But would to God," said he, "that I wist not where were that traitor Sir Mordred that has caused all this mischief."

13   And so they met according to their plan, and they fully agreed to everything. And wine was served and they drank together. Then suddenly, a snake came out of a little bush and stung a knight in the foot. And when the knight felt himself stung, he looked down and saw the snake. And he quickly drew his sword to slay the snake, meaning no other harm.

14   And when both armies saw that sword drawn, they blew bugles, trumpets, and horns, and shouted grimly. And so both armies charged each other. And King Arthur mounted his horse and said, "Alas, this unhappy day!" And so he rode to his army, and Sir Mordred rode to his.

15   And never since has there been seen a sadder battle in a Christian land. For there was rushing and riding, lunging and striking, and many grim words passed between men, and many deadly strokes as well.

16   But King Arthur kept riding through Sir Mordred's army many times. He did so very nobly, as a noble king should do, and he never, ever showed fear. And Sir Mordred did his duty that day, and put himself in great peril.

17   And thus they fought all day long, and never stopped till the noble knights were laid upon the cold earth. And they fought on and on till it was nearly night, and by then a hundred thousand were dead upon the field.

18   King Arthur went completely mad with rage when he saw so many of his people slain. And then he looked around and could see no more of his army. Of all his good knights, only two were left. One was Sir Lucan the Butler, and the other his brother Sir Bedivere. And even they were seriously wounded.

19   "Mercy, Jesus!" said the king. "Where are all my noble knights now? Alas, that I should ever see this bitter day! For now I have reached my end. But I wish to God that I knew where that traitor Sir Mordred was, who caused all this mischief."

20 Then King Arthur looked about and was ware where stood Sir Mordred leaning upon his sword among a great heap of dead men.

21 "Now give me my spear," said King Arthur unto Sir Lucan, "for yonder I have espied the traitor that all this woe hath wrought."

22 "Sir, let him be," said Sir Lucan, "for he is unhappy. And if ye pass this unhappy day ye shall be right well revenged upon him. And, good lord, remember ye of your night's dream, and what the spirit of Sir Gawain told you tonight, and yet God of his great goodness hath preserved you hitherto. And for God's sake, my

23 lord, leave off by this, for, blessed be God, ye have won the field: for yet we been here three on-live, and with Sir Mordred is not one on-live. And therefore if ye leave off now, this wicked day of destiny is past."

20   Then King Arthur looked around and saw Sir Mordred leaning upon his sword among a great heap of dead men.

21   "Now give me my spear," King Arthur said to Sir Lucan. "For yonder I see the traitor who brought all this woe."

22   "Sir, let him be," said Sir Lucan, "for he is unhappy. And if you live through this unhappy day, you will be well revenged upon him. And, good lord, remember your dream last night, and what the spirit of Sir Gawain told you. And yet, God in his great goodness has saved you for the time being.

23   "And for God's sake, my lord, let this go. For blessed be God, you have won the field. For there are still three of us alive, and Mordred has not one alive. And so if you let this go for now, this wicked day of destiny will pass."

24   "Now, tide me death, tide me life," said the King, "now I see him yonder alone, he shall never escape mine hands. For at a better avail shall I never have him."

25   "God speed you well!" said Sir Bedivere.

26   Then the King got his spear in both his hands and ran toward Sir Mordred, crying and saying, "Traitor, now is thy deathday come!"

27   And when Sir Mordred saw King Arthur he ran until him with his sword drawn in his hand, and there King Arthur smote Sir Mordred under the shield, with a thrust of his spear, throughout the body more than a fathom. And when Sir Mordred felt

24   "Let either death or life befall me now," said the king. "I see him yonder alone, and he shall never escape my hands. For I shall never have a better chance against him."

25   "God give you good fortune!" said Sir Bedivere.

26   Then the king took his spear in both his hands and ran toward Sir Mordred, crying out, "Traitor, the day of your death has come!"

27   And when Sir Mordred saw King Arthur, he ran toward him with his sword drawn in his hand. And King Arthur struck Sir Mordred under the shield with a thrust of his spear, pushing it through his body more than six feet.

Arthur and Mordred in Mutually Fatal Combat by Arthur Rackham

28   that he had his death's wound, he thrust himself
with the might that he had up to the burr of King
Arthur's spear, and right so he smote his father King
Arthur with his sword holden in both his hands,
upon the side of the head, that the sword pierced the
helmet and the casing of the brain. And therewith
Sir Mordred dashed down stark dead to the earth.

29   And noble King Arthur fell in a swough to the
earth, and there he swooned oftentimes, and Sir
Lucan and Sir Bedivere ofttimes heaved him up. And
so, weakly betwixt them, they led him to a little
chapel not far from the seaside, and when the King
was there, him thought him reasonably eased. Then
30 heard the people cry in the field. "Now go thou, Sir
Lucan," said the King, "and do me to wit what
betokens that noise in the field."

31   So Sir Lucan departed, for he was grievously
wounded in many places. And so as he walked he saw
and harkened by the moonlight how that pillagers
and robbers were come into the field to pill and to
rob many a full noble knight of brooches and
bracelets and of many a good ring and many a rich
jewel. And who that were not dead all out there they
slew them for their harness and their riches. When
32 Sir Lucan understood this work, he came to the King
as soon as he might and told him all what he had
heard and seen. "Therefore by my read," said Sir
Lucan, "it is best that we bring you to some town."

33   "I would it were so," said the King, "but I may not
stand, my head works so. Ah, Sir Lancelot," said King
Arthur, "this day have I sore missed thee. And alas
that ever I was against thee, for now have I my
death, whereof Sir Gawain me warned in my dream."

34   Then Sir Lucan took up the King the t'one party
and Sir Bedivere the other party; and in the lifting up

28   And then Sir Mordred felt that he had his death's wound. So with the strength he had left, he thrust himself up to the hand guard of King Arthur's spear. And with his sword in both hands, he struck his father, King Arthur, on the side of the head. The sword pierced the helmet and the casing of the brain. And then Sir Mordred fell down to the earth, stone dead.

29   And noble King Arthur fainted to the earth, and he swooned many more times, and Sir Lucan and Sir Bedivere helped him up every time. And so, although they were both weak themselves, they led him to a little chapel not far from the seaside. And when the king was there, he felt reasonably eased.

30   Then they heard people cry in the field. "Go now, Sir Lucan," said the king. "And find out for me what that noise in the field means."

31   So Sir Lucan departed, although he was grievously wounded in many places. And as he walked, he looked and listened in the moonlight. Thieves and robbers had come into the field to steal and rob many noble knights of brooches, bracelets, and many good rings and rich jewels. And they slew those who were not dead for their armor and riches.

32   When Sir Lucan saw what was happening, he came to the king right away and told him all he had heard and seen. "So my advice is this," said Sir Lucan. "It is best that we take you to some town."

33   "I wish it were possible," said the king, "but I cannot stand, my head hurts so. Ah, Sir Lancelot," added King Arthur, "I miss you badly today. And alas, I wish I'd never been against you, for now I am going to die, just as Sir Gawain warned me in my dream."

34   Then Sir Lucan took up the king on one side, and Sir Bedivere took him up on the other. And as they

the King swooned and in the lifting Sir Lucan fell in a swoon that part of his guts fell out of his body, and therewith the noble knight's heart burst. And when the King awoke he beheld Sir Lucan how he lay foaming at the mouth and part of his guts lay at his feet.

35   "Alas," said the King, "this is to me a full heavy sight to see this noble duke so die for my sake, for he would have helped me that had more need of help than I. Alas that he would not complain him for his heart was so set to help me. Now Jesu have mercy upon his soul."

36   Then Sir Bedivere wept for the death of his brother.

37   "Now leave this mourning and weeping gentle knight," said the King, "for all this will not avail me. For wit thou well, and might I live myself, the death of Sir Lucan would grieve me evermore. But my time

38 passeth on fast," said the King. "Therefore," said King Arthur unto Sir Bedivere, "take thou here Excalibur my good sword and go with it to yonder water's side; and when thou comest there I charge thee throw my sword in that water and come again and tell me what thou sawest there."

39   "My lord," said Sir Bedivere, "your commandment shall be done, and I shall lightly bring you word again."

40   So Sir Bedivere departed. And by the way he beheld that noble sword, that the pommel and the haft was all precious stones. And then he said to himself, "If I throw this rich sword in the water, thereof shall never come good, but harm and loss." And then

41 Sir Bedivere hid Excalibur under a tree. And so, as soon as he might, he came again unto the King and said he had been at the water and had thrown the sword into the water.

42   "What saw thou there?" said the King.

43   "Sir," he said, "I saw nothing but waves and winds."

did, the king swooned. And Sir Lucan swooned too, and some of his guts fell out of his body, and then the noble knight's heart burst. And when the king awoke, he saw how Sir Lucan lay foaming at the mouth with some of his guts at his feet.

35   "Alas," said the king, "this is a terrible sight, to see this noble duke die for my sake. For he tried to help me, when he needed help more than I. Alas, he would not complain, for his heart was so set on helping me. Now Jesus have mercy on his soul."

36   Then Sir Bedivere wept for the death of his brother.

37   "Now quit this mourning and weeping, gentle knight," said the king. "For this will not help me. For you can be sure, if I could live myself, the death of Sir Lucan would grieve me forever.

38   "But my time passes fast," added the king. "So take Excalibur, my good sword, and go to the side of the water yonder. And when you get there, I order you to throw it in the water and come back and tell me what you saw there."

39   "My lord," said Sir Bedivere, "what you command shall be done, and I shall quickly bring you word again."

40   So Sir Bedivere departed. And on his way, he looked at that noble sword, its handle all decorated with precious stones. And then he said to himself, "If I throw this rich sword in the water, good will never come of it—just harm and loss."

41   And so Sir Bedivere hid Excalibur under a tree. As then, as soon as he could, he came again to the king. He said he had been at the water and had thrown the sword in the water.

42   "What did you see there?" said the king.

43   "Sir," he said, "I saw nothing but waves and winds."

44   "That is untruly said of thee," said the King. "And therefore go thou lightly again and do my commandment; as thou art to me loved and dear, spare not, but throw it in."

45   Then Sir Bedivere returned again and took the sword in his hand. And yet him thought sin and shame to throw away that noble sword. And so eft he hid the sword and returned again and told the King that he had been at the water and done his commandment.

46   "What sawest thou there?" said the King.

47   "Sir," he said, "I saw nothing but waters wap and waves wan."

48   "Ah, traitor unto me and untrue," said King Arthur, "now hast thou betrayed me twice. Who would have weened that thou that has been to me so loved and dear, and thou art named a noble knight, and would betray me for the riches of this sword. But

49 now go again lightly, for thy long tarrying putteth me in great jeopardy of my life, for I have taken cold. And but if thou do now as I bid thee, if ever I may see thee I shall slay thee mine own hands, for thou wouldest for my rich sword see me dead."

50   Then Sir Bedivere departed and went to the sword and lightly took it up, and so he went to the water's side; and there he bound the girdle about the hilts, and threw the sword as far into the water as he might. And there came an arm and an hand above the water and took it and clutched it, and shook it thrice and brandished; and then vanished away the hand with the sword into the water. So Sir Bedivere came again to the King and told him what he saw.

44   "Then you speak falsely," said the king. "And so go quickly again and do as I command. Because I love you and hold you dear, don't spare it, but throw it in."

45   Then Sir Bedivere took the sword in his hand and returned again. And he still thought it a sin and a shame to throw away that noble sword. And so he hid the sword again and returned to the king. He told him that he had been to the water and had done as he was commanded.

46   "What did you see there?" said the king.

47   "Sir," he said, "I saw nothing but the waters lap and the waves grow pale."

48   "Ah, you are a traitor to me, and untrue," said King Arthur. "Now you have betrayed me twice. Who would have thought it? You have been so loved and dear to me, and are called a noble knight, and yet you would betray me for the riches of this sword.

49   "But go again quickly, for your long delay puts my life in great danger, and I grow cold. And unless you do as I tell you, I will slay you with my own hands if I ever see you again. For you wish to see me dead because of my rich sword."

50   Then Sir Bedivere departed and quickly took up the sword, and then he went to the water's side. There he tied the belt [by which Arthur wore the sword] around the handle. Then he threw the sword as far into the water as he could. And an arm and a hand came out of the water and clutched it, shaking and waving it three times. Then the hand vanished with the sword into the water. So Sir Bedivere went back to the king and told him what he saw.

51   "Alas," said the King, "help me hence, for I dread
me I have tarried overlong."

52   Then Sir Bedivere took the King upon his back
and so went with him to that water's side. And when
they were at the water's side, even fast by the bank
floated a little barge with many fair ladies in it; and
among them all was a queen; and all they had black
hoods, and all they wept and shrieked when they saw
King Arthur.

53   "Now put me into that barge," said the King; and
so he did softly. And there received him three ladies
with great mourning, and so they set them down.
And in one of their laps King Arthur laid his head,

54   and then the queen said, "Ah, my dear brother, why
have ye tarried so long from me? Alas, this wound on
your head hath caught overmuch cold." And anon
they rowed fromward the land, and Sir Bedivere
beheld all the ladies go froward him.

55   Then Sir Bedivere cried and said, "Ah, my lord
Arthur, what shall become of me, now ye go from me
and leave me here alone among mine enemies?"

56   "Comfort thyself," said the King, "and do as well
as thou mayest, for in me is no trust for to trust in.
For I must into the vale of Avilion to heal me of my
grievous wound. And if thou hear nevermore of me,
pray for my soul."

57   But ever the queen and ladies wept and shrieked,
that it was pity to hear. And as soon as Sir Bedivere
had lost sight of the barge he wept and wailed, and
so took the forest and went all that night.

58   And in the morning he was ware, betwixt two
bare woods, of a chapel and an hermitage. Then was
Sir Bedivere glad, and thither he went, and when he
came into the chapel he saw where lay an hermit
groveling on all fours, close thereby a tomb was new

51 "Alas," said the king, "help me to go there, for I fear that I have delayed too long."

52 Then Sir Bedivere took the king on his back and carried him to the water's side. And when they got there, a little barge with many fair ladies on it floated nearby. Among them was a queen. They all had black hoods, and they all wept and shrieked when they saw King Arthur.

53 "Now put me on that barge," said the king. And Sir Bedivere did so gently. And the three ladies greeted him with great mourning as they sat down around him. And King Arthur laid his head in one of their laps.

54 And then the queen said, "Ah, my dear brother, why have you stayed so long from me? Alas, this wound on your head has grown too cold." And soon they rowed away from the land, and Sir Bedivere saw all the ladies going away from him.

55 Then Sir Bedivere called out, "Ah, my lord Arthur! What shall become of me, now that you have gone from me, leaving me here alone among my enemies?"

56 "Comfort yourself," said the king, "and do as well as you can. For you cannot depend upon me now. I must go to the valley of Avalon to heal from my grievous wound. And if you never hear more of me, pray for my soul."

57 But the queen and ladies kept weeping and shrieking, and it was pitiful to hear. As soon as Sir Bedivere lost sight of the barge, he wept and wailed. Then he went to the forest and stayed there all that night.

58 And in the morning, he found a chapel and a hermit's home between two barren woods. Sir Bedivere was glad, and he went inside the chapel, where he saw a hermit crawling on all fours. Close by was a newly dug grave.

59   dug. When the hermit saw Sir Bedivere he knew him well, for he was but little tofore Bishop of Canterbury, that Sir Mordred put to flight.

60   "Sir," said Sir Bedivere, "what man is there here interred that you pray so fast for?"

61   "Fair son," said the hermit. "I wot not verily but by guessing. But this same night, at midnight, here came a number of ladies and brought here a dead corpse and prayed me to inter him. And here they offered an hundred tapers, and gave me a thousand gold coins."

62   "Alas," said Sir Bedivere, "that was my lord King Arthur, which lieth here buried in this chapel."

63   Then Sir Bedivere swooned, and when he awoke he prayed the hermit that he might abide with him still, there to live with fasting and prayers:

64   "For from hence will I never go," said Sir Bedivere, "by my will, but all the days of my life here to pray for my lord Arthur."

65   "Sir, ye are welcome to me," said the hermit, "for I know you better than ye think that I do: for ye are Sir Bedivere the Bold, and the full noble duke Sir Lucan the Butler was your brother."

66   Then Sir Bedivere told the hermit all as you have heard tofore, and so he stayed with the hermit that was beforehand Bishop of Canterbury. And there Sir Bedivere put upon him poor clothes, and served the hermit full lowly in fasting and in prayers.

67   Thus of Arthur I find no more written in books that been authorized, neither more of the very certainty of his death heard I nor read, but thus was he led away in a ship wherein were three queens; that one was King Arthur's sister, Queen Morgan le Fay, the other was the Queen of North Galis, and the third was the Queen of the Waste Lands.

59   When the hermit saw Sir Bedivere, he knew him
well. For not long before, he had been the Bishop of
Canterbury, but had been forced to flee by Sir Mordred.

60   "Sir," said Sir Bedivere, "who is buried there, for
whom you pray so strongly?"

61   "Fair son," said the hermit, "I can only guess. But
this very night at midnight, a number of ladies came
and brought a corpse, and they begged me to bury
him. And they brought a hundred candles and gave
me a thousand gold coins."

62   "Alas," said Sir Bedivere, "it is my lord King
Arthur who lies buried in this chapel."

63   Then Sir Bedivere swooned. And when he awoke,
he begged the hermit to let him stay there with him
to fast and pray:

64   "For I will never leave here by my own will," said
Sir Bedivere. "I will spend all the days of my life
here, praying for my lord Arthur."

65   "Sir, you are welcome by me," said the hermit.
"For I know you better than you think I do. You are
Sir Bedivere the Bold, and the noble duke Sir Lucan
the Butler was your brother."

66   Then Sir Bedivere told the hermit all that you
have heard already. And he stayed with the hermit
who had once been the Bishop of Canterbury. And Sir
Bedivere wore poor clothes and served the hermit
humbly in fasting and prayers.

67   I find no other books written about Arthur, and I
have neither heard nor read anything more concerning whether he really died or not. But he was,
indeed, led away in a ship carrying three queens.
One was King Arthur's sister, Queen Morgan le Fay;
the second was the Queen of North Galis; and the
third was the Queen of the Waste Lands.

68   Now more of the death of King Arthur could I never find, but that these ladies brought him to his grave, and such one was interred there which the hermit bare witness that was once Bishop of Canterbury. But yet the hermit knew not in certain that he was verily the body of King Arthur; for this tale Sir Bedivere, a knight of the Table Round, made it to be written.

69   Yet some men say in many parts of England that King Arthur is not dead, but carried by the will of our Lord Jesu into another place; and men say that he shall come again, and he shall win the Holy Cross. Yet I will not say that it shall be so, but rather I would say: here in this world he changed his life. And many men say that there is written upon the tomb this:

HIC IACET ARTHURUS, REX
QUONDAM, REXQUE FUTURUS

68   I never found anything more concerning the death of King Arthur, except that these ladies brought him to his grave. And the hermit who was once the Bishop of Canterbury witnessed someone's burial there. Even so, the hermit did not know for certain if this was truly King Arthur's body. This story has come down to us from Sir Bedivere, a knight of the Round Table.

69   Yet some men in many parts of England say that King Arthur is not dead, but was carried by the will of our Lord Jesus to another place. And some men say that he shall come again and win the Holy Cross. And yet, I will not say that it shall be so. But rather I will say that he changed his life here in this world. And many men say that this is written on his tomb:

HERE LIES ARTHUR, WHO WAS ONCE KING,
AND WILL BE KING AGAIN.

Arthur in Avalon (detail) by Sir Edward Burne-Jones

Unit Two

The Renaissance
(1485–1660)

Queen Elizabeth I

*T*he exciting period called the Renaissance began in Italy in the mid-1300s. Interestingly, the word *renaissance* was seldom used during the period itself. It was in the 1900s that historians really began to call those earlier days by that name.

Henry VII

Renaissance means "rebirth" in French. It was, indeed, a time of exciting change. During the medieval period, literacy had been restricted to a very few. During the Renaissance, more and more people could read and write, so literature flourished. Amazing advances were also made in visual art, science, philosophy, and political thought.

The Renaissance is said to have reached the British Isles in 1485, the year Henry VII became king of England. This was also the year that William Caxton published Malory's *Le Morte d'Arthur* on England's first printing press.

Printing was one of the greatest wonders of the Renaissance. Books were no longer a handmade rarity, and knowledge became available to many more people.

The English Renaissance reached its peak during the reign of Queen Elizabeth I, from 1558 until 1603. Elizabeth herself was an extremely well-educated monarch and an able poet in her own right. She was also a devoted patron of arts and ideas.

Her reign produced many of England's greatest authors—including Sir Thomas Wyatt, Edmund Spenser, Christopher Marlowe, Sir Walter Raleigh, and William Shakespeare.

London was the center of literary activity. It was a small city by today's standards, so many of these writers knew one another. They exchanged and commented on one another's manuscripts; they met in places like the Mermaid Tavern to discuss ideas; and they sometimes quarreled bitterly.

Not surprisingly, all this activity produced a feeling of literary adventure. England had not had a single great poet since Chaucer a century and a half earlier. The Elizabethan writers were determined to change that—and they did.

They read and imitated Chaucer with reverence. They also studied poets of the European continent, borrowing ideas, techniques, and forms. The 14-line sonnet, originally an Italian form, became popular in England during the Renaissance.

Many of London's greatest authors wrote for the theater. Indeed, the Elizabethan age produced some of the greatest plays the world has ever seen. Even so, play writing was not then considered fully respectable. So even professional playwrights like Marlowe, Jonson, and Shakespeare wrote and published nondramatic poetry.

Metaphysical Poets

A small group of Elizabethan authors became known in later years as "metaphysical poets." These included John Donne and Andrew Marvell. Metaphysics is the study of the deeper nature of reality. So the metaphysical poets often probed philosophical questions and also touched on politics, psychology, and science.

But their poetry was far from dry or vague. Instead, it is full of concrete, vivid images. Metaphysical poets were especially fond of a figure of speech called the *conceit*. A conceit is a kind of comparison, like a metaphor or simile. But unlike most figures of speech, conceits can be long and detailed.

One example is John Donne's "A Valediction: Forbidding Mourning," included in this unit. Donne uses the poem's last 12 lines to compare two lovers to the points of a drawing compass.

Most Elizabethan poets used conceits from time to time. But the metaphysical poets used them far more often.

Cavaliers and Puritans

Elizabeth's successor, King James I, was an able ruler, but his reign was troubled and uneasy. A growing pessimism found its way into English literature. Shakespeare wrote his darkest tragedies, *King Lear, Othello,* and *Macbeth*, during James' reign.

When James I died in 1625, his son Charles took the throne. Charles I did not have his father's leadership abilities, and the political situation worsened. In 1642, civil war broke out in England between King Charles and Parliament (England's governing body). Soldiers and courtiers loyal to King Charles were known as Cavaliers.

Cavalier poets like Robert Herrick and Richard Lovelace often wrote about love and pleasure. In poems like "To Lucasta, on Going to the Wars" (included in this unit), they also praised such old-fashioned values as honor, chivalry, and loyalty to one's king.

In 1649, the royalists lost the Civil War, and King Charles I was beheaded. A brief period called the Commonwealth began. During this time, England had no king. In 1653, Oliver Cromwell became Lord Protector of England.

Cromwell was a Puritan who believed that religion must be rid of all corruption. His reign was marked by strict religious belief and a concern for public morality. During his dictatorship, the theaters were closed.

Needless to say, the Cavalier poets did not fare well in the Commonwealth. But this did not mean an end to fine poetry. John Milton, who worked in Cromwell's government, was a devoted Puritan and a truly great poet.

Milton published his great religious epic, *Paradise Lost,* in 1667. By then, Cromwell had died and the Commonwealth had ended. Charles II, the son of Charles I, had returned to England from exile and was the new king. The Restoration, a new period in English history and literature, was beginning.

Unit Two Author Biographies

Sir Thomas Wyatt (1503–1542)

Sir Thomas Wyatt was a skilled soldier, musician, and poet. During his travels in Europe, he studied poetry in other languages. He introduced the sonnet to England, where it became extremely popular. "Whoso List to Hunt" is one of his most popular verses.

Edmund Spenser (1552?–1599)

Edmund Spenser wrote his first published works when he was 16 years old. By the time of his death, he was considered the most important poet in England. His greatest work was the huge epic poem *The Faerie Queen*, which was admired by Queen Elizabeth.

Sonnet 30, which appears in this unit, is part of a collection of eighty-nine sonnets entitled *Amoretti* (little love poems). These sonnets describe Spenser's courtship to a woman named Elizabeth Boyle.

Christopher Marlowe (1564–1593)

Christopher Marlowe was the most important English dramatist before Shakespeare. In plays like *Tamburlane* (Parts I and II), *Dr. Faustus*, and *Edward II*, Marlowe paved the way for a generation of great playwrights.

Marlowe also wrote important nondramatic poems. His unfinished *Hero and Leander* is one of the great narrative poems of its time.

At one point Marlowe served as a spy for the English government. He also developed a reputation for atheism and unruly behavior. At the age of 29, he was stabbed to death, reportedly in a quarrel over a tavern bill. But some scholars believe that his death was a government assassination.

Sir Walter Raleigh (1552?–1618)

Sir Walter Raleigh fought as a soldier in France, Ireland, and Spain, and explored parts of America. He was also deeply involved in the politics of his age.

For a time, he was a favorite courtier of Queen Elizabeth. But he fell from her favor when he secretly married. Upon discovering his marriage, Elizabeth imprisoned Raleigh and his wife.

Raleigh and his wife were released, but his fortunes grew even shakier after Queen Elizabeth's death. He was charged with treason against James I, and was eventually executed.

None of Raleigh's poems were published during his life. Instead, they were circulated in hand-written copies. In those days, it was considered undignified for a courtier like Raleigh to publish poetry.

William Shakespeare (1564–1616)

William Shakespeare is generally regarded as the greatest author in the English language. He was born in the village of Stratford, where he started a family at the age of 18. He eventually moved to London and became active in the theater. But he kept his family in Stratford and died there.

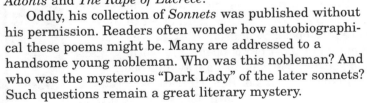

Shakespeare is most famous as the author of plays such as *The Taming of the Shrew*, *Romeo and Juliet*, *Julius Caesar*, *Hamlet*, and *Macbeth*. He also published two long narrative poems, *Venus and Adonis* and *The Rape of Lucrece*.

Oddly, his collection of *Sonnets* was published without his permission. Readers often wonder how autobiographical these poems might be. Many are addressed to a handsome young nobleman. Who was this nobleman? And who was the mysterious "Dark Lady" of the later sonnets? Such questions remain a great literary mystery.

John Donne (1572?–1631)

John Donne was a Catholic for much of his life. Eventually, Donne converted to Anglicanism (the official religion of England) and became an Anglican priest.

Donne's early writings are mostly love poems. His later works are generally concerned with religious matters. In some of his poems, romantic and religious feeling blend together. In "A Valediction: Forbidding Mourning," the speaker describes his love for a woman in deeply spiritual terms.

Most of Donne's writings are intensely personal. For example, Meditation 17 (also in this unit) was written when Donne was dangerously ill. At the sound of a tolling bell, he genuinely wondered if he was about to die.

Ben Jonson (1573–1637)

Ben Jonson was the stepson of a bricklayer and practiced that trade for a time during his youth. He had little formal education, but more than made up for it in reading and study.

He and William Shakespeare were close friends. Shakespeare acted in Jonson's first play, *Every Man in His Humor*. But Jonson could be critical of his fellow playwright. He felt that Shakespeare's plays were sometimes carelessly written and showed a lack of learning. Even so, Jonson wrote a poem honoring Shakespeare's memory for an edition of his friend's plays.

Jonson's best plays are comedies such as *Volpone, or the Fox* and *The Alchemist*. He was also one of the most respected poets of his time.

Robert Herrick (1591–1674)

Robert Herrick was one of several poets who called themselves "sons of Ben" because they were influenced by Jonson. Herrick was a clergyman, but most of his poems are worldly, light, and sensual. He was also a Cavalier poet.

Like other sons of Ben, Herrick explored the theme of *carpe diem* (Latin for "seize the day"). His poems often remind us of how fleeting and precious life is.

Andrew Marvell (1621–1678)

During his life, Andrew Marvell was better known as a politician than as a poet. He became a member of Parliament during the reign of Oliver Cromwell, and his political career continued after Cromwell's fall.

Marvell's "To His Coy Mistress," included in this unit, is a metaphysical poem that explores the nature of time and mortality. It is also a carpe diem poem that urges living life to the fullest.

Richard Lovelace (1618–1658)

A Cavalier poet, Richard Lovelace wrote "To Lucasta, on Going to the Wars" when he was about to fight in the English Civil War. After Cromwell took power, Lovelace spent much time in prison and died in poverty.

Lovelace's sufferings produced phrases and sayings that remain well-known today. While in prison, he wrote a poem in which he famously declared, "Stone walls do not a prison make / Nor iron bars a cage."

John Milton (1608–1674)

John Milton was a deeply religious poet whose greatest work, *Paradise Lost*, explores the ways of God in the world.

When Oliver Cromwell took power, Milton served in his government. When Cromwell died and the monarchy was restored, Milton was arrested and lived under the threat of execution. He survived this difficult time, partly with the help of his friend Andrew Marvell.

This unit includes Milton's sonnet "How Soon Hath Time," which expresses the poet's anxiety at turning 23. In fact, Milton was already quite an accomplished poet by then. He wrote his first truly great poem, "On the Morning of Christ's Nativity," at the age of 21.

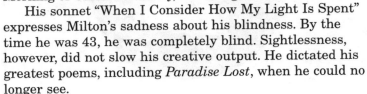

His sonnet "When I Consider How My Light Is Spent" expresses Milton's sadness about his blindness. By the time he was 43, he was completely blind. Sightlessness, however, did not slow his creative output. He dictated his greatest poems, including *Paradise Lost*, when he could no longer see.

Whoso List to Hunt

Sir Thomas Wyatt

*W*hoso list to hunt, I know where is an hind,
But as for me, alas, I may no more.
The vain travail hath wearied me so sore
I am of them that farthest cometh behind.
5   Yet may I, by no means, my wearied mind
Draw from the deer, but as she fleeth afore,
Fainting I follow. I leave off therefore,
Since in a net I seek to hold the wind.

Who list her hunt, I put him out of doubt,
10   As well as I, may spend his time in vain.
And graven with diamonds in letters plain
There is written, her fair neck round about,
"*Noli me tangere*, for Caesar's I am,
And wild for to hold, though I seem tame."

Anne Boleyn

Whoso List to Hunt

Sir Thomas Wyatt

The Literal Meaning of the Poem

If anyone wishes to hunt (**whoso list to hunt**), I know where a female deer (**hind**) can be found, says the speaker of this poem. But, he continues, I am tired of the useless work (**vain travail**) of hunting, and so I am in the group of hunters who follow last. Even though my tired mind still weakly (**fainting**) pursues the fleeing deer, I will give up the actual hunt, which is like trying to hold wind in a net.

The speaker goes on to tell the listener (**I put him out of doubt**) that hunting the deer is useless because round the deer's neck hang these words carved with diamonds: "Touch me not (***Noli me tangere***), for I belong to Caesar. And I am too wild to hold, though I seem tame."

The Symbolic Meaning of the Poem

The "hind" of this poem refers to Anne Boleyn, a wife of King Henry VIII (**Caesar**). At one time, Boleyn may have been Wyatt's mistress. Not surprisingly, this poem was not published while Wyatt was alive.

Sonnet 30

Edmund Spenser

*M*y love is like to ice, and I to fire;
How comes it then that this her cold so great
Is not dissolved through my so hot desire,
But harder grows the more I her entreat?
5 Or how comes it that my exceeding heat
Is not delayed by her heart frozen cold,
But that I burn much more in boiling sweat,
And feel my flames augmented manifold?
What more miraculous thing may be told
10 That fire which all thing melts, should harden ice,
And ice which is congealed with senseless cold,
Should kindle fire by wonderful device?
Such is the power of love in gentle mind,
That it can alter all the course of kind.

Sonnet 30

Edmund Spenser

*M*y beloved is like ice; I am like fire.
So why is it that her great coldness
is not melted by my hot desire,
but only grows harder the more I beg for her love?
5   And why is it that my great heat
is not cooled by her cold, frozen heart?
I only burn much more and boil in my sweat,
and feel my flames increase again and again.
Can anything be more miraculous?
10 For fire, which melts all things, now hardens ice;
and ice, although thickened with numbing cold,
stirs up fire by some amazing trick.
Such is the power of love over a gentle mind,
that it can change the very ways of nature.

Fair Is My Love by Edwin Austin Abbey

The Passionate Shepherd to His Love

Christopher Marlowe

*C*ome live with me, and be my love,
And we will all the pleasures prove
That valleys, groves, hills, and fields,
Woods, or steepy mountain yields.

5   And we will sit upon the rocks,
Seeing the shepherds feed their flocks
By shallow rivers, to whose falls
Melodious birds sing madrigals.

And I will make thee beds of roses,
10   And a thousand fragrant posies,
A cap of flowers, and a kirtle,
Embroidered all with leaves of myrtle.

A gown made of the finest wool
Which from our pretty lambs we pull,
15   Fair linèd slippers for the cold,
With buckles of the purest gold.

A belt of straw and ivy buds,
With coral clasps and amber studs,
And if these pleasures may thee move,
20   Come live with me, and be my love.

The shepherd swains shall dance and sing
For thy delight each May morning.
If these delights thy mind may move,
Then live with me, and be my love.

The Passionate Shepherd to His Love

Christopher Marlowe

*C*ome live with me and be my love,
and we will experience all the pleasures
to be found in valleys, groves, hills, fields,
woods, or steep mountainsides.

5   And we will sit upon the rocks
watching shepherds feed their flocks
by shallow rivers. And to those rivers' waterfalls,
tuneful birds will sing madrigals.[1]

And I will make you beds out of roses
10   and a thousand sweet-smelling posies,
and also a cap made of flowers, and a dress
stitched with myrtle[2] leaves.

I'll make you a gown from the finest wool
pulled from our pretty lambs—
15   and for cold weather, beautifully lined slippers
with buckles of the purest gold.

I'll make you a belt from straw and ivy buds
with coral clasps and amber buttons.
And if these pleasures appeal to you,
20   come live with me and be my love.

The shepherd boys will dance and sing
for your entertainment each May morning.
If these delights appeal to you,
then live with me and be my love.

---

1 **madrigals:** songs for several voices
2 **myrtle:** a type of evergreen bush

The Nymph's Reply to the Shepherd

Sir Walter Raleigh

*I*f all the world and love were young,
And truth in every shepherd's tongue,
These pretty pleasures might me move
To live with thee and be thy love.

5 But Time drives flocks from field to fold,
When rivers rage and rocks grow cold,
And Philomel becometh dumb;
The rest complains of cares to come.

The flowers do fade, and wanton fields
10 To wayward winter reckoning yields;
A honey tongue, a heart of gall
Is fancy's spring, but sorrow's fall.

Thy gowns, thy shoes, thy beds of roses,
Thy cap, thy kirtle, and thy posies.
15 Soon break, soon wither, soon forgotten,
In folly ripe, in reason rotten.

Thy belt of straw and ivy buds,
Thy coral clasps and amber studs,

The Nymph's[1] Reply to the Shepherd

Sir Walter Raleigh

*I*f all the world and love were young,
and if every shepherd spoke the truth,
these pretty pleasures might persuade me
to live with you and be your love.

5   But Time drives flocks from the pen
in the season of floods and cold stones,
and the nightingale becomes silent.
All other living things complain of troubles to come.

The flowers fade, and the splendid fields
10   surrender themselves to thoughtless winter.
A tongue of honey with a cruel heart
is like a dream in spring, sorrow in fall.

Your gowns, shoes, beds of roses,
cap, dress, and posies
15   are soon broken, withered, and forgotten.
They seem ripe in our foolishness, rotten in our
    reason.

Your belt of straw and ivy buds,
your coral clasps and amber buttons—

---

1 **nymph:** a minor nature goddess in Greek mythology; in
this instance, a young girl

All these in me no means can move
20   To come to thee and be thy love.

But could youth last and love still breed,
Had joys no date, nor age no need,
Then these delights my mind might move
To live with thee and be thy love.

none of these can persuade me
20   to come to you and be your love.

But if youth were to last and love always grew,
and if joys never faded and no one grew old,
then these delights might persuade me
to live with you and be your love.

The Hireling Shepherd by William Holman Hunt

Sonnet 29

William Shakespeare

When, in disgrace with Fortune and
    men's eyes,
I all alone beweep my outcast state,
And trouble deaf heaven with my bootless
    cries,
And look upon myself and curse my fate,
5   Wishing me like to one more rich
    in hope,
Featured like him, like him with friends
    possessed,
Desiring this man's art, and that man's
    scope,
With what I most enjoy contented
    least;
Yet in these thoughts myself almost despising,
10   Haply I think on thee, and then my state,
Like to the lark at break of day arising
From sullen earth, sings hymns at
    heaven's gate;
  For thy sweet love remembered such wealth brings
  That then I scorn to change my state with kings.

Sonnet 29

William Shakespeare

When I fall out of favor (**disgrace**) with Fortune
   and men,
I weep alone over my outcast condition
And trouble deaf heaven with useless (**bootless**)
   cries,
And I look at myself and curse my fate.
5 I wish I were like a man I know who has more to
   hope for—
That I had another man's good looks, and yet
   another's friends.
I desire this man's abilities (**art**), that man's power
   (**scope**),
And am least happy with the things I usually enjoy
   most.
But then, when I almost hate myself,
10 I luckily think about you. And then I feel
Like a lark when the sun rises
From the gloomy (**sullen**) earth, singing hymns at
   heaven's gate.
   For remembering your sweet love brings me such
      wealth
   That I wouldn't change places with a king.

Sonnet 116

William Shakespeare

*L*et me not to the marriage of true minds
Admit impediments. Love is not love
Which alters when it alteration finds,
Or bends with the remover to remove.

5   Oh no! It is an ever-fixèd mark
That looks on tempests and is never shaken.
It is the star to every wandering bark,
Whose worth's unknown, although his height be
    taken.

Love's not Time's fool, though rosy lips and cheeks
10 Within his bending sickle's compass come.
Love alters not with his brief hours and weeks,
But bears it out even to the edge of doom.
    If this be error and upon me proved,
    I never writ, nor no man ever loved.

Sonnet 116

William Shakespeare

In a church wedding, the preacher typically asks
if anyone objects to the marriage. This sonnet is
phrased as an answer to this question. The speaker
does not wish to object (**Admit impediments**) to a
marriage of "true minds."

Love is not true love, he says, if it is changeable
or unfaithful. Instead, it is like a landmark (**an ever-
fixèd mark**) for a sailor to guide his ship (**wandering
bark**). Or it is like a star that serves as a sailor's
guide. The star's altitude is measured to decide a
ship's course, but its value cannot be measured.

Love is not Time's plaything (**fool**), even if temptation comes within a lover's reach (**bending sickle's
compass**). Indeed, true love endures (**bears it out**)
until Judgment Day (**the edge of doom**).

"If I am proved wrong in saying this," the speaker
concludes, "I never wrote a word, and no man ever
loved."

Sonnet 130

William Shakespeare

*M*y mistress' eyes are nothing like the sun,
Coral is far more red than her lips' red.
If snow be white, why then her breasts are dun,
If hairs be wires, black wires grow on her head.
5 I have seen roses damasked, red and white,
But no such roses see I in her cheeks.
And in some perfumes is there more delight
Than in the breath that from my mistress reeks,
I love to hear her speak, yet well I know
10 That music hath a far more pleasing sound.
I grant I never saw a goddess go,
My mistress, when she walks, treads on the ground.
    And yet, by Heaven, I think my love as rare
    As any she belied with false compare.

Sonnet 130

William Shakespeare

In Shakespeare's time, darkness of skin and hair was considered unattractive. Not surprisingly, poets often compared their lovers to sunlight, snow, and other bright things. Such comparisons grew somewhat boring.

In this sonnet, the speaker's beloved is not a typical beauty. Her "eyes are nothing like the sun," her lips are not red like coral, and her breasts are dark (**dun**), not snow-white. He describes her hair as looking like "black wires."

Her cheeks do not look like streaked (**damasked**) roses, and her breath is not sweet like perfume. And although the speaker loves to hear her voice, he knows "that music has a far more pleasing sound." Far from walking with the airy footsteps of a goddess, the speaker's beloved "treads on the ground."

"And yet, by Heaven," the speaker concludes, "I think my love is as precious as any woman described with false comparisons."

This is one of many sonnets in which Shakespeare speaks of a "Dark Lady." In other sonnets, the speaker's love for her is mixed with disgust, and she proves unfaithful to him. One of the great mysteries of the sonnets is whether the Dark Lady was a real person loved by Shakespeare. If so, who was she?

A Valediction: Forbidding Mourning

John Donne

*A*s virtuous men pass mildly away,
  And whisper to their souls, to go,
Whilst some of their sad friends do say,
  The breath goes now, and some say, no:

5 So let us melt, and make no noise,
    No tear-floods, nor sigh-tempests move,
  'Twere profanation of our joys
    To tell the laity our love.

Moving of th' earth brings harms and fears,
10   Men reckon what it did and meant,
  But trepidation of the spheres,
    Though greater far, is innocent.

Dull sublunary lovers' love
    (Whose soul is sense) cannot admit

A Valediction:[1]
Forbidding Mourning

John Donne

*G*ood men die quietly,
   Whispering to their souls to go,
While some of their sad friends watch on and say,
   "He's gone now," and others say, "No."

5   Like them, let us melt away from each other quietly
      Without floods of tears or storms of sighs.
    It would show disrespect (**profanation**) to our love
      To speak of it to those (**the laity**) who cannot
        understand.

Earthquakes cause both harm and fear,
10   And men wonder why they come and what they
        mean.
But changes that happen in the heavens (**trepida-
tions of the spheres**)
    Cause no harm, even though they are much
      greater.

The love of dull, sublunary[2] lovers
    Is purely physical (of the **senses**). So these lovers
      cannot accept

---

1 **valediction:** farewell
2 **sublunary:** beneath the moon—and changeable like the
moon

15   Absence, because it doth remove
        Those things which elemented it.

But we by a love, so much refined,
    That ourselves know not what it is,
Interassurèd of the mind,
20   Care less eyes, lips, and hands to miss.

Our two souls therefore, which are one,
    Though I must go, endure not yet
A breach, but an expansion,
    Like gold to airy thinness beat.

25   If they be two, they are two so
        As stiff twin compasses are two,
Thy soul the fixed foot, makes no show
        To move, but doth, if th' other do.

And though it in the center sit,
30   Yet when the other far doth roam,
It leans, and hearkens after it,
    And grows erect, as that comes home.

Such wilt thou be to me, who must
    Like th' other foot, obliquely run;
35   Thy firmness makes my circle just,
        And makes me end, where I begun.

15 Each other's absence, because absence removes
   Everything their love is made **(elemented)** of.

But our love is so fine
   That we cannot understand it ourselves.
When our very minds are mingled **(Interassurèd)**,
20   It is less important that our eyes, lips, and hands
      are not together.

And so our two souls are one.
   And though I must go away, our souls do not suffer
A break. Instead, they expand
   Like a sheet of gold beaten to the thinness of air.

25 If our souls are two, they are two in the way
   That a drawing compass has two points.
Your soul is the fixed point, and it does not seem
   To move. But it *does* move if the other point
      moves.

Your point sits in the center of the circle
30   And leans and watches the other point
When it roams far way.
   Then it stands straight again when the other
      point comes back.

You will be like this to me, for I must
   Move away, like the other point.
35 Your faithfulness **(firmness)** will make the circle I
      draw perfect **(just)**,
   And so I will end just where I started.

Meditation 17

John Donne

*Nunc lento
sunitu dicunt,
Morieris.*

1   *P*erchance he for whom this bell tolls, may be so ill, as that he knows not it tolls for him; and perchance I may think myself so much better than I am, as that they who are about me, and see my state, may have caused it to toll for me, and I know not that. The
2   Church is catholic, universal, so are all her actions; all that she does belongs to all. When she baptizes a child, that action concerns me; for that child is thereby connected to that Head which is my Head too, and engrafted into that body,

3   whereof I am a member. And when she buries a man, that action concerns me: All mankind is of one Author, and is one volume; when one man dies, one chapter is not torn out of the book, but translated into a better language; and every chapter must be so

4   translated; God employs several translators; some pieces are translated by age, some by sickness, some by war, some by justice; but God's hand is in every translation; and his hand shall bind up all

Meditation 17

John Donne

Now, this bell that tolls softly
for another says to me, "You must die."

1   *P*erhaps the man for whom this bell tolls is so ill
that he does not know it tolls for him. And perhaps I
think myself much more well than I am. So perhaps
the people around me see how sick I am, and have
caused it to toll for me, and I don't realize it.

2   The church is broad and limitless, and so are all
her actions. All that she does belongs to everyone.
When she baptizes a child, that action concerns me.
For that child becomes connected to that head[1] which
is my head too. He joins that body of which I am also
a part.

3   And when the church buries a man, that action
also concerns me. All mankind has one author and is
one book. When one man dies, a chapter is not torn
out of the book. Instead, it is translated into a better
language.[2] And every chapter must be so translated.

4   God uses several translators. Some pieces are
translated by old age, some by sickness, some by war,
some by justice. But God's hand is in every translation. And his hand will bind together all our

---

1 **head:** Christ
2 **translated into a better language:** Donne compares
   going to heaven to translating a book. He then describes
   heaven as a library.

our scattered leaves again, for that Library where every book shall lie open to one another: As therefore

5   the bell that rings to a sermon, calls not upon the preacher only, but upon the congregation to come; so this bell calls us all: but how much more me, who am brought so near the door by this sickness. There was

6   a contention as far as a suit (in which both piety and dignity, religion and estimation, were mingled), which of the religious orders should ring to prayers first in the morning; and it was determined, that they should ring first that rose earliest. If we

7   understand aright the dignity of this bell that tolls for our evening prayer, we would be glad to make it ours, by rising early, in that application, that it might be ours, as well as his, whose indeed it is. The bell

8   doth toll for him that thinks it doth; and though it intermit again, yet from that minute, that that occasion wrought upon him, he is united to God. Who

9   casts not up his eye to the sun when it rises? but who takes off his eye from a comet when that breaks out? Who bends not his ear to any bell, which upon any occasion rings? but who can remove it from that bell, which is passing a piece of himself out of this world?

10   No man is an island, entire of itself; every man is a piece of the continent, a part of the main; if a clod be washed away by the sea, Europe is the less, as well as if a promontory were, as well as if a manor of thy

11   friends or of thine own were; any man's death diminishes me, because I am involved in mankind; and therefore never send to know for whom the bell tolls; it tolls for thee. Neither can we call this a begging of

scattered pages again. And we will go to that library where all books shall lie open to one another.

5   And so the bell that rings for a sermon does not call only the preacher. It also calls his flock to come. This bell calls us all. But it calls to me most of all, because I have been brought so near death by this sickness.

6   I know of a quarrel that turned into a lawsuit. In it, faith and dignity, religion and self-esteem were all mixed together. It had to do with which monastery should ring the prayer bells first in the morning. It was decided that the monastery that rose earliest should ring first.

7   If we fully understand the dignity of this bell tolling for our evening prayer, we will gladly rise early to ring it. Then it will belong to us, as well as to the man for whom it is meant.

8   The bell tolls for any man who thinks it tolls for him. And even though the bell may stop again, a man is united with God from the moment he realizes this.

9   Who does not turn his eye toward the sun when it rises? Who can stop looking at a comet once it appears? Who does not turn to listen to any bell, no matter what it rings for? And who cannot think that it marks the passing of a piece of himself from this world?

10   No man is an island, complete in itself. Every man is a piece of the continent, a part of the mainland. If a piece of dirt is washed away by the sea, Europe is made smaller, just as it would be if a whole hill were washed away—or a house belonging to your friends, or your own house.

11   Any man's death makes me smaller, because I am part of mankind. So never send someone to find out for whom the bell tolls. It tolls for you.

12   misery or a borrowing of misery, as though we were not miserable enough of ourselves, but must fetch in more from the next house, in taking upon us the misery of our neighbors. Truly it were an excusable

13   covetousness if we did; for affliction is a treasure, and scarce any man hath enough of it. No man hath affliction enough that is not matured, and ripened by it, and made fit for God by that affliction. If a man

14   carry treasure in bullion, or in a wedge of gold, and have none coined into current monies, his treasure will not defray him as he travels. Tribulation is treasure in the nature of it, but it is not current money in the use of it, except we get nearer and nearer our

15   home, Heaven, by it. Another man may be sick too, and sick to death, and this affliction may lie in his bowels, as gold in a mine, and be of no use to him; but this bell, that tells me of his affliction, digs out, and applies that gold to me; if by this consideration

16   of another's danger I take mine own into contemplation, and so secure myself by making my recourse to my God, who is our only security.

12   In saying all this, we are not begging or borrowing misery. Are we not miserable enough already? Must we fetch more misery from the next house, and take upon us the misery of our neighbors?

13   But truthfully, we would be excusable in our envy if we did. For suffering is a treasure, and hardly any man has enough of it. If a man suffers enough, his suffering matures and ripens him, and he is made more fit for God by it.

14   Suppose a man carries his treasure in bars of gold and has none coined into money. His treasure will not pay his way as he travels. Trouble is treasure by its very nature. But it is not really money, except when we use it to get nearer and nearer our home, heaven.

15   Perhaps another man is sick too, and sick to death. This illness may lie in his bowels, as gold lies in a mine, and be of no use to him. But this bell that tells me of his illness digs out his gold and makes it useful to me.

16   Someone else's danger makes me think carefully about my own. And so I bring myself safety by asking for help from God, who is our only safety.

Death Be Not Proud

John Donne

*D*eath be not proud, though some have
    callèd thee
Mighty and dreadful, for though art not so,
For those whom thou think'st thou dost overthrow,
Die not, poor Death, nor yet canst thou kill me.
5   From rest and sleep, which but thy pictures be,
Much pleasure, then from thee, much more must
    flow,
And soonest our best men with thee do go,
Rest of their bones, and soul's
    delivery.
Though art slave to fate, chance, kings, and
    desperate men,
10   And dost with poison, war, and sickness dwell,
And poppy, or charms can make us sleep as well,
And better than thy stroke; why swell'st thou then?
One short sleep past, we wake eternally,
And death shall be no more; Death, thou shalt die.

Death Be Not Proud

John Donne

*D*eath, do not be proud, even though some have called you
Mighty and dreadful, for you are not so.
Those whom you think you kill **(overthrow)**
Do not die, poor Death. Nor can you kill me.
5 Rest and sleep are but images of you,
But they give much pleasure, and you must give even more.
The best men go with you easily,
Resting their bones and freeing their souls from their bodies.
You are a slave to fate, chance, kings, and murderous men,
10 And you live with poison, war, and sickness.
Opium and magic can make us sleep as well as you—
Or even better. So why do you swell with pride?
When one short sleep is over, we will wake eternally,[1]
And death will be no more. Death, you will die.

---

1 **wake eternally:** Donne refers to the Christian idea of
Judgment Day, when all the dead will be resurrected.

On My First Son

Ben Jonson

*F*arewell, thou child of my right hand, and joy;
　My sin was too much hope of thee, loved boy:
Seven years thou wert lent to me, and I thee pay,
　Exacted by thy fate, on the just day.

5　Oh, could I lose all father now! for why
　　Will man lament the state he should envy—
　To have so soon 'scaped world's and flesh's rage,
　　And if no other misery, yet age?

　Rest in soft peace, and asked, say, "Here doth lie
10　　Ben Jonson his best piece of poetry;
　For whose sake henceforth all his vows be such
　　As what he loves may never like too much."

On My First Son

Ben Jonson

Ben Jonson lost two children to the plague—a daughter and a son. He wrote poems about both deaths. In this poem, he says farewell to his son, whom he calls "child of my right hand." This a translation from Hebrew of the boy's name, Benjamin.

The boy died on his seventh birthday. Seven years was the amount of time typically given to pay back a loan. So Jonson compares the boy's life to a loan. "Forced by fate, I pay you back on the exact day," he says.

He wishes he could end his feeling of fatherhood (**lose all father**). He finds it strange that he should grieve, when his son's fate is truly enviable. After all, Benjamin has escaped trouble and sickness (**world's and flesh's rage**) and also old age.

He asks his son to rest in peace. He also asks him to tell visitors to his grave that he is Ben Jonson's "best piece of poetry." As for Jonson, he vows never to love anyone in quite the same way he loved his son.

Song: To Celia

Ben Jonson

*D*rink to me only with thine eyes,
    And I will pledge with mine;
Or leave a kiss but in the cup,
    And I'll not look for wine.
5   The thirst that from the soul doth rise
    Doth ask a drink divine;
But might I of Jove's nectar sup,
    I would not change for thine.
I sent thee late a rosy wreath,
10   Not so much honoring thee
As giving it a hope, that there
    It could not withered be.
But thou thereon didst only breathe,
    And sent'st it back to me;
15   Since when it grows, and smells, I swear,
    Not of itself but thee.

Song: To Celia

Ben Jonson

*S*imply drink to me with your eyes,
    And I will promise faithfulness with mine.
Or put nothing in the cup but a kiss,
    And I'll not wish there was wine in it.
5   The thirst felt by the soul
    Longs for a divine drink.
But even if I could sip from Jove's nectar,[1]
    I would not exchange it for yours.
Lately, I sent you a wreath of roses—
10   Not so much to honor you
As in the hope
    That it would never wither.
You merely breathed on it
    And sent it back to me.
15   Since then it keeps growing—and I swear that it smells
    Not like flowers, but like you.

1 **Jove's nectar:** In Roman mythology, Jove was the ruler of the gods. The gods drank nectar to keep them immortal.

To the Virgins to Make Much of Time

Robert Herrick

*G*ather ye rosebuds while ye may,
　　Old time is still a-flying;
And this same flower that smiles today
　　Tomorrow will be dying.

5　　The glorious lamp of heaven, the sun,
　　　The higher he's a-getting,
The sooner will his race be run,
　　And nearer he's to setting.

That age is best which is the first,
10　　When youth and blood are warmer:
But being spent, the worse, and worst
　　Times still succeed the former.

Then be not coy, but use your time,
　　And, while ye may, go marry;
15　For, having lost but once your prime,
　　You may forever tarry.

To the Virgins to Make Much of Time

Robert Herrick

*G*ather rosebuds while you can,
    For time is always passing.
And this same flower that blooms today
    Will be dying tomorrow.

5   That glorious lamp of heaven,
        The sun, rises in the sky.
    But the higher he goes, the sooner his race is run,
        And the closer he is to setting.

The best time of life is the earliest,
10   When youth and blood are warm.
But once youth is gone, worse and worse
    Is the time that follows.

So don't be coy, use your time well,
    And marry while you can.
15   For once you've lost your youth,
      You might wait for marriage forever.

To His Coy Mistress

Andrew Marvell

*H*ad we but world enough, and time,
This coyness, Lady, were no crime.
We would sit down, and think which way
To walk, and pass our long love's day.
5   Thou by the Indian Ganges' side
Shouldst rubies find; I by the tide
Of Humber would complain. I would
Love you ten years before the Flood,
And you should, if you please, refuse
10 Till the conversion of the Jews.
My vegetable love should grow
Vaster than empires and more slow;
An hundred years should go to praise
Thine eyes, and on thy forehead gaze;
15 Two hundred to adore each breast,
But thirty thousand to the rest;
An age at least to every part,
And the last age should show your heart.
For, Lady, you deserve this state,
20 Nor would I love at lower rate.
        But at my back I always hear
Time's wingèd chariot hurrying near;
And yonder all before us lie

To His Coy Mistress

Andrew Marvell

*I*f we had enough space and time,
Lady, your coyness would be no crime.
We would sit down and think about which way
To walk, and how to pass our long day in love.
5   You would find rubies
By the side of the Indian Ganges, while I
Would complain on the Humber's shore.[1]
I would love you for ten years before the flood,
And if you wished to, you could refuse me
10   Till the conversion of the Jews.[2]
My plant-like love would grow
Greater and more slowly than empires.
I would take a hundred years to praise
Your eyes and gaze on your forehead,
15   Then take two hundred to adore each breast,
And 30,000 more for the rest of you.
Each part would take an age,
And the last age would show your heart.
For, lady, you deserve all this attention,
20   Nor do I wish to give you less love.
     But at my back, I always hear
The winged chariot of time hurrying near.
And spread out before us yonder

---

1 **You would . . . Humber's shore:** The Ganges is a great river in India; the Humber is a much smaller one where Marvell grew up. Rubies were once used as charms to preserve virginity.

2 **flood . . . Jews:** The biblical flood destroyed all humankind except for Noah's family. Christians in Marvell's time believed that all Jews would convert to Christianity before the end of the world.

Deserts of vast eternity.
25 Thy beauty shall no more be found,
Nor, in thy marble vault, shall sound
My echoing song; then worms shall try
That long-preserved virginity,
And your quaint honor turn to dust,
30 And into ashes all my lust:
The grave's a fine and private place,
But none, I think, do there embrace.
    Now therefore, while the youthful hue
Sits on thy skin like morning dew,
35 And while thy willing soul transpires
At every pore with instant fires,
Now let us sport us while we may,
And now, like amorous birds of prey,
Rather at once our time devour
40 Than languish in his slow-chapped power.
Let us roll all our strength and all
Our sweetness up into one ball,
And tear our pleasures with rough strife
Through the iron gates of life;
45 Thus, though we cannot make our sun
Stand still, yet we will make him run.

Are eternity's vast deserts.
25 Your beauty will not be found
In your marble funeral vault, nor will my echoing song
Be heard there. Then worms will try to take
Your long-guarded virginity.
Your old-fashioned honor will turn to dust,
30 And my lust will turn to ashes.
The grave is a fine and private place,
But I do not think anyone embraces there.
    Right now, a youthful color
Sits on your skin like morning dew,
35 And your willing soul breathes
Out quick fires from your every pore.
So let us enjoy each other while we can
And behave like loving birds of prey,
Devouring time instead of
40 Allowing time to slowly chew us up.
Let us roll up all our strength
And sweetness into a cannonball,
And take pleasure in using it to tear through
The iron gates of life.
45 So even though we cannot make our sun
Stand still, we will make him run.

To Lucasta, on Going to the Wars

Richard Lovelace

*T*ell me not, sweet, I am unkind,
    That from the nunnery
Of thy chaste breast and quiet mind
    To war and arms I fly.

5   True, a new mistress now I chase,
    The first foe in the field;
And with a stronger faith embrace
    A sword, a horse, a shield.

Yet this inconstancy is such
10   As you too shall adore;
I could not love thee, dear, so much,
    Loved I not honor more.

To Lucasta, on Going to the Wars

Richard Lovelace

In this poem addressed to his sweetheart, the speaker compares going to war to taking another lover. He describes his sweetheart's company as pure and virtuous—a kind of "nunnery." He now leaves to

chase a "new mistress"—"the first foe in the field." And with greater faithfulness than he has ever shown to his sweetheart, he will embrace "a sword, a horse, a shield."

Even so, he tells his sweetheart that she should cherish this unfaithfulness. It reflects well on his love for her. "I could not love you so much, dear," he says, "if I did not love honor more."

How Soon Hath Time

John Milton

*H*ow soon hath Time, the subtle thief of youth,
    Stoln on his wing my three and twentieth year!
    My hasting days fly on with full career,

    But my late spring no bud or blossom show'th.
5 Perhaps my semblance might deceive the truth,
    That I to manhood am arrived so near,
    And inward ripeness doth much less appear,

    That some more timely-happy spirits endu'th.
Yet be it less or more, or soon or slow,

10   It shall be still in strictest measure even
    To that same lot, however mean or high,
Toward which Time leads me, and the will of Heaven;
    All is, if I have grace to use it so,
    As ever in my great Taskmaster's eye.

How Soon Hath Time

John Milton

*T*ime, that cunning thief of youth,
has flown away with my 23rd year so quickly!
My hurried (**hasting**) days fly by with full speed
    (**career**),
but my late spring brings forth no bud or blossom.[1]
5   Perhaps my appearance (**semblance**) is deceiving
and doesn't show that I'm so close to manhood.
Perhaps my inner maturity (**ripeness**) doesn't show
    itself as much
as it does in those who have done more at my age.
But whether my growth is less or more, or fast or
    slow,
10   it will always be adequate.
I will fulfill my fate (**lot**), however low or high,
toward which time and the will of heaven lead me.
All is eternal in my great taskmaster's[2] eye,
and I only need faith (**grace**) to accept this.

1 **my late spring brings forth no bud or blossom:** The
speaker means that he has not accomplished what he
had hoped to at his age (his "late spring").

2 **great taskmaster's:** God's

When I Consider How My Light Is Spent

John Milton

When I consider how my light is spent
    Ere half my days, in this dark world and wide,
    And that one talent which is death to hide,
    Lodged with me useless, though my soul more bent
5   To serve therewith my Maker, and present
    My true account, lest he returning chide;
    "Doth God exact day-labor, light denied?"
    I fondly ask; but Patience to prevent
That murmur, soon replies, "God doth not need
10   Either man's work or his own gifts; who best
    Bear his mild yoke, they serve him best. His state
Is kingly. Thousands at his bidding speed
    And post o'er land and ocean without rest:
    They also serve who only stand and wait."

When I Consider How My Light Is Spent

John Milton

In this sonnet, Milton explores his feelings about his own blindness. He has "spent" his eyesight before his life is half over. How can he, a poet, fulfill his duty to God when he cannot see?

He remembers a story told by Jesus in the book of Matthew (25:14–30). In it, a master gave his servant a coin **(talent)** and expected him to invest it wisely for him. Instead, the servant buried the coin, for which he was driven away by his master.

Milton compares himself to the servant, even though he is much more eager to serve his own master, God. His sight, like the coin, is hidden and useless, and he fears that God will criticize **(chide)** him. Milton wonders, "Does God expect me to work, even when I have no light?"

But Milton's inner voice **(Patience)** prevents him from making such a complaint against God and answers: "God does not need a man's work or gifts. A man serves God best by quietly bearing his troubles **(mild yoke)**. God lives a kingly life, and thousands of angels rush over land and sea obeying his orders without rest. But others serve him by simply standing and waiting."

INTRODUCTION TO
Paradise Lost

John Milton always wanted to write a great epic poem. His original idea was to tell a story about England, perhaps using stories of King Arthur.

By the time he set about writing his epic in the 1650s, Milton was completely blind and had to dictate his work. He had also changed his mind about his epic's topic. Instead of English myth and history, he turned toward religion.

According to Christian belief, humankind had suffered a terrible fall from perfect happiness. Adam and Eve, the first people, originally lived blissfully in the Garden of Eden. But God ordered them not to eat from a certain tree in the garden. Its fruit would give them the knowledge of good and evil.

Urged by an evil serpent, Adam and Eve disobeyed and ate the fruit. God had no choice but to bring death and suffering into the world. The world's first couple had to leave Eden forever.

This story has stirred up many questions since it was first told. Why was it a crime for Adam and Eve to eat from the tree? Why did God have no choice but to end their perfect happiness? And why did Jesus Christ have to die to save humankind from that original fall?

A devout Puritan, Milton decided to take on all these questions and more. In his epic, he planned to do nothing less than "justify the ways of God to men."

Milton's religious ideas were very original, and he did not agree with his fellow Puritans on everything. Puritans, who followed the teachings of French thinker John Calvin, believed in *predestination*. According to this idea, God had already decided who would be saved and who would be damned. People could do nothing to change what God had already planned for them.

Milton did not accept predestination, believing instead that people had free will. Salvation was a choice that human

Paradise Lost by John Medina

beings could make for themselves. So although *Paradise Lost* reflects Puritan beliefs, it allows humanity more freedom than Puritanism usually did.

Milton's story starts before the fall of Adam and Eve—and even before the biblical creation. As the poem begins, Satan is writhing in hell. He and his fellow rebel angels have been cast out of heaven for warring against God. It is Satan who will urge Adam and Eve to disobey God.

There was surely no doubt in Milton's mind that Satan was evil. Even so, Milton couldn't help portraying Satan as a complex and tragic character. Satan has noble qualities, including strength, courage, intelligence, and skill at leadership. Some later English poets, including William Blake and Percy Bysshe Shelley, suggested that Satan was the true hero of *Paradise Lost*.

from **Paradise Lost**

John Milton

*O*f man's first disobedience,
    and the fruit
Of that forbidden tree whose mortal taste
Brought death into the world, and all our woe,
With loss of Eden, till one greater Man

5   Restore us, and regain the blissful seat,
Sing, Heavenly Muse, that on the secret top
Of Oreb, or of Sinai, didst inspire
That shepherd who first taught the chosen seed
In the beginning how the heavens and earth

10   Rose out of Chaos: or, if Sion hill
Delight thee more, and Siloa's brook that flowed
Fast by the oracle of God, I thence
Invoke thy aid to my adventurous song,
That with no middle flight intends to soar

15   Above th' Aonian mount, while it pursues
Things unattempted yet in prose or rhyme.
And chiefly thou, O Spirit, that dost prefer
Before all temples th' upright heart and pure,
Instruct me, for thou know'st; thou from the first

from Paradise Lost

John Milton

*S*ing, Heavenly Muse,[1] of man's first disobedience,
    and the fruit
Of that forbidden tree whose deadly taste
Brought death and woe into the world.
Sing of how Eden was lost to us until Jesus Christ
    (one greater Man)

5   Regains that happy place for us again.
On the secret mountain tops
Of Horeb and Sinai, you inspired
Moses to teach the Jews **(the chosen seed)**
How the heavens and earth rose out of Chaos

10   In the beginning. Or perhaps Mount Zion
Delights you more, and Siloa's brook that flowed
Fast by the Temple.[2] If so, by their names
I ask your help for my adventurous song.
For I intend to make no trifling **(middle)** flight

15   Above Mount Helicon[3] in pursuit
Of things not yet attempted in prose or rhyme.
So teach me, Spirit—
You who prefer an upright and pure heart
To all temples. Teach me, for you know all. You were
    present

1 **Muse:** The ancient epics of Homer and Virgil began with the poet asking for the help of one of the Muses, the goddesses of artistic inspiration.

2 **Horeb ... the temple:** Horeb and Sinai were mountains where Moses spoke with God. Mount Zion, Siloa's brook, and the Temple were all in Jerusalem. According to Greek and Roman mythology, Chaos existed before the creation of the world.

3 **Mount Helicon:** a mountain in Greece where the Muses were thought to live

20   Wast present, and with mighty wings
        outspread
  Dovelike sat'st brooding on the vast
        abyss,
  And mad'st it pregnant: what in me
        is dark
  Illumine; what is low, raise and support;
  That to the height of this great
        argument
25   I may assert Eternal Providence,

  And justify the ways of God to men.
      Say first (for Heaven hides nothing from thy
        view,
  Nor the deep tract of Hell), say first what cause
  Moved our grand parents, in that happy state,
30   Favored of Heaven so highly, to
        fall off
  From their Creator, and transgress
        his will
  For one restraint, lords of the world
        besides?
  Who first seduced them to that foul
        revolt?
      Th' infernal serpent; he it was, whose guile,
35   Stirred up with envy and revenge, deceived
  The mother of mankind, what time his pride
  Had cast him out from Heaven, with all
        his host
  Of rebel angels, by whose aid aspiring
  To set himself in glory above his peers,
40   He trusted to have equaled the
        Most High,
  If he opposed; and with ambitious aim
  Against the throne and monarchy of God

20 At the beginning, and you spread your mighty, dove-
      like wings
   As you sat brooding over the vast nothingness
      (**abyss**),
   Then gave it shape (**mad'st it pregnant**). Whatever is
      dark in me,
   Make light. Whatever is low in me, raise and support.
   Help me rise to the height of this great subject
      (**argument**)
25 So I can praise God's plan for the universe
      (**Providence**)
   And show men the justice of God's ways.
         Neither heaven nor the deepest parts (**tract**) of
            hell
   Can hide anything from you. So speak first of
   Adam and Eve, born to happy lives
30 And favored so highly by heaven. Why did they fall
      out
   With their creator? Why did they disobey
      (**transgress**) his will
   In one small matter, when they could have been lords
      of the world?
   Who first persuaded (**seduced**) them to that foul
      revolt?
         It was the infernal serpent.[4] His cunning (**guile**)
35 Was stirred up with envy and revenge, so he lied
   To the mother of mankind. Because of his pride,
   He had already been cast out of heaven, with all his
      army
   Of rebel angels. With their aid, he had hoped
   To set himself above his equals in glory.
40 Indeed, he expected to have been a match for God
      himself
   If they should fight. So with the ambitious aim
   Of seizing the throne and kingship of God,

---

4 **infernal serpent:** According to the book of Genesis, Eve
   was tempted to eat the fruit of the Tree of Knowledge by
   a serpent. Milton will later explain that this serpent was
   actually Satan.

Raised impious war in Heaven and battle
    proud,
With vain attempt. Him the Almighty Power
45   Hurled headlong flaming from th'
        ethereal sky
With hideous ruin and combustion down
To bottomless perdition, there
    to dwell
In adamantine chains and
    penal fire,
Who durst defy th' Omnipotent to arms.
50   Nine times the space that measures day and
        night
To mortal men, he with his horrid crew
Lay vanquished, rolling in the fiery gulf
Confounded though immortal. But his
    doom
Reserved him to more wrath; for now the thought
55   Both of lost happiness and lasting pain
Torments him; round he throws his baleful eyes,
That witnessed huge affliction and dismay,
Mixed with obdùrate pride and
    steadfast hate.
At once, as far as angels ken, he views
60   The dismal situation waste and wild:
A dungeon horrible, on all sides round
As one great furnace flamed; yet from those flames
No light, but rather darkness visible
Served only to discover sights of woe,
65   Regions of sorrow, doleful shades,
    where peace
And rest can never dwell, hope never comes
That comes to all, but torture without end
Still urges, and a fiery deluge, fed
With ever-burning sulphur unconsumed:
70   Such place Eternal Justice had prepared
For those rebellious; here their prison ordained

He started an unholy (**impious**) war in Heaven.
    Satan fought proudly,
But in vain. The almighty power

45 Hurled him headfirst and flaming from heaven
    (**ethereal sky**).
Down he fell horribly, all on fire,
To bottomless damnation (**perdition**). There he was
    to live
In unbreakable (**adamantine**) chains and punishing
    (**penal**) fire
For having dared defy God with arms.

50   For nine times the time that mortal men
        call
Day and night, Satan and his horrid crew
Lay defeated, rolling in the fiery deep,
Baffled (**confounded**) but immortal. But Satan's
    doom
Meant only more suffering, for now he was tortured

55 By thoughts of both his lost happiness
And lasting pain. He looked around with deadly eyes,
Seeing great suffering and dismay,
Feeling a mixture of stubborn (**obdurate**) pride and
    determined hate.
As far as angels can see, he viewed

60 The dismal scene, wasted and wild.
It was a horrible dungeon—a great, flaming furnace
On all sides. And yet, those flames gave
No light, but rather a visible darkness
Which served only to show sights of woe,

65 Regions of sorrow, and sad shadows (**doleful
    shades**). Peace
And rest can never live there. Hope, that comes to all,
Is never there. But torture without end
Always afflicts (**still urges**)—and a rain of fire fed
With ever-burning, endless sulfur.

70 Such a place eternal justice had prepared
For those who rebelled. It was a prison fixed

In utter darkness and their portion set
As far removed from God and light of Heaven
As from the center thrice to th' utmost pole.
75 O how unlike the place from whence they fell!
There the companions of his fall, o'erwhelmed
With floods and whirlwinds of tempestuous fire,
He soon discerns; and, weltering by his side,
One next himself in power, and next in crime,
80 Long after known in Palestine, and
        named
Beëlzebub. To whom th' arch-enemy,
And thence in Heaven called Satan, with bold words
Breaking the horrid silence thus began:
    "If thou beëst he—but O how fallen!
        how changed
85 From him who in the happy realms of light
Clothed with transcendent brightness didst
        outshine
Myriads, though bright! if he whom mutual league,
United thoughts and counsels, equal hope
And hazard in the glorious enterprise,
90 Joined with me once, now misery hath joined
In equal ruin; into what pit thou seest
From what height fallen, so much the stronger
        proved
He with his thunder: and till then who knew
The force of those dire arms? Yet not
        for those,
95 Nor what the potent Victor in his rage
Can else inflict, do I repent or change,
Though changed in outward luster, that fixed
        mind
And high disdain, from sense of
        injured merit,
That with the Mightiest raised me to contend,
100 And to the fierce contention brought along
Innumerable force of spirits armed,

In utter darkness, and their part was set
Twice as far below the earth
As God and the light of Heaven are above it.

75   Oh, how unlike the place they fell from!
Satan soon could see the comrades who had fallen
With him, overwhelmed with floods and whirlwinds
Of stormy fire. And writhing (**weltering**) at his side
Was one who was next in power and in crime.

80   Long afterwards, he was known in Palestine by the
       name of
Beëlzebub.[5] Satan, whose very name
Means "enemy," broke the horrid silence
With these bold words:

     "Are you really he? Oh, how you've fallen! How
       you've changed!

85   Once, in happy worlds of light,
You were dressed in perfect (**transcendent**)
       brightness, and you outshone
Countless other bright beings! You sided with me,
Became my comrade. We shared thoughts and advice,
And our hopes and risks in this glorious plan

90   Were equal. But now misery has joined us
In equal ruin. You see what a pit we've fallen into,
And from what a height, because God proved so
       much stronger
With his thunder. Till then, who knew
The strength of those grim arms? And yet I won't
       repent or change—

95   Not because of our fall, nor anything else
Our powerful victor can do to us in his rage.
My outward brilliance is gone, but I still have a fixed
       mind
And high pride that come from unrewarded worth
       (**injured merit**).
I raised myself up to fight with the mightiest

100   In fierce battle, and brought along
An armed force of countless spirits

5   **Beëlzebub:** "God of Flies"

That durst dislike his reign, and me preferring,
His utmost power with adverse power opposed
In dubious battle on the plains of Heaven,
105   And shook his throne. What though the field be lost?
All is not lost: the unconquerable will,
And study of revenge, immortal hate,
And courage never to submit or yield:
And what is else not to be overcome?
110   That glory never shall his wrath or might
Extort from me. To bow and sue for grace
With suppliant knee, and deify
     his power
Who from the terror of this arm so late
Doubted his empire—that were low
     indeed;
115   That were an ignominy and shame beneath
This downfall; since, by fate, the strength
     of gods
And this empyreal substance
     cannot fail;
Since, through experience of this great event,
In arms not worse, in foresight much
     advanced,
120   We may with more successful hope
     resolve
To wage by force or guile eternal war,
Irreconcilable to our grand Foe,
Who now triùmphs, and in th' excess of joy
Sole reigning holds the tyranny of Heaven."
125   So spake th' apostate angel, though
       in pain,
Vaunting aloud, but racked with deep despair;
And him thus answered soon his bold
     compeer:
       "O prince, O chief of many thronèd powers,
That led th' embattled seraphim to war

That disliked his reign and preferred me.
We attacked his utmost power with all we had
In doubtful battle on the plains of heaven

105 And shook his throne. So what if the field is lost?
All is not lost. I still have my unconquerable will,
My pursuit (**study**) of revenge, my undying hate,
And my courage never to surrender.
And what else do I have to lose?

110 His might and anger will never force me
To give up my glory. I will not bow and beg for mercy
On a humble (**suppliant**) knee, nor worship (**deify**)
    his power—
Not after this arm of mine so recently frightened him
Into fearing for his empire. That would be low
    indeed—

115 A disgrace (**ignominy**) and shame even worse than
This downfall. Because of fate, I am strong and made
    of
An indestructible (**empyreal**) substance; my body can
    never die.
And the experience of this event
Has left me no poorer in arms and much richer in
    foresight.

120 So we can decide to wage war, either by force or
    cleverness,
With better hope than before.
We will never make peace with our grand foe,
Who now triumphs. He rejoices too much
As he reigns alone in tyranny over heaven."

125   So spoke the renegade (**apostate**) angel, though
        in pain,
Boasting aloud, but torn with deep despair.
Then his bold partner and comrade (**compeer**)
    answered him thus:
    "Oh, prince, chief of many royal (**throned**) armies,
You led the desperate angels (**seraphim**) to war

130 Under thy conduct, and in dreadful
      deeds
Fearless, endangered Heaven's perpetual King,
And put to proof his high supremacy,
Whether upheld by strength, or chance, or fate!
Too well I see and rue the dire
      event
135 That with sad overthrow and foul defeat
Hath lost us Heaven, and all this mighty host
In horrible destruction laid thus low,
As far as gods and heavenly essences
Can perish: for the mind and spirit remains
140 Invincible, and vigor soon returns,
Though all our glory extinct, and happy state
Here swallowed up in endless misery.
But what if he our Conqueror (whom I now
Of force believe almighty, since no less
145 Than such could have o'erpowered such force as ours)
Have left us this our spirit and
      strength entire,
Strongly to suffer and support our
      pains,
That we may so suffice his vengeful ire,
Or do him mightier service as his
      thralls
150 By right of war, whate'er his business be,
here in the heart of Hell to work in fire,
Or do his errands in the gloomy deep?
What can it then avail though yet we feel
Strength undiminished, or eternal being
155 To undergo eternal punishment?"
      Whereto with speedy words th' arch-fiend replied:
"Fallen cherub, to be weak is miserable,
Doing or suffering: but of this be sure,
To do aught good never will be our task,
160 But ever to do ill our sole delight,
As being the contrary to his high will

130   Under your orders (**conduct**). And your dreadful,
          fearless deeds
      Endangered heaven's eternal king.
      You put his high authority to the test (**to proof**),
      Whether he kept it by strength, chance, or fate!
      I see too well this terrible outcome (**event**), and
          regret it.
135   Our sad overthrow and foul defeat
      Have lost us heaven. And this whole mighty army
      Is laid low in horrible destruction,
      Even though gods and heavenly beings (**essences**)
      Can never truly die. For the mind and spirit remain
140   Indestructible, and our strength soon returns,
      Even though our glory is dead, and our happiness
      Is swallowed up here in endless misery.
      I now believe our conqueror
      To be almighty, indeed. He couldn't have overpowered
145   A force like ours if he were less.
      And what good is it that he has left our spirit and
          strength whole?
      We can only suffer and withstand (**support**) our
          pains more strongly,
      And so better satisfy (**suffice**) his vengeful anger.
      Or perhaps he means for us to serve him mightily as
          slaves (**thralls**)
150   He's won in war. He might have business
      Here in the heart of hell, and want us to work in fire
      Or do his errands in the gloomy deep.
      So how does it help us to feel
      As strong as ever, or that we'll live forever
155   Only to undergo eternal punishment?"
              Satan replied with these quick words:
      "Fallen angel, it is miserable to be weak,
      Whether we attack or suffer. But be sure of this—
      It will never be our task to do anything (**ought**) good.
160   Always to do ill will be our sole delight,
      Because it is against the high will of him

Whom we resist. If then his providence
Out of our evil seek to bring forth good,
Our labor must be to pervert that end,
165 And out of good still to find means of evil;
Which ofttimes may succeed, so as perhaps
Shall grieve him, if I fail not, and disturb
His inmost counsels from their destined
    aim.
But see! the angry Victor hath recalled
170 His ministers of vengeance and pursuit
Back to the gates of Heaven; the sulphurous hail,
Shot after us in storm, o'erblown hath laid
The fiery surge that from the precipice
Of Heaven received us falling; and the thunder,
175 Winged with red lightning and impetuous rage,
Perhaps hath spent his shafts, and ceases now
To bellow through the vast and boundless deep.
Let us not slip th' occasion, whether
    scorn
Or satiate fury yield it from our Foe.
180 Seest thou yon dreary plain, forlorn and wild,
The seat of desolation, void of light,
Save what the glimmering of these livid flames
Casts pale and dreadful? Thither let us tend
From off the tossing of these fiery waves;
185 There rest, if any rest can harbor there;
And reassembling our afflicted powers,
Consult how we may henceforth most offend
Our enemy, our own loss how repair,
How overcome this dire calamity,
190 What reinforcement we may gain from hope,
If not, what resolution from despair."
    Thus Satan talking to his nearest mate
With head uplift above the wave, and eyes
That sparkling blazed; his other parts besides
195 Prone on the flood, extended long and large

Whom we resist. If it is God's plan (**providence**)
To bring forth good out of our evil,
We must work to ruin (**pervert**) his plan,
165   And always find ways to bring evil out of good.
We may often succeed, and so perhaps
We'll grieve him. If I'm not mistaken, we'll prevent
His deepest wishes (**inmost counsels**) from coming
     true.
But look! The angry victor has called
170   His vengeful, pursuing army
Back to the gates of heaven. The hail of sulfur
That was shot at us has calmed (**laid**)
The fiery waves (**surge**) into which we've fallen
From heaven's heights. And the thunder,
175   With wings of red lightning and violent rage,
Seems to have used up all its arrows. It has stopped
Booming through the vast, bottomless depths.
Let's not miss this chance (**slip th' occasion**), whether
     it comes
From our foe's scorn or satisfaction.
180   Do you see that dreary plain, sad and wild,
A desolate place without light
Except for the dreadful glimmering
Of those pale flames? Let's move toward it
From these tossing, fiery waves.
185   We will rest, if any rest can be found there,
And gather our beaten troops (**powers**).
Then we can discuss how to best attack
Our enemy, mend our losses,
And overcome this awful disaster.
190   There we'll see if there is any hope for us—
And if not, what firmness can come from our despair."
       So said Satan to his closest mate,
With his head above the water and his eyes
Sparkling and blazing. The rest of him
195   Lay prone along the waves. He stretched out long
     and large,

Lay floating many a rood, in bulk as huge
As whom the fables name of monstrous size,
Titanian or Earth-born, that warred on Jove,
Briareos or Typhon, whom the den
200 By ancient Tarsus held, or that sea
     beast
Leviathan, which God of all his works
Created hugest that swim th' ocean-stream.
Him, haply, slumbering on the
     Norway foam,
The pilot of some small night-foundered skiff,
205 Deeming some island, oft, as seamen tell,
With fixèd anchor in his scaly rind
Moors by his side under the lee,
     while night
Invests the sea, and wishèd morn
     delays:
So stretched out huge in length the arch-fiend lay,
210 Chained on the burning lake; nor ever thence
Had risen or heaved his head, but that the will
And high permission of all-ruling Heaven
Left him at large to his own dark designs,
That with reiterated crimes he might
215 Heap on himself damnation, while he sought
Evil to others, and enraged might see
How all his malice served but to bring forth
Infinite goodness, grace, and mercy shown
On man by him seduced, but on himself
220 Treble confusion, wrath, and vengeance poured.
     Forthwith upright he rears from off the pool
His mighty stature; on each hand the
     flames
Driven backward slope their pointing spires, and
     rolled

For yards and yards. He was as huge
As anything old stories called monstrous in size—
For example, the Titan Briareos,
Or the Giant Typhon, now held in a cave
200   Near ancient Tarsus. Or else he was like that sea
     beast
Called Leviathan, the largest thing
God ever made to swim in the ocean.[6]
Leviathan might be dozing on the waves near
     Norway
When the pilot of some small boat overtaken by night
205   Would think him an island. Seamen often tell
Of fixing an anchor in his scaly hide.
Then they stay fastened to him away from the wind,
     while night
Covers (**invests**) the sea and precious morning is
     delayed.
So Satan was stretched out, huge in length,
210   Chained on the burning lake. He never
So much as raised or tossed his head without the will
And permission of all-ruling heaven.
For God left him at large to do his dark deeds,
So that Satan might heap more damnation on himself
215   With repeated (**reiterated**) crimes. He'd seek
Evil for others, only to be enraged by failure.
All his cruelty only served to bring forth
Infinite goodness, grace, and mercy
For the men he snared. But for himself,
220   He only tripled his confusion, rage, and punishment.
     At once, he raised his mighty form upright
From the water. On each side of him, he drove the
     flames backward,
Sloping in their pointed spires. The billows rolled,

6   **Titan Briareos . . . Ocean:** In Greek and Roman
mythology, the Titans (including Briareos) ruled the universe before Jove (Zeus) and the Olympian gods. The
Giants (including Typhon) rebelled against Jove. Typhon
was sometimes said to live near Tarsus, a city on the
coast of what is now Turkey. Leviathan is a huge sea
creature mentioned in the Bible.

In billows, leave i' th' midst a horrid vale.
225 Then with expanded wings he steers his flight
Aloft, incumbent on the dusky air,
That felt unusual weight; till on dry land
He lights, if it were land that ever
    burned
With solid, as the lake with liquid fire,
230 And such appeared in hue; as when the
    force
Of subterranean wind transports a hill
Torn from Pelorus or the shattered side
Of thundering Etna, whose combustible
And fuelèd entrails thence conceiving
    fire,
235 Sublimed with mineral fury, aid the
    winds,
And leave a singèd bottom all involved
With stench and smoke: such resting found the sole
Of unblest feet. Him followed his next
    mate,
Both glorying to have 'scaped the Stygian flood
240 As gods, and by their own recovered strength,
Not by the sufferance of supernal
    power.
    "Is this the region, this the soil, the clime,"
Said then the lost archangel, "this
    the seat
That we must change for Heaven? this mournful
    gloom
245 For that celestial light? Be it so, since he
Who now is sovereign can dispose and bid
What shall be right: farthest from him is best,
Whom reason hath equaled, force hath made
    supreme

Leaving a horrid valley in the middle.
225 Then he spread his wings and flew
Upward, lying (**incumbent**) on the dark air,
Which felt unusually heavy. At last, he lighted
On dry land—if you could call it land that burned
    with solid fire,
Just as the lake had burned with liquid fire.
230 The fire burned many colors. The land looked like
    Pelorus
Or the shattered side of thundering Etna
When underground winds
Blast and tear whole hills away from them.[7]
At such times, the earth's fiery and explosive interior
    creates fire
235 Which is vaporized (**sublimed**) by sheer heat. This
    fire helps the winds
To singe the ground and wrap it
In stench and smoke. In such a place rested the soles
Of Satan's unblessed feet, and Beelzebub followed
    him.
Both rejoiced to have escaped the Styx's tide[8]
240 Like true gods—by their own recovered strength,
And not by permission (**sufferance**) of heavenly
    (**supernal**) power.
    "Is this the region, the soil, the climate, the home
That we must exchange for heaven?" asked the lost
    but mighty angel then.
"Must we have mournful gloom

245 Instead of starry light? Let it be so.
He who is now king can choose and decide
What shall be right. It is best to be farthest from him.
In reason, he was merely our equal; it took force to
    place him

7 **Pelorus, Etna:** Pelorus is a cape in Sicily; Etna is a vol-
    cano in Sicily.
8 **Styx's tide:** According to Greek and Roman mythology,
    the Styx was a river in the Underworld.

Above his equals. Farewell, happy fields,
250 Where joy forever dwells! Hail, horrors! hail,
Infernal world! and thou, profoundest Hell,
Receive thy new possessor, one who brings
A mind not to be changed by place or time.
The mind is its own place, and in itself
255 Can make a Heaven of Hell, a Hell of Heaven.
What matter where, if I be still the same,
And what I should be, all but less
    than he
Whom thunder hath made greater? Here
    at least
We shall be free; th' Almighty hath not built
260 Here for his envy, will not drive
    us hence.
Here we may reign secure; and in my choice
To reign is worth ambition, though in Hell:
Better to reign in Hell than serve in Heaven.
But wherefore let we then our faithful friends,
265 Th' associates and copartners of our loss,
Lie thus astonished on th' oblivious
    pool,
And call them not to share with us their part
In this unhappy mansion, or once more
With rallied arms to try what may be yet
270 Regained in Heaven, or what more lost in Hell?"

above us. Farewell, happy fields,
250 where joy lives forever! Welcome, horrors! Welcome,
fiery world! Deepest hell,
meet your new owner—one who brings
a mind not to be changed by place or time.
The mind is its own place, and by itself
255 can make a heaven of hell, a hell of heaven.
What does it matter where I am? I am still the same,
and what I should be. And I am still second
only to God,
who is greater only because of his thunder. Here
at least
we shall be free. The almighty has not built here
260 and does not envy this place, so he will not drive
us away.
Here we may rule safely. And in my view,
to rule is worthy of ambition, even though in hell.
Better to reign in hell than serve in heaven.
But why do we neglect our faithful friends,
265 the comrades and partners in our loss,
letting them lie stunned (**astonished**) in pools of
forgetfulness?
Let us call them to share with us their part
in this unhappy home. Let us learn together
what may be gained with renewed fighting
270 in heaven—or what more may be lost in hell."

Unit Three
The Restoration and the Enlightenment
(1660–1798)

The Restoration

In 1660, Charles II returned to England after 11 years of exile, and the English Restoration (which refers to the restoration of the monarchy) began. A tolerant, pleasure-loving man, Charles II became known as the "Merry Monarch."

Under Oliver Cromwell's rule, the English Commonwealth had been strict and puritanical. Swearing, drunkenness, and stage plays were outlawed. Aristocrats lost much of their power. The Restoration reversed all that. Public morality loosened, new theaters opened, and aristocrats regained their old privilege.

Politically, Charles II was not a remarkably successful king. But as a promoter of culture, he accomplished a great deal. Architects like Sir Christopher Wren designed magnificent new buildings. Painters like Sir Godfrey Kneller raised English art to new greatness. John Dryden was considered the greatest poet of the Restoration. He also wrote plays, as did Thomas Otway and William Wycherley.

Newton and Locke

Perhaps the most exciting developments in 17th-century England were in science and philosophy. In 1687, the English physicist Isaac Newton published his *Principia*, possibly the most important scientific paper ever written. In it, Newton set down laws of gravitation and motion.

When it appeared, the *Principia* made the world itself seem more understandable. Newton's universe appeared to work something like a clock set in motion by God. What could be more rational and elegant?

Bristol Docks and Quay by Philip van Dijk

Newton's friend, the philosopher John Locke, took a similar view of human nature. His *An Essay Concerning Human Understanding*, published in 1690, described the mind in mechanical terms.

Such ideas produced a great deal of optimism. Suddenly, there seemed little that humans couldn't learn or achieve. Thinkers spoke of the "Great Chain of Being." According to this idea, the world was a well-ordered place in which every creature had a proper role.

Samuel Pope expressed the optimism of his day in a famous couplet:

> Nature and Nature's laws lay hid in night:
> God said, Let Newton be! and all was light.

The Enlightenment

The Restoration did not end political instability in England. When Charles II died, his brother James became king. James II angered Parliament by trying to restore Catholicism as England's official religion. He also wanted absolute power.

James II was removed from the throne in 1689. He was replaced by William of Orange and his wife, Mary (James' daughter). William and Mary signed the English Bill of Rights, which greatly limited the power of monarchs.

These events were called the Glorious Revolution. To the English, it suddenly seemed as if the ideas of Newton and Locke had found their way into politics.

Indeed, Locke himself wrote *Two Treatises on Government*, defending the Glorious Revolution. Locke held that government was a social contract between rulers and subjects. Rulers could only govern by the people's consent.

After the Glorious Revolution, England's period of intellectual adventure continued. In both England and Europe, the Enlightenment (sometimes called the Age of Reason) was well under way.

18th-Century Literature

During the 18th century, the novel became a popular literary form thanks to works such as *Pamela* by Samuel Richardson and *Tom Jones* by Henry Fielding. Samuel

Pope was thought the greatest poet of the time, and Samuel Johnson the greatest man of letters.

Some thinkers began to ask probing questions about the Enlightenment. For example, if human reason was so powerful, why did people so seldom put it to good use? Why did injustice continue in the world?

Pope, Johnson, and Jonathan Swift turned to *satire* as a way to point out the world's evils. A *satire* is a work that ridicules human faults and errors. Pope, Johnson, and Swift also made brilliant use of *epigrams*. An *epigram* is a brief statement that wittily sums up an important idea. Pope's couplet about Newton is an example of a verse epigram.

Samuel Johnson created memorable prose epigrams. "A very small part of the year is spent by choice," he once wrote. Elsewhere, he observed, "The natural flights of the human mind are not from pleasure to pleasure, but from hope to hope."

The Waning of the Enlightenment

As the 18th century wore on, contradictions began to appear in Enlightenment thought. Locke's ideas held that monarchs did *not* rule by divine right, and that all men were equal. If so, how could men fit into their proper places on the Great Chain of Being? By what right did one group of people oppress another?

Some people also grew wary of the Enlightenment's fondness for rationality. Were feelings and emotions of no value? Could it be true that the human mind was little more than a machine?

Some writers began to grapple with these questions. In his novel *Tristram Shandy*, Laurence Sterne portrayed the untidiness of human experience. And in his poem "Elegy Written in a Country Churchyard," included in this unit, Thomas Gray praised common people. Gray's verse came more from the heart than from the head.

In a way, the ideas of the Enlightenment led to its own end. The Great Chain of Being would be smashed to pieces by two revolutions inspired by the Enlightenment. One began in America in 1776, the other in France in 1789. The Age of Reason would soon wane, and Romanticism would begin.

Unit Three Author Biographies

Samuel Pepys (1633–1703)

Samuel Pepys, whose last name is pronounced "peeps," was a tailor's son. From his humble beginnings, he became one of the most powerful men in England.

As secretary of the admiralty, he helped make the English Navy the strongest in the world. He served in Parliament, the governing body of England. He was also president of the Royal Society, the British scientific circle, and was friends with Sir Isaac Newton.

He kept his famous *Diary* from 1660 through 1669, writing it in shorthand. He never intended it to be published, but parts of it began to appear in print in 1825.

Alexander Pope (1688–1744)

Alexander Pope grew up a Catholic in Protestant England, so he had little access to formal education. However, he was a precocious young man who educated himself and began writing fine poetry while still in his teens.

He was only four feet, six inches tall, somewhat deformed, and suffered from poor health throughout his life. But he was a bold and energetic writer. He was also a shrewd and sometimes ruthless judge of other people's writing. His *An Essay on Criticism* is an extremely clever poem about literary style.

His best poetry is noted for its satirical wit, especially in "mock epics" like *The Rape of the Lock* and *The Dunciad*.

Jonathan Swift (1667–1745)

Jonathan Swift was perhaps the greatest satirist of the English language. He was born in Ireland to English parents and received his education there. He lived much of his life in England, where he wrote numerous poems, pamphlets, and satirical pieces.

His *A Tale of the Tub* ridicules British religious differences. In his *The Battle of the Books*, he takes sides with ancient, classical learning over newer and more fashionable ideas. His *Journal to Stella* is a vivid description of his life in London.

A clergyman as well as a writer, Swift became dean of St. Patrick's Cathedral in Dublin, Ireland, in 1713 and lived there for the rest of his life.

James Boswell (1740–1795)

James Boswell was born and educated in Scotland. In 1760, he went to London, where he studied law and took part in the city's intellectual life. When he was 22 years old, he met Samuel Johnson, who was then 53. They became devoted friends.

Boswell published his *The Life of Samuel Johnson, LL.D.* in 1791, several years after Johnson's death. Much of this great biography records actual conversations with Johnson.

Boswell made himself look somewhat foolish in the *Life* in order to make Johnson seem even more brilliant. But in the 20th century, Boswell's personal diaries were discovered and published. They revealed that Boswell was a remarkable intellect in his own right.

Thomas Gray (1716–1771)

The most famous poem by Thomas Gray is "Elegy Written in a Country Churchyard." Gray also wrote some lighter verse, such as "Ode on the Death of a Favorite Cat, Drowned in a Tub of Gold Fishes."

After some of his later poems were harshly criticized, Gray almost stopped writing altogether. He died at the age of 55, and was buried in the churchyard he described in his famous "Elegy."

INTRODUCTION TO
The Diary

From 1664 until 1666, London suffered its most terrible attack of the Black Death, now called the bubonic plague. Perhaps 75,000 people died. But if Londoners thought that things couldn't get worse, they were in for a shock. On September 2, 1666, a fire broke out which destroyed much of the city.

As Samuel Pepys explained in his famous *Diary*, the fire began with a tiny accident. The king's baker, Thomas Farrinor, failed to put out his oven at the end of his work day. His house caught fire, and soon the whole neighborhood went up in flames.

A strong, dry wind spread the fire far and wide. Little could be done to stop it. In those days, firefighters had little to work with except buckets of water. Gunpowder was also used to destroy houses in hopes of giving the flames less to feed on. These methods helped, but the fire continued to rage for four days.

When the fire was over, about four-fifths of London was destroyed. More than 13,000 houses were lost, along with many churches and public buildings. Most of the city had to be rebuilt entirely.

Pepys' friend, the architect Sir Christopher Wren, did a great deal to restore London's glory. The old St. Paul's Cathedral was destroyed by the fire. In its place, Wren designed the magnificent new St. Paul's Cathedral that stands in its place today.

At the time of the fire, Samuel Pepys lived in Seething Lane, in the eastern part of London. His house was near the Tower, London's ancient prison-fortress, and London Bridge, which crossed the River Thames. This was the area where the fire broke out. So Pepys' eyewitness account covers the fire almost from the beginning.

His diary entry for September 2 also introduces us to some of the most important men in London, including King Charles II himself. Charles' brother, the Duke of York, would become King James II after Charles' death. Sir William Batten and Sir William Penn were leading admirals of the day. Pepys' account also includes politicians, neighbors, servants, and maids.

Amazingly, only 16 people died in the fire. Even more amazingly, the plague almost came to an end. Londoners did not know why.

It wasn't until almost the end of the 19th century that the truth was understood. Scientists then learned that the bubonic plague was spread by fleas carried by rats. By the time the Great Fire of London was over, not enough rats survived to carry the plague. Despite the hardship and destruction the fire caused, it almost certainly saved more lives than it took.

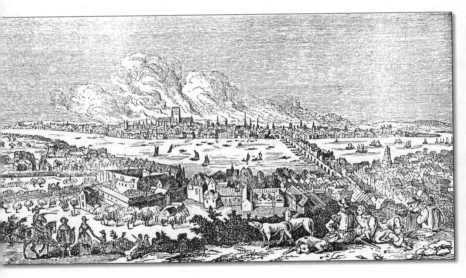

from **The Diary**

Samuel Pepys

edited by
Robert Latham and William Matthews

The Fire of London

1 *Sept. 2, 1666.* (Lord's day.) Some of our maids sitting up late last night to get things ready against our feast today, Jane called us up about three in the morning, to tell us of a great fire they saw in the city. So I rose and slipped on my night-gown, and went to

2 her window, and thought it to be on the back side of Mark Lane at the farthest; but, being unused to such fires as followed, I thought it far enough off; and so went to bed again and to sleep. About seven rose

3 again to dress myself, and there looked out at the window, and saw the fire not so much as it was and farther off. So to my closet to set things to rights after yesterday's cleaning. By and by Jane comes and

4 tells me that she hears that above 300 houses have been burned down tonight by the fire we saw, and

from The Diary

1 *S*ept. 2, 1666. (Lord's day.)[1] Some of our maids sat
up late last night to get things ready for our feast
today. Jane woke us up about three in the morning to
tell us of a great fire they saw in the city. So I rose,
slipped on my nightgown, and went to her window.

2   I thought the fire was no farther away than the
back side of Mark Lane. But I was not used to fires
like the one that followed, so I thought it far enough
off. I went to bed again and slept.

3   About seven, I rose again to get dressed. I looked
out the window, and the fire did not look as large as
it had, and it seemed farther off. So I went to my
bedroom to put things in order after yesterday's
cleaning.

4   Jane soon came. She told me that she had heard
that more than 300 houses had been burned down

---

1 **Lord's day:** Sunday

that it is now burning down all Fish Street, by
London Bridge. So I made myself ready presently,
and walked to the Tower, and there got up upon one
5   of the high places, Sir J. Robinson's little son going
up with me; and there I did see the houses at that
end of the bridge all on fire, and an infinite great fire
on this and the other side the end of the bridge;
which, among other people, did trouble me for poor
little Michell and our Sarah on the bridge. So down,
6   with my heart full of trouble, to the Lieutenant of the
Tower, who tells me that it begun this morning in the
King's baker's house in Pudding Lane, and that it
hath burned St. Magnus's Church and most part of
Fish Street already. So I down to the waterside, and
7   there got a boat and through bridge, and there saw a
lamentable fire. Poor Michell's house, as far as the
Old Swan, already burned that way, and the fire
running farther, that in a very little time it got as
far as the steel yard, while I was there. Everybody

8   endeavoring to remove their goods, and flinging into
the river or bringing them into lighters that lay off;
poor people staying in their houses as long as till the
very fire touched them, and then running into boats,
or clambering from one pair of stairs by the waterside to another. And among other things, the poor
9   pigeons, I perceive, were loth to leave their houses,
but hovered about the windows and balconies till
they were, some of them burned, their wings, and fell

10   down. Having stayed, and in an hour's time seen the
fire rage every way, and nobody, to my sight, endeavoring to quench it, but to remove their goods, and
leave all to the fire, and having seen it get as far as
the steel yard, and the wind mighty high and driving
it into the city; and everything, after so long a

that night by the fire we had seen. She said it was now burning all along Fish Street, by London Bridge. So I got ready quickly and walked to the Tower.

5   I went up in one of the high places there, along with Sir J. Robinson's little son. From there, I could see the houses at that end of the bridge all on fire. All the way to the bridge, the fire seemed unbelievably great. Among other people, I worried for poor little Mitchell and our Sarah on the bridge.

6   My heart full of worry, I went down to see the Lieutenant of the Tower. He told me that the fire had begun that morning in the house of the King's baker in Pudding Lane. It had already burned St. Magnus' Church and most of Fish Street.

7   I went down to the waterside and got a boat. I passed through the bridge and saw a terrible fire. From poor Mitchell's house all the way to the Old Swan,[2] everything had been burned. The fire ran farther, and while I watched, it got as far as the steel yard.

8   Everybody was trying to save their goods. They threw them into the river or put them on barges that carried them off. Poor people stayed in their houses until the fire actually touched them. Then they ran to the boats, or else they climbed up and down the stairs by the waterside.

9   Among other things, I saw that the poor pigeons did not want to leave their houses. They hovered near the windows and balconies until some of them burned their wings and fell down.

10   I stayed there for an hour and saw the fire rage in all directions. I could see nobody trying to put it out. People only tried to save their goods and leave the rest to burn. I saw it get as far as the steel yard. The strong, high wind was driving it into the city.

---

2 **Old Swan:** stairs leading to the river on the north bank of the Thames

11 drought, proving combustible, even the very stones of churches, and among other things the poor steeple by which pretty Mrs. — — — lives, and whereof my old schoolfellow Elborough is parson, taken fire in the very top, and there burned till it fell down. I to

12 Whitehall (with a gentleman with me who desired to go off from the Tower, to see the fire, in my boat), and there up to the King's closet in the chapel, where people come about me, and I did give them an account dismayed them all, and word was carried in to the King. So I was called for, and did tell the King and Duke of York what I saw, and that unless his Majesty did command houses to be pulled down noth-

13 ing could stop the fire. They seemed much troubled, and the King commanded me to go to my Lord Mayor from him, and command him to spare no houses, but to pull down before the fire every way. The Duke of

14 York bid me tell him that if he would have any more soldiers he shall; and so did my Lord Arlington afterwards, as a great secret. Here meeting with

15 Captain Cocke, I in his coach, which he lent me, and Creed with me to Paul's, and there walked along Watling Street, as well as I could, every creature coming away loaden with goods to save, and here and there sick people carried away in beds. Extraordinary good goods carried in carts and on backs. At last met

16 my Lord Mayor in Canning Street, like a man spent, with a handkerchief about his neck. To the King's message he cried, like a fainting woman, "Lord! what can I do? I am spent: people will not obey me. I have been pulling down houses; but the fire overtakes us

11   After so long a dry spell, everything was flammable—even the stones of the churches. I looked toward the steeple that pretty Mrs. ——— lived by, and where my old schoolmate Elborough was parson. It caught fire at the very top, then burned until it fell down.

12   A gentleman wanted to leave the Tower and see the fire in my boat. So we went to Whitehall,[3] and then to the King's rooms. I was called for, and I told the King and the Duke of York what I had seen. I told His Majesty that he must command houses to be torn down. Otherwise, nothing could stop the fire.

13   They seemed very worried, and the King commanded me to go to the Lord Mayor right away. I was to command him to spare no houses, but to tear them all down wherever there was fire.

14   The Duke of York asked me to tell the Mayor that he could have more soldiers if he needed them. Lord Arlington told me the same thing afterwards, very secretively.

15   Then I met with Captain Cocke, who lent me his coach, and Creed and I rode in it to [St.] Paul's [Cathedral]. Once there, I walked along Watling Street as well as I could. Everybody was rushing away carrying goods to save. Here and there, sick people were carried away in beds. People carried precious goods in carts and on their backs.

16   At last, I met the Lord Mayor in Canning Street. He looked quite exhausted and had a handkerchief around his neck. I gave him the King's message. Then he exclaimed like a fainting woman, "Lord, what can I do? I am exhausted. People will not obey me. I have been tearing down houses, but the fire overtakes us faster than we can do it."

---

3 **Whitehall:** In Pepys' time, Whitehall was the royal palace. It was in the western part of London and safely away from the fire.

17   faster than we can do it." That he needed no more
      soldiers; and that, for himself, he must go and refresh
      himself, having been up all night. So he left me, and I
      him, and walked home, seeing people all almost dis-
      tracted, and no manner of means used to quench the

18   fire. The houses, too, so very thick thereabouts, and
      full of matter for burning, as pitch and tar, in
      Thames Street; and warehouses of oil, and wines, and
      brandy, and other things. Here I saw Mr. Isaake
19   Houblon, the handsome man, prettily dressed and
      dirty, at his door at Dowgate, receiving some of his
      brothers' things, whose houses were on fire; and, as
      he says, have been removed twice already; and he
      doubts (as it soon proved) that they must be in a
      little time removed from his house also, which was a
      sad consideration. And to see the churches all filling
20   with goods by people who themselves should have
      been quietly there at this time. By this time it was

21   about twelve o'clock; and so home. Soon as dined, and
      walked through the city, the streets full of nothing
      but people and horses and carts loaden with goods,
      ready to run over one another, and removing goods
      from one burned house to another. They now remov-
22   ing out of Canning Street (which received goods in
      the morning) into Lumbard Street, and farther; and
      among others I now saw my little goldsmith, Stokes,
      receiving some friend's goods, whose house itself was

23   burned the day after. I to Paul's Wharf, where I had
      appointed a boat to attend me, and took in Mr.
      Carcasse and his brother, whom I met in the street,
      and carried them below and above bridge to and
      again to see the fire, which was now got farther, both
      below and above, and no likelihood of stopping it.

17 He said he needed no more soldiers. As for himself, he said he needed to go and refresh himself, for he had been up all night. So we left each other, and I walked home. Along the way, I saw that people had almost gone mad, and nothing was being done to put out the fire.

18 The houses were very thick in the Thames Street area, and they were made of flammable materials such as pitch and tar. There were also warehouses full of oil, wine, brandy, and other things.

19 At his door at Dowgate, I saw the handsome Mr. Isaake Houblon, prettily dressed but dirty. He was gathering some things for his brothers, whose houses were on fire. He said he had moved those things twice already. And he guessed that they soon would have to be moved from his house all over again. It was a sad thought, but it soon proved true.

20 People should have been quietly in church at that time. Instead, they were filling the churches with goods.

21 It was about 12 o'clock by the time I reached home. I ate, then walked through the city. The streets were full of nothing but people, horses, and carts piled with goods. They were ready to run over each other as they moved goods from one burned house to another.

22 They had taken goods to Canning Street in the morning, then to Lumbard Street and farther away. Among others, I saw Stokes, my little goldsmith, gathering some friend's goods. That friend's house burned the next day.

23 I went to Paul's Wharf, where I had ordered a boat to wait for me. I had met Mr. Carcasse and his brother in the street, and we rowed below and above the bridge again and again to see the fire. It had gone much farther, both above and below, and there was no likelihood of it being stopped.

24　Met with the King and Duke of York in their barge,
and with them to Queen-hithe, and there called Sir
Richard Browne to them. Their order was only to pull

25　down houses apace, and so below bridge at the waterside; but little was or could be done, the fire coming
upon them so fast. Good hopes there was of stopping

26　it at the Three Cranes above, and at Buttolph's
Wharf below bridge, if care be used; but the wind carries it into the city, so as we know not by the
waterside what it do there. River full of lighters and

27　boats taking in goods, and good goods swimming in
the water, and only I observed that hardly one lighter
or boat in three that had the goods of a house in, but
there was a pair of virginals in it. Having seen as

28　much as I could now, I away to Whitehall by appointment, and there walked to St. James's Park, and
there met my wife and Creed and Wood and his wife,
and walked to my boat; and there upon the water
again, and to the fire up and down, it still increasing,

29　and the wind great. So near the fire as we could for
smoke; and all over the Thames, with one's face in
the wind, you were almost burned with a shower of
firedrops. This is very true; so as houses were burned
by these drops and flakes of fire, three or four, nay,
five or six houses, one from another. When we could

30　endure no more upon the water, we to a little alehouse on the Bankside, over against the Three
Cranes, and there stayed till it was dark almost, and
saw the fire grow; and, as it grew darker, appeared

24   I met with the King and the Duke of York in their barge. I went with them to Queen-hithe, where they called Sir Richard Browne to come to them.

25   The only order they gave him was to tear down houses quickly, and to do the same thing below the bridge at the waterside. But little was done, nor could be done. The fire was coming upon them too fast.

26   There was good hope of stopping the fire at the Three Cranes above the bridge, and at Buttolph's Wharf below it, if care was taken. But the wind carried the fire into the city. We at the waterside did not know what it might do there.

27   The river was full of barges and boats carrying goods, and many precious goods were floating in the water. I observed many barges and boats with goods aboard. Hardly one out of three barges didn't also have a pair of harpsichords in it.

28   I had seen as much as I could now, so I went to keep an appointment in Whitehall. From there, I walked to St. James' Park, where I met my wife, Creed, and Wood and his wife. We walked to my boat and were soon on the water again, looking at the fire up and down. It was still growing, and the wind was great.

29   We got as near to the fire as we could because of the smoke. All over the Thames, with one's face in the wind, you were almost burned with a shower of sparks. This is the truth. And houses were burned by these sparks and flakes of fire—three or four, no, five or six houses, one after another.

30   When we could not stand being on the water anymore, we went to a little alehouse on the Bankside, across the river from the Three Cranes.[4] We stayed there until it was almost dark, watching the fire grow.

4 **Bankside ... Three Cranes:** The Bankside is the south side of the Thames, where the fire did not reach. Like the Old Swan, the Three Cranes was a stairway to the river.

31 more and more, and in corners and upon steeples, and between churches and houses, as far as we could see up the hill of the city, in a most horrid malicious bloody flame, not like the fine flame of an

32 ordinary fire. Barbary and her husband away before us. We stayed till, it being darkish, we saw the fire as only one entire arch of fire from this to the other side the bridge, and in a bow up the hill for an arch of above a mile long: it made me weep to see it. The

33 churches, houses, and all on fire and flaming at once; and a horrid noise the flames made, and the cracking of houses at their ruin. So home with a sad heart,

34 and there find everybody discoursing and lamenting the fire; and poor Tom Hater come with some of his few goods saved out of his house, which is burned upon Fish Street Hill. I invited him to lie at my

35 house, and did receive his goods, but was deceived in his lying there, the news coming every moment of the growth of the fire; so as we were forced to begin to pack up our own goods, and prepare for their removal; and did by moonshine (it being brave dry, and moonshine, and warm weather) carry much of

36 my goods into the garden, and Mr. Hater and I did remove my money and iron chests into my cellar, as thinking that the safest place. And got my bags of

37 gold into my office, ready to carry away, and my chief papers of accounts also there, and my tallies into a box by themselves. So great was our fear, as Sir W.

38 Batten hath carts come out of the country to fetch away his goods this night. We did put Mr. Hater, poor man, to bed a little; but he got but very little rest, so much noise being in my house, taking down of goods.

31   As it grew darker, we saw more and more fire in corners and on steeples, and between churches and houses. The fire stretched as far as we could see up the hill of the city. It was a most horrid, cruel, and bloody flame, not like the fine flame of an ordinary fire.

32   Barbary and her husband went away before we did. We stayed till it was darkish, when the fire was just one whole arch from this side of the bridge to the other. The arch formed a bow more than a mile long up the hill.

33   It made me weep to see it. Churches and houses were all flaming at once. The flames made a horrid noise as the houses crackled into ruins.

34   Then we went home with a sad heart. There we found everybody discussing and grieving over the fire. And poor Tom Hater came with a few goods he had saved from his house, which had burned on Fish Street Hill.

35   I invited him to sleep at my house, and I took in his goods. But he wasn't able to sleep there, because news came every moment of the fire's growth. So we were forced to begin packing up our own goods, preparing for their removal.

36   We did so by moonlight. (It had been extremely dry, warm weather, with a bright moon.) We carried many of my goods into the garden. Mr. Hater and I took my money and iron chests into my cellar, thinking that the safest place.

37   I took my bags of gold into my office, ready to carry away. I also put my chief accounting papers there, and my tallies[5] into a box by themselves.

38   Our fear was very great. Sir W. Batten had carts come in out of the country to carry away his goods that night. We did put Mr. Hater to bed for a little while, poor man. But he got very little rest because of all the noise in my house, with all the moving of goods.

5   **tallies:** wooden sticks used in accounting

39 *3rd.* About four o'clock in the morning, my Lady Batten sent me a cart to carry away all my money, and plate, and best things, to Sir W. Rider's at Bednall Green. Which I did, riding myself in my nightgown in the cart; and, Lord! to see how the

40 streets and the highways are crowded with people running and riding, and getting of carts at any rate

41 to fetch away things. I find Sir W. Rider tired with being called up all night, and receiving things from several friends. His house full of goods, and much of Sir W. Batten's and Sir W. Pen's. I am eased at my heart to have my treasure so well secured. Then

42 home, with much ado to find a way, nor any sleep all this night to me nor my poor wife.

39   *3rd.* At about four o'clock in the morning, Lady Batten sent me a cart. It was for carrying away all my money, silver, and best things to Sir W. Rider's at Bednall Green. I rode in the cart myself in my nightgown.

40   And, Lord! How the streets and highways were crowded with people running and riding! Everybody was getting carts to carry away their things.

41   I found Sir W. Rider tired from being kept up all night and gathering things from several friends. His house was full of goods, much of it belonging to Sir W. Batten and Sir W. Penn. I am relieved in my heart to have my valuables so safe.

42   Then we went home, finding the way with much difficulty. There will be no sleep tonight for me or my poor wife.

from An Essay on Man

Alexander Pope

*K*now then thyself, presume not God to scan;
The proper study of mankind is man.

Placed on this isthmus of a middle state,
A being darkly wise, and rudely great:

5 With too much knowledge for the skeptic side,
With too much weakness for the Stoic's pride,

He hangs between; in doubt to act, or rest;
In doubt to deem himself a god, or beast;
In doubt his mind or body to prefer;
10 Born but to die, and reasoning but to err;
Alike in ignorance, his reason such,
Whether he thinks too little, or too much:
Chaos of thought and passion, all confused;
Still by himself abused, or disabused;
15 Created half to rise, and half to fall;
Great lord of all things, yet a prey to all;
Sole judge of truth, in endless error hurled:
The glory, jest, and riddle of the world!

from An Essay on Man

Alexander Pope

"**K**now yourself," the speaker begins, echoing the Greek philosophers Socrates and Plato. "Do not pry into (**scan**) God, for the proper study of mankind is man."

Man lives in a realm somewhere below the angels and above the beasts (**this isthmus of a middle state**). He is dim in his wisdom (**darkly wise**) and crude in his greatness (**rudely great**).

The ancient skeptics claimed that man could know very little. The ancient stoics said that man should bear both pain and pleasure patiently. But, the speaker says, we are wiser than the skeptics claim, yet also weaker than the stoics say.

Man "hangs between," always in doubt, whether acting or resting. Is he a god or a beast? Should he be more concerned with his mind or his body? Man is "born only to die, and his reasoning leads him into error." It doesn't matter if man thinks too little or too much. For he is a confused mass (**Chaos**) of thought and passion.

He is always either deceiving himself (**by himself abused**) or finding out the truth (**disabused**). He is "created half to rise, and half to fall." He rules things, yet things also rule him. He is the "sole judge of truth, yet he falls into endless error." He is, in short, "the glory, joke, and riddle of the world!"

These lines sound rather pessimistic. But as a whole, *An Essay on Man* is an optimistic poem. Man is small, but he has an important place in the Great Chain of Being. And although we humans can know very little, we can be sure of one thing: God has made this the best of all worlds.

INTRODUCTION TO

The Rape of the Lock

Early in the 18th century, Lord Petre, a young English nobleman, fell in love with Miss Arabella Fermor. In a reckless moment, Lord Petre cut off a lock of Arabella's hair. Arabella was furious, and a feud broke out between her family and Lord Petre's.

John Caryll, a friend of both families, was anxious to restore peace. He asked Alexander Pope to write a poem making light of the whole business. So Pope wrote "an heroic-comical" poem called *The Rape of the Lock*.

It certainly seemed a silly subject for a poem. To make the most of this silliness, Pope wrote it in the grandest possible style. For example, here are lines 7 through 10 of its first canto (section):

> Say what strange motive, Goddess! could compel
> A well-bred lord to assault a gentle belle?
> Oh, say what stranger cause, yet unexplored,
> Could make a gentle belle reject a lord?

These lines might remind of you of the opening verses of Milton's *Paradise Lost*. Like Milton, Pope calls upon a Muse (Goddess) for poetic inspiration. In fact, Pope was imitating Milton's epic, and also the ancient epics of Homer and Virgil. So *The Rape of the Lock* is often described as a mock epic.

It is a very good *parody*—a comical imitation of another kind of writing. But it is also something more. In it, Pope satirized the shallow manners of London society. And like a good stand-up comic today, Pope knew that the best way to tell a joke was with a per-fectly straight face.

In Canto I, Pope introduces his heroine, the beauti-ful but rather vain and empty-headed Belinda.

In Canto II, Belinda is on her way up the River Thames to Hampton Court, the royal palace. There she expects to make a good impression at court. In Canto III, Belinda encounters the Baron, who cuts off a lock of her hair. The following excerpts start at the beginning of Canto III.

Like much of Pope's work (including *An Essay on Man*), *The Rape of the Lock* is written in a form called *heroic couplets*. A *heroic couplet* is a rhymed pair of lines. Each line typically has ten syllables and five accents.

The Rape of the Lock by Aubrey Beardsley

from
The Rape of the Lock

Alexander Pope

from Canto III

*C*lose by those meads, forever crowned with flowers,
Where Thames with pride surveys his rising towers,
There stands a structure of majestic frame,
Which from the neighboring Hampton takes its
    name.
5 Here Britain's statesmen oft the fall foredoom
Of foreign tyrants, and of nymphs at home;
Here thou, great Anna! whom three realms obey,
Dost sometimes counsel take—and sometimes tea.
    Hither the heroes and the nymphs resort,
10 To taste awhile the pleasures of a court;
In various talk th' instructive hours they passed,
Who gave the ball, or paid the visit last;
One speaks the glory of the British queen,
And one describes a charming Indian screen;
15 A third interprets motions, looks, and eyes;
At every word a reputation dies.
Snuff, or the fan, supply each pause of chat,
With singing, laughing, ogling, and all that.
    Meanwhile, declining from the noon of day,
20 The sun obliquely shoots his burning ray;
The hungry judges soon the sentence sign,

from

The Rape of the Lock

Alexander Pope

from Canto III

A grand palace
named Hampton Court
stands near flower-filled meadows,
and the River Thames looks up proudly at its rising
    towers.
5   Here Britain's statesmen often predict the fall
of foreign tyrants—and also of young ladies at home.
And you, great Queen Anne, ruler of all Britain,
sometimes accept advice here—and sometimes tea.
    Heroes and maidens come here
10 to learn what pleasures can be found at court.
They pass many useful hours in all kinds of talk—
discussing who gave a ball, or who last paid a visit.
One person describes the British queen's glory,
while another describes a charming Indian screen.
15 Yet another studies movements, looks, and eyes.
And a reputation dies at every word.
Snuff[1] or fans are used to fill up pauses,
and there is singing, laughing, flirting, and all that.
    The sun slipped down from its noontime height
20 and shot its burning ray sideways.
Hungry judges were signing sentences quickly,

---

1 **snuff:** a powdered tobacco inhaled through the nose or
pressed on the gums

And wretches hang that jurymen
    may dine. . . .
Belinda now, whom thirst of fame invites,
Burns to encounter two adventurous knights,
25 At ombre singly to decide their
    doom;
And swells her breast with conquests yet to come. . . .
The nymph exulting fills with shouts the sky;
The walls, the woods, and long canals
    reply.
    Oh thoughtless mortals! ever blind to
      fate,
30 Too soon dejected and too soon elate.
Sudden, these honors shall be snatched away,
And cursed forever this victorious day.
    For lo! the board with cups and spoons is crowned,
The berries crackle, and the mill turns round;
35 On shining altars of Japan they raise
The silver lamp; the fiery spirits blaze:
From silver spouts the grateful liquors glide,
While China's earth receives the smoking tide.
At once they gratify their scent and taste,
40 And frequent cups prolong the rich repast.
Straight hover round the fair her airy band;
Some, as she sipped, the fuming liquor fanned,
Some o'er her lap their careful plumes
    displayed,
Trembling, and conscious of the rich brocade.
45 Coffee (which makes the politician wise,
And see through all things with his
    half-shut eyes)
Sent up in vapors to the Baron's brain
New stratagems, the radiant lock to gain.
Ah, cease, rash youth! desist ere 'tis too late,
50 Fear the just gods, and think of Scylla's fate!

hanging unlucky men so that jurymen could get on
    with their meals. . . .
Belinda had come desiring fame,
burning to meet two adventurous knights.

25 At a card game for three, she planned to decide their
    fates,
and her breast swelled over her expected conquests. . . .
She filled the sky with rejoicing shouts,
and the walls, woods, and long canals replied with
    echoes.
    Oh, unthinking mortals! You are always blind to
        fate!

30 Too quickly you become either sad or joyful.
All honors will soon be snatched away,
and this victorious day will be cursed forever.
    The table was set with cups and spoons.
The coffee beans crackled in the grinder.

35 Fiery spirits blazed in silver lamps
set on little Japanese tables.
Floods of hot coffee flowed freely from silver spouts
into earthen china cups.
Taste and smell were both delighted,

40 and pleasure continued cup after cup.
Belinda's band of sprites hovered around her.
Some fanned the steaming coffee as she sipped,
while others spread their trembling feathers over her
    lap
to protect the fine fabric of her dress.

45 Coffee makes the politician wise
so he can see through all things with his
    half-shut eyes.
Its vapors sent new schemes to the Baron's brain,
telling him to get the glowing lock.
Ah, stop, reckless youth! Stop before it is too late!

50 Fear the just gods, and think of Scylla's fate![2]

> 2 **Scylla:** In classical mythology, the princess Scylla cut
> the hair of her father, King Nisus. She was punished by
> being turned into a bird.

Changed to a bird, and sent to flit in air,
She dearly pays for Nisus' injured hair!
    But when to mischief mortals bend their will,
How soon they find fit instruments of ill!
55 Just then, Clarissa drew with tempting grace
A two-edged weapon from her shining case;
So ladies in romance assist their knight,
Present the spear, and arm him for the fight.
He takes the gift with reverence, and extends
60 The little engine on his fingers' ends;
This just behind Belinda's neck he spread,
As o'er the fragrant steams she bends her head.

Swift to the lock a thousand sprights repair,
A thousand wings, by turns, blow back the hair;
65 And thrice they twitched the diamond in her ear;
Thrice she looked back, and thrice the foe
    drew near.
Just in that instant, anxious Ariel sought
The close recesses of the virgin's thought;
As on the nosegay in her breast reclined,
70 He watched th' ideas rising in her mind,
Sudden he viewed, in spite of all her art,
An earthly lover lurking at her heart.
Amazed, confused, he found his power expired,
Resigned to fate, and with a sigh retired.
75   The peer now spreads the glittering *forfex* wide,
T' enclose the lock; now joins it, to divide.
Even then, before the fatal engine closed,
A wretched sylph too fondly interposed;
Fate urged the shears, and cut the sylph in twain,
80 (But airy substance soon unites again).
The meeting points the sacred hair dissever
From the fair head, forever and forever!

She dearly paid for cutting Nisus' hair
by being turned into a bird, sent flitting in the air.
    But when mortals decide on mischief,
how soon they find the tools to do it!
55 Just then, Clarissa[3] gracefully drew
a pair of scissors from her shining case,
in the same way a lady in a romance helps her knight
by giving him a spear, arming him for a fight.
He took the gift respectfully, and spread
60 the scissors open with his fingers.
He held them just behind Belinda's neck
as she bent her head toward the coffee's sweet-
        smelling steam.
A thousand sprites rushed to the lock,
blowing back her hair with their wings
65 and twitching her diamond earring three times.
She looked back three times, and the foe drew nearer
        each time.
At that moment, anxious Ariel lay
among the flowers on her breast.
He looked into the virgin's deepest thoughts,
70 watching ideas rising in her mind.
In spite of all her efforts, he suddenly saw
an earthly lover lurking in her heart.[4]
Frightened and confused, his power gone,
Ariel surrendered to fate and left with a sigh.
75   Then the Baron spread the glittering scissors wide
around the lock, then closed them to cut it off.
Just before the fatal blades closed,
an unlucky Sylph foolishly stepped between them.
Fate closed the scissors, cutting the Sylph in half—
80 (although airy bodies soon grow back again).
The scissor blades removed the sacred hair
from the fair head forever!

---

3 **Clarissa:** a friend of the Baron's
4 **In spite . . . her heart:** Because Belinda is attracted to
    the Baron, Ariel can do nothing to help her.

Then flashed the living lightning from her eyes,
And screams of horror rend th' affrighted
    skies.
85   Not louder shrieks to pitying Heaven are cast,
When husbands, or when lapdogs breathe their last;
Or when rich china vessels fallen from high,
In glittering dust, and painted fragments lie!
        "Let wreaths of triumph now my temples
            twine,"
90   The victor cried, "the glorious prize is mine!
While fish in streams, or birds delight in air,
Or in a coach and six the British fair,
As long as *Atalantis* shall be read,
Or the small pillow grace a lady's bed,
95   While visits shall be paid on solemn days,
When numerous wax lights in bright order blaze,
While nymphs take treats, or assignations give,
So long my honor, name, and praise
    shall live!
What time would spare, from steel receives its date,
100   And monuments, like men, submit to fate! . . ."
Steel could labor of the gods destroy,
And strike to dust the imperial towers of Troy;
Steel could the works of mortal pride confound,
And hew triumphal arches to the ground.
105   What wonders then, fair nymph! thy hairs should
        feel
The conquering force of unresisted steel?

Then living lightning flashed from her eyes,
and her screams of horror tore through the frightened
   skies.
85 No louder shrieks are raised to pitying heaven
when husbands or lapdogs die—
nor even when expensive china cups fall from on high
and break into glittering dust and painted pieces!
   "Let my forehead be crowned with wreaths of
     triumph!"
90 the victor cried. "The glorious prize is mine!
My honor, name, and praise shall live
as long as fish delight in streams, or birds in air,
or British ladies in coaches drawn by six horses;
or as long as *Atalantis*[5] shall be read
95 and small pillows lie on ladies' beds;
or as long as formal evening visits are paid
with many brightly lit wax candles;
or as long as young ladies take snacks or meet their
   lovers!
What time might save has been destroyed by steel,
100 and monuments must surrender to fate, like men!"
Steel could destroy something built by the gods,
And even turn the imperial towers of Troy into dust.
Steel could ruin the works of proud mankind,
And topple triumphal arches to the ground.
105 So is it any wonder, fair lady, that your hair should
   feel
The fierce power of unchallenged steel?

*In Canto IV, a furious Belinda demands that
her beau, Sir Plume, rescue her stolen lock of
hair. Plume, however, fails to convince the
Baron to return the curl.*

*At the beginning of Canto V, Clarissa, the
young woman who supplied the Baron with
the scissors, tries to end the uproar. Instead,
tempers become even more heated.*

5 **Atalantis:** *The New Atalantis* was a rather scandalous
   memoir that was popular in Pope's time.

from Canto V

"To arms, to arms!" the fierce virago cries,
And swift as lightning to the combat flies.
All side in parties, and begin th' attack;
Fans clap, silks rustle, and tough
    whalebones crack;
5   Heroes' and heroines' shouts confus'dly rise,
And bass and treble voices strike the skies.
No common weapons in their hands are found,
Like gods they fight, nor dread a mortal wound. . . .
    See, fierce Belinda on the Baron flies,
10   With more than usual lightning in her eyes:
Nor feared the chief th' unequal fight to try,
Who sought no more than on his foe to die.
But this bold lord with manly strength
    endued,
She with one finger and a thumb subdued:
15   Just where the breath of life his nostrils drew,
A charge of snuff the wily virgin threw;
The gnomes direct, to every atom just,
The pungent grains of titillating dust.
Sudden with starting tears each eye o'erflows,
20   And the high dome re-echoes to
    his nose.
    "Now meet thy fate," incensed Belinda cried,
And drew a deadly bodkin from her side. . . .
    "Boast not my fall," he cried, "insulting foe!
Thou by some other shalt be laid as low.
25   Nor think, to die dejects my lofty mind:
All that I dread is leaving you behind!
Rather than so, ah, let me still survive,
And burn in Cupid's flames—but burn alive."
    "Restore the lock!" she cries; and all around
30   "Restore the lock!" the vaulted roofs rebound.
Not fierce Othello in so loud a strain

from **Canto V**

"*T*o arms, to arms!" the fierce virago[6] cried,
and flew into battle as swift as lightning.
Everyone took sides and began the attack.
Fans snapped shut, silks rustled, and tough
    whalebones[7] cracked.
5 The shouts of heroes and heroines rose wildly,
and low and high voices reached the skies.
They had no ordinary weapons in their hands
and fought like gods, not fearing a mortal wound. . . .
    How fiercely Belinda flew at the Baron,
10 with even more lightning in her eyes than usual!
Nor did the Baron fear to join in this unequal fight,
for he wanted nothing more than to be killed by his foe.
But though this bold lord was filled with manly
    strength,
she tamed him with just one finger.
15 The wily virgin threw a wad of snuff
straight toward his nostrils.
The sprites directed every atom
of the peppery grains of stinging dust.
Suddenly, each eye overflowed with bursting tears,
20 and his sneeze echoed from the top of his head to
    his nose.
    "Now meet your fate!" furious Belinda cried,
drawing a deadly hairpin from her side. . . .
    "Don't boast of my defeat, insulting foe!" he cried.
"You will be defeated by some other suitor.
25 And don't suppose I'm sad at the thought of death.
The only thing I dread is giving you up!
Instead of that, let me
burn in the flames of love—but burn alive."
    "Give back the lock!" she cried. And the high roof
30 echoed all around, "Give back the lock!"
Even fierce Othello never roared so loudly

6 **virago:** a loud, threatening woman; here, a friend of
    Belinda's named Thalestris
7 **whalebones:** used to stiffen women's corsets

Roared for the handkerchief that caused his pain.
But see how oft ambitious aims are crossed,
And chiefs contend till all the prize is lost!
35   The lock, obtained with guilt, and kept with pain,
In every place is sought, but sought in vain:
With such a prize no mortal must be blessed,
So Heaven decrees! with Heaven who can contest?
    Some thought it mounted to the lunar sphere,
40   Since all things lost on earth are treasured there.
There heroes' wits are kept in ponderous vases,
And beaux' in snuffboxes and tweezer
    cases.
There broken vows and deathbed alms are found,
And lovers' hearts with ends of riband bound. . . .
45   But trust the Muse—she saw it
       upward rise,
Though marked by none but quick, poetic eyes: . . .
A sudden star, it shot through liquid air,
And drew behind a radiant trail of hair. . . .
    Then cease, bright nymph! to mourn thy
      ravished hair,
50   Which adds new glory to the shining sphere!
Not all the tresses that fair head can boast,
Shall draw such envy as the lock you lost.
For, after all the murders of your eye,
When, after millions slain, yourself shall die;
55   When those fair suns shall set, as set they must,
And all those tresses shall be laid in dust,
This lock, the Muse shall consecrate to fame,
And midst the stars inscribe Belinda's name.

for the handkerchief that caused his pain.[8]
But ambitious aims are often defeated,
and warriors fight on till the prize is lost!
35 The lock, guiltily gotten and painfully kept,
was looked for everywhere, but couldn't be found.
Heaven had declared that no mortal must be blessed
with such a prize. And who can argue with Heaven?
Some thought the lock climbed up to the moon,
40 since all things lost on earth are treasured there.[9]
Heroes' wits are kept there in heavy vases,
and wits of fancy lords in snuffboxes and tweezer
cases.
Broken vows and deathbed offerings are found there,
and lovers' hearts tied together with ribbons. . . .
45 But trust the Muse, who says she saw it
rise upward,
unseen except by people with quick, poetic eyes: . . .
A comet, shooting through clear air,
followed by a radiant trail of hair. . . .
So young lady, stop mourning for your
stolen hair,
50 which adds new glory to the skies!
Not all the hair upon your head
shall draw as much envy as the lock you lost.
Someday, after you've slain millions
of young men with your eyes, you'll die yourself.
55 Someday, those very eyes of yours must close,
and all your hairs will lie in the grave.
But even then, the Muse will bless this lock with fame,
writing among the stars Belinda's name.

---

8 **Othello . . . pain:** In Shakespeare's tragedy *Othello*, the
title character gives a handkerchief to his wife,
Desdemona. The play's villain, Iago, steals the handkerchief to convince Othello that Desdemona is unfaithful.

9 **moon . . . treasured there:** It used to be said that all
lost things ended up on the moon.

INTRODUCTION TO
Gulliver's Travels

"Satire is a sort of glass [mirror], wherein beholders do generally discover everybody's face but their own . . ." So wrote Jonathan Swift in his preface to a work called *The Battle of the Books*.

Many satirists, like Swift, feel that their audiences deliberately miss their point. Seeing themselves ridiculed in satire, readers may persuade themselves that they are really reading about other people. So not surprisingly, satirists often wind up wondering if human beings can be improved at all.

Gulliver's Travels is Swift's most comical satire—and also his angriest. Its full title is *Travels into Several Remote Nations of the World. In Four Parts. By Lemuel Gulliver, First a Surgeon, and then a Captain of Several Ships*.

Each of the novel's four parts describes one of Gulliver's voyages. In Book I, Gulliver is shipwrecked on the island of Lilliput, where he encounters a race of tiny people. The following excerpts are from this part of the book.

Alert readers of Swift's time would have realized that Lilliput was much like England. Like Englishmen (at least as Swift saw them), the Lilliputians are small, vain, and foolish.

Many other facets of Lilliputian life also suggest England. For example, Lilliput's enemies live on another island called Blefuscu. Blefuscu is clearly meant to remind readers of England's traditional enemy, France.

Lilliput has two political parties that violently disagree with each other. One political party wears high heels, while another wears low heels. Swift meant the "High-Heels" to represent the Tories, England's conservative party. The "Low-Heels" represent the Whigs, England's liberal party.

Lilliputians are also torn over which end of an egg to break before eating it. Officially, Lilliputians are only allowed to break their eggs at the little end. But "Big-Endians" are ready to die for their belief that eggs must be broken at the large end. Here, Swift was commenting on the conflict between Protestants and Catholics in England.

Throughout the first part of *Gulliver's Travels*, Swift makes similar references to British monarchs, politicians, and history.

In Book II, Gulliver makes a voyage to Brobdingnag, a world of giants. There he finds human faults and imperfections hugely magnified.

In Book III, he travels to a flying island called Laputa, where the people seem to be extremely wise. Actually, they are only foolish and impractical. In parts of this section, Swift satirizes the Royal Society for what he thought to be its misplaced faith in science.

In Book IV, Gulliver arrives in the land of the Houyhnhms. At long last, he has found a race of wise, intelligent, and gentle creatures. Alas, the Houyhnhms are not human. They are horses. The Houyhnhms are often troubled by rude, ugly, brutal creatures called Yahoos. The Yahoos are, of course, people.

Gulliver loves the Houyhnhms and wishes to live with them always. But to them, he is only a slightly more civilized Yahoo. So they send him back to England, where he lives the rest of his days a bitter, angry man.

Since *Gulliver's Travels* was first published in 1726, readers have been shocked by its final chapters. In them, Swift's bitterness seems to know no bounds. And for once, it is difficult for any reader not to recognize his or her own face in Swift's satirical mirror.

Here Swift is asking some very troubling questions. Is there any hope for the human race? And in a world where humans behave like beasts, can only beasts be human?

from Gulliver's Travels

Jonathan Swift

from Chapter I: A Voyage to Lilliput

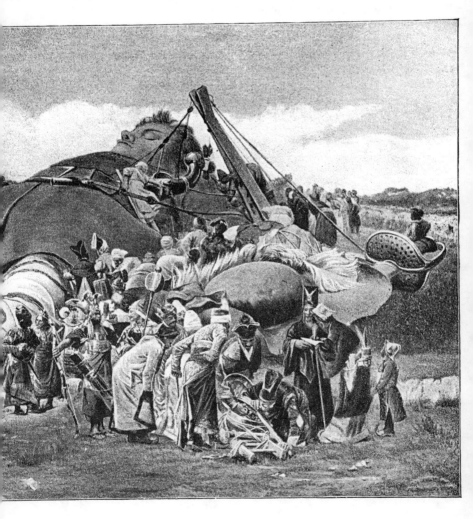

1   *I* lay down on the grass, which was very short and soft, where I slept sounder than ever I remember to have done in my life, and, as I reckoned, above nine hours; for when I awaked, it was just daylight. I

2   attempted to rise, but was not able to stir: For as I happened to lie on my back, I found my arms and legs were strongly fastened on each side to the ground; and my hair, which was long and thick, tied down in the same manner. I likewise felt several slender ligatures across my body, from my armpits to my thighs. I could

3   only look upward; the sun began to grow hot, and the light offended my eyes. I heard a confused noise about me, but in the posture I lay, could see nothing except the sky.

4   In a little time I felt something alive moving on my left leg, which advancing gently forward over my breast, came almost up to my chin; when bending my eyes downward as much as I could, I perceived it to be a human creature not six inches high, with a bow and arrow in his hands, and a quiver at his back. In

5   the meantime, I felt at least forty more of the same kind (as I conjectured) following the first. I was in the utmost astonishment, and roared so loud, that they all ran back in a fright; and some of them, as I was afterward told, were hurt with the falls they got by leaping from my sides upon the ground. However,

6   they soon returned, and one of them, who ventured so far as to get a full sight of my face, lifting up his hands and eyes by way of admiration, cried out in a shrill, but distinct voice, *Hekinah degul*: The others repeated the same words several times, but then I knew not what they meant. I lay all this while, as the

7   reader may believe, in great uneasiness: At length, struggling to get loose, I had the fortune to break the strings, and wrench out the pegs that fastened my

1   *I* lay down in the grass, which was very short and soft, and I slept more soundly than I ever remember having done in my life. I suppose I slept more than nine hours, for when I awoke, it was just daylight.

2   I tried to rise, but I was not able to stir. I was on my back, and now I found my arms and legs strongly tied to the ground on each side. My long, thick hair was tied down in the same manner. I also felt several slender cords across my body from my armpits to my thighs.

3   I could only look upward. The sun began to grow hot, and the light hurt my eyes. I heard some confused noises around me. But in my position, I could see nothing but the sky.

4   In a little while, I felt something alive moving on my left leg. It approached gently forward over my chest and came almost up to my chin. I bent my eyes downward as much as I could. I then saw that it was a human creature not six inches high. He had a bow and arrow in his hands, and a quiver on his back.

5   In the meantime, I guessed that I felt at least forty more of the same kind of people following the first. I was completely astonished, and I roared so loudly that they all ran back in fright. I was told afterward that some of them were hurt by the falls they took by leaping from my sides to the ground.

6   However, they soon returned. One of them dared to come near enough to get a full view of my face. He lifted up his hands in amazement, and cried out in a shrill, clear voice, *"Hekinah degul!"*[1] The others repeated the same words several times, but I did not yet know what they meant.

7   The reader may well believe that I had been lying very uneasily all this time. After a while, I struggled to get loose. I was lucky enough to break the strings

1   *Hekinah degul*: Scholars have often wondered if there is any meaning to Swift's made-up Lilliputian words. It has been suggested that *hekinah degul* means "What in the devil!"

8 left arm to the ground; for, by lifting it up to my face, I discovered the methods they had taken to bind me, and at the same time with a violent pull, which gave me excessive pain, I a little loosened the strings that tied down my hair on the left side, so that I was just able to turn my head about two inches.

9 But the creatures ran off a second time, before I could seize them; whereupon there was a great shout in a very shrill accent, and after it ceased, I heard one of them cry aloud, *Tolgo phonac*; when in

10 an instant I felt above an hundred arrows discharged on my left hand, which pricked me like so many needles; and besides, they shot another flight into the air, as we do bombs in Europe, whereof many, I suppose, fell on my body (though I felt them not), and some on my face, which I immediately covered with my left hand. When this shower of arrows was over, I

11 fell a-groaning with grief and pain, and then striving again to get loose, they discharged another volley larger than the first, and some of them attempted with spears to stick me in the sides; but, by good luck, I had on me a buff jerkin, which they could not pierce. I thought it the most prudent method to lie

12 still, and my design was to continue so till night, when, my left hand being already loose, I could easily free myself: And as for the inhabitants, I had reason to believe I might be a match for the greatest armies they could bring against me, if they were all of the same size with him that I saw. But fortune disposed otherwise of me.

13 When the people observed I was quiet, they discharged no more arrows; but, by the noise increasing, I knew their numbers were greater; and about four yards from me, over against my right ear, I heard a

14 knocking for above an hour, like that of people at work; when turning my head that way, as well as the

and yank out the pegs that fastened my left arm to the ground. By lifting my arm up to my face, I understood the method they had used to bind me.

8   Then I gave my head a violent pull, which caused me great pain. This loosened the strings that tied down my hair on the left side a little. I was able to turn my head about two inches.

9   The creatures ran away a second time before I could seize them. Then there was a great deal of shouting in a very shrill tone. After it stopped, I heard one of them cry aloud, *"Tolgo phonac!"*

10   And at that instant, I felt a hundred arrows shot at my left hand. They pricked me like so many needles. And then they shot another flight into the air, as we do bombs in Europe. I guess that many of them fell on my body, although I did not feel them. Some fell on my face, which I immediately covered with my left hand.

11   When this shower of arrows was over, I groaned with sorrow and pain. When I tried again to get loose, they shot another volley larger than the first. Some of them tried to stick spears in my sides. But by good luck, I was wearing a leather jacket that they couldn't pierce.

12   I thought it wisest to lie still, and I planned to do so until night. Since my left hand was already loose, I thought I could easily free myself then. And I wasn't much worried about the natives. I thought myself a match for the greatest armies they could bring against me, if they were all the same size as the men I had seen. But fortune had other plans for me.

13   When the people saw that I was quiet, they shot no more arrows. But by the increasing noise, I knew that their numbers were greater.

14   I heard a knocking for more than an hour, as if people were working. The knocking was about four

pegs and strings would permit me, I saw a stage
erected, about a foot and a half from the ground,
capable of holding four of the inhabitants, with two
or three ladders to mount it: From whence one of
them, who seemed to be a person of quality, made me

15   a long speech, whereof I understood not one syllable.
But I should have mentioned, that before the principal person began his oration, he cried out three
times, *Langro dehul san* (these words and the former
were afterward repeated and explained to me).

16   Whereupon immediately about fifty of the inhabitants came and cut the strings that fastened the left
side of my head, which gave me the liberty of turning
it to the right, and of observing the person and ges-
ture of him who was to speak. He appeared to be of a
17   middle age, and taller than any of the other three
who attended him, whereof one was a page who held
up his train, and seemed to be somewhat longer than
my middle finger; the other two stood one on each

18   side to support him. He acted every part of an orator,
and I could observe many periods of threatenings,
and others of promises, pity, and kindness.

19   I answered in a few words, but in the most submissive manner, lifting up my left hand, and both my
eyes to the sun, as calling him for a witness; and
being almost famished with hunger, having not eaten
a morsel for some hours before I left the ship. I found
the demands of nature so strong upon me, that I
could not forbear showing my impatience (perhaps
against the strict rules of decency) by putting my finger frequently on my mouth, to signify that I wanted
20   food. The *Hurgo* (for so they call a great lord, as I
afterward learnt) understood me very well. He

yards away from me, opposite my right ear. I turned my head that way, as much as the pegs and strings would allow. I saw that a stage had been built about a foot and a half off the ground. It was large enough to hold four of the natives, with two or three ladders to climb it.

15   A man was standing on the stage, and he seemed to be a nobleman. He gave me a long speech, and I didn't understand a syllable. But I should have mentioned something. Before this leader began his speech, he cried out three times, *"Langro dehul san!"* These and the other words I had heard were later repeated and explained to me.

16   Right then, about fifty natives came and cut the strings that fastened the left side of my head. This left me free to turn it to the right. I could then observe the figure and manner of the man who was speaking.

17   He looked middle-aged, and was taller than the other three who stood with him. One was a page who held up his cloak and seemed to be somewhat longer than my middle finger. The other two stood on each side to support the leader.

18   He certainly enjoyed making speeches. I could guess that he made many threats. But at other moments, he made promises and showed pity and kindness.

19   I answered with a few words, but in the mildest manner. I lifted up my left hand and my eyes to the sun, as if calling upon it as a witness. I had not eaten a bite since some hours before I had left the ship. The natives were making great demands on me, and I could not help showing some impatience. Perhaps rather impolitely, I often put my finger on my mouth, showing that I wanted food.

20   I later learned that they called a great lord a *Hurgo*. This *Hurgo* understood me very well. He

descended from the stage, and commanded that several ladders should be applied to my sides, on which
21 above an hundred of the inhabitants mounted and walked toward my mouth, laden with baskets full of meat, which had been provided and sent thither by the King's orders, upon the first intelligence he
22 received of me. I observed there was the flesh of several animals, but could not distinguish them by the taste. There were shoulders, legs, and loins, shaped like those of mutton, and very well dressed, but smaller than the wings of a lark. I ate them by two or three at a mouthful, and took three loaves at a time, about the bigness of musket bullets. They
23 supplied me as fast as they could, showing a thousand marks of wonder and astonishment at my bulk and appetite.

I then made another sign that I wanted drink. They found by my eating, that a small quantity would not suffice me; and being a most ingenious people, they slung up with great dexterity one of their largest hogsheads, then rolled it toward my
24 hand, and beat out the top; I drank it off at a draft, which I might well do, for it hardly held half a pint, and tasted like a small wine of Burgundy, but much more delicious. They brought me a second hogshead, which I drank in the same manner, and made signs for more, but they had none to give me. When I had
25 performed these wonders, they shouted for joy, and danced upon my breast, repeating several times as they did at first, *Hekinah degul*. They made me a sign that I should throw down the two hogsheads, but first warned the people below to stand out of the way, crying aloud, *Borach mivola*, and when they saw the vessels in the air, there was an universal shout of *Hekinah degul*. I confess I was often tempted, while
26 they were passing backward and forward on my body, to seize forty or fifty of the first that came in my reach, and dash them against the ground. But the

came down from the stage and ordered several ladders to be put at my sides.

21   About a hundred natives climbed the ladders and walked toward my mouth. They were carrying baskets full of food. The King had ordered these to be brought when I had first spoken to him.

22   I saw that there was meat of several animals, but I could not tell them apart by taste. There were shoulders, legs, and loins, all shaped like those of mutton. They were very well prepared, but smaller than a lark's wings. I ate two or three of them at a mouthful. I also swallowed three loaves of bread at a time, about the size of musket bullets.

23   The natives fed me as fast as they could. They showed a thousand signs of wonder and astonishment at my size and hunger. Then I made another sign that I wanted drink. They had found by my eating that a small amount would not do. Because they were very clever people, they brought along one of their largest barrels. They rolled it toward my hand and knocked out the top.

24   I drank it at a swallow—which was easy to do, for it hardly held half a pint. It tasted like cheap wine from Burgundy, but much more delicious. They brought me a second barrel, which I drank in the same way. Then I made signs for more, but they had none to give me.

25   After I had performed these wonders, they shouted for joy and danced upon my chest. They repeated several times those earlier words, *"Hekinah degul."* Then they made me a sign to throw down the two barrels. But first, they warned the people below to stand out of the way, crying, *"Borach mivola!"* When they saw the barrels in the air, everyone shouted, *"Hekinah degul!"*

26   They kept passing back and forth on my body. I confess that I was often tempted to seize the first forty or fifty that came in my reach and dash them

remembrance of what I had felt, which probably might not be the worst they could do, and the promise of honor I made them, for so I interpreted
27 my submissive behavior, soon drove out those imaginations. Besides, I now considered myself as bound by the laws of hospitality to a people who had treated me with so much expense and magnificence.

However, in my thoughts, I could not sufficiently
28 wonder at the intrepidity of these diminutive mortals, who durst venture to mount and walk on my body, while one of my hands was at liberty, without trembling at the very sight of so prodigious a creature as I must appear to them.

29 After some time, when they observed that I made no more demands for meat, there appeared before me a person of high rank from his Imperial Majesty. His Excellency, having mounted on the small of my right leg, advanced forward up to my face, with about a
30 dozen of his retinue. And producing his credentials under the Signet Royal, which he applied close to my eyes, spoke about ten minutes, without any signs of anger, but with a kind of determinate resolution;

against the ground. But I remembered how I had felt when they had attacked me. And that was probably not the worst they could do.

27   I also felt that I had made a promise of honor by my mild behavior. So I put such ideas out of my mind. Besides, I now felt bound by the laws of hospitality to a people who had treated me with such expense and generosity.

28   Still, I could not help wondering at the bravery of these tiny mortals. They had dared to climb and walk on my body while one of my hands was free. And they never trembled at the sight of a creature as huge as I must have seemed to them.

29   After a while, they saw that I stopped asking for meat. Then a person of high rank was sent to me from His Imperial Majesty. This official climbed on the small of my right leg and walked up to my face, with about a dozen followers.

30   He took out official papers, stamped with the royal seal, and held them close to my eyes. He spoke for about ten minutes with no sign of anger, but with

often pointing forward, which, as I afterward found,
was toward the capital city, about half a mile distant,
whither it was agreed by his Majesty in council that
I must be conveyed. I answered in few words, but to
31   no purpose, and made a sign with my hand that was
loose, putting it to the other (but over his
Excellency's head for fear of hurting him or his train)
and then to my own head and body, to signify that I
desired my liberty. It appeared that he understood
32   me well enough, for he shook his head by way of dis-
approbation, and held his hand in a posture to show
that I must be carried as a prisoner. However, he
made other signs to let me understand that I should
have meat and drink enough, and very good treatment. Whereupon I once more thought of attempting
33   to break my bonds; but again, when I felt the smart
of their arrows, upon my face and hands, which were
all in blisters, and many of the darts still sticking in
them, and observing likewise that the number of my
enemies increased, I gave tokens to let them know
34   that they might do with me what they pleased. Upon
this, the *Hurgo* and his train withdrew, with much
civility and cheerful countenances.
35   Soon after I heard a general shout, with frequent
repetitions of the words, *Peplom selan*, and I felt
great numbers of people on my left side relaxing the
cords to such a degree, that I was able to turn upon
my right, and to ease myself with making water;
36   which I very plentifully did, to the great astonishment of the people, who conjecturing by my motions
what I was going to do, immediately opened to the
right and left on that side, to avoid the torrent which
fell with such noise and violence from me. But before
37   this, they had daubed my face and both my hands
with a sort of ointment very pleasant to the smell,
which in a few minutes removed all the smart of
their arrows. These circumstances, added to the
refreshment I had received by their victuals and

tough firmness. He often pointed forward. I later learned that this was toward the capital city, about a half a mile away. His Majesty and his advisors had decided that I must be taken there.

31   I answered in a few words, but it was no use. So I made a sign with my free hand, putting it to the other hand (being careful not to hurt the official or his followers). Then I pointed to my own head and body, showing that I wanted my liberty.

32   He appeared to understand me well enough, for he shook his head with disapproval. He held his hand in a way that showed I must be carried as a prisoner. However, he made other signs to show me that I would have enough food and drink, and very good treatment.

33   I thought again of trying to break my bonds. But I still felt the pain of their arrows on my face and hands, which were all blistered. Many of the darts were still sticking in me. I also saw that the number of my enemies had increased.

34   So I gave signs to them that they could do what they pleased with me. The *Hurgo* and his followers left with great politeness and happy faces.

35   I soon heard a shout among the people around me. They often repeated the words, *"Peplom selan."* Then I felt great numbers of people on my left side loosen the cords. I was soon able to turn on my right side and was able to comfort myself by making water.

36   I did so very plentifully, to the great amazement of the people. They had guessed what I was going to do by my movements. So the crowd had immediately parted to the right and left on that side, avoiding the noisy and violent downpour that fell from me.

37   But before this, they had smeared my face and hands with a sort of ointment. It had a very pleasant smell, and in a few minutes it took away all the pain of their arrows.

38   drink, which were very nourishing, disposed me to sleep. I slept about eight hours, as I was afterward assured; and it was no wonder, for the physicians, by the Emperor's order, had mingled a sleeping potion in the hogshead of wine. . . .

39   My gentleness and good behavior had gained so far on the Emperor and his court, and indeed upon the army and people in general, that I began to conceive hopes of getting my liberty in a short time. I took all possible methods to cultivate this favorable

40   disposition. The natives came by degrees to be less apprehensive of any danger from me. I would sometimes lie down, and let five or six of them dance on my hand. And at last the boys and girls would venture to come and play at hide-and-seek in my hair. I

41   had now made a good progress in understanding and speaking their language. The Emperor had a mind one day to entertain me with several of the country shows, wherein they exceed all nations I have known, both for dexterity and magnificence. I was diverted

42   with none so much as that of the rope dancers, performed upon a slender white thread, extended about two foot, and twelve inches from the ground. Upon which I shall desire liberty, with the reader's patience, to enlarge a little.

43   This diversion is only practiced by those persons who are candidates for great employments, and high favor, at court. They are trained in this art from their youth, and are not always of noble birth, or liberal

44   education. When a great office is vacant, either by death or disgrace (which often happens), five or six of those candidates petition the Emperor to entertain his Majesty and the court with a dance on the rope, and whoever jumps the highest without falling, succeeds in the office. Very often the chief ministers themselves are commanded to show their skill, and to convince the Emperor that they have not lost their

38   All this made me sleepy, along with the nourishing food and drink I had already received. I was later told that I slept about eight hours. And this was no wonder. For at the Emperor's order, the physicians had mixed a sleeping potion in the barrel of wine. . . .

39   My gentleness and good behavior impressed the emperor and his court—and indeed, the army and people in general. So I began to hope that I might soon be set free. I did everything I could to make this happen.

40   Little by little, the natives became less afraid of me. I would sometimes lie down and let five or six of them dance on my hand. And boys and girls would dare to come and play hide-and-seek in my hair.

41   I had made good progress in understanding and speaking their language. One day, the emperor decided to entertain me with several country shows. For skill and splendor, these outdid any shows I had ever seen in any nation.

42   I was most impressed by the tightrope dancers. They performed on a slender white thread, stretched about two feet long, 12 inches off the ground. With the reader's patience, I'll take the liberty to tell more about this.

43   This sport is only practiced by candidates for great positions and high favor at court. They are trained for it from their youth, and they are not always of noble birth or wide education.

44   Sometimes a great office falls vacant, either by death or disgrace (which often happens). Then five or six candidates ask to entertain His Majesty and the court with a dance on the rope. Whoever jumps highest without falling takes office. Very often, even chief officials are ordered to show their skill and convince the Emperor that they have not lost their skill.

45 faculty. Flimnap, the Treasurer, is allowed to cut a
caper on the straight rope, at least an inch higher
than any other lord in the whole empire. I have seen
him do the summerset several times together upon a
trencher fixed on the rope, which is no thicker than a
common packthread in England. My friend Reldresal,

46 principal Secretary for Private Affairs, is, in my opinion, if I am not partial, the second after the
Treasurer; the rest of the great officers are much
upon a par.

47   These diversions are often attended with fatal
accidents, whereof great numbers are on record. I
myself have seen two or three candidates break a
limb. But the danger is much greater when the min-

48 isters themselves are commanded to show their
dexterity; for, by contending to excel themselves and
their fellows, they strain so far, that there is hardly
one of them who hath not received a fall, and some of

49 them two or three. I was assured that a year or two
before my arrival, Flimnap would have infallibly
broke his neck, if one of the King's cushions, that
accidentally lay on the ground, had not weakened the
force of his fall.

50   There is likewise another diversion, which is only
shown before the Emperor and Empress, and first
minister, upon particular occasions. The Emperor
lays on the table three fine silken threads of six
inches long. One is blue, the other red, and the third
green. These threads are proposed as prizes for those
persons whom the Emperor hath a mind to distinguish by a peculiar mark of his favor. The ceremony

51 is performed in his Majesty's great chamber of state,
where the candidates are to undergo a trial of dexterity very different from the former, and such as I have
not observed the least resemblance of in any other
country of the Old or the New World. The Emperor

52 holds a stick in his hands, both ends parallel to the
horizon, while the candidates advancing one by one,

45   Flimnap, the Treasurer, is allowed to dance on a rope at least an inch higher than any other lord in the whole empire. I have seen him do several somersaults on a wooden platter fixed to a rope. The rope was no thicker than English twine.

46   If I'm not biased, I believe my friend Reldresal, chief Secretary for Private Affairs, is second to the Treasurer in skill. The rest of the great officers are pretty much equal to one another.

47   These entertainments often lead to fatal accidents, and there are many on record. I myself have seen two or three candidates break a limb. But the danger is much greater when the ministers are

48   ordered to show their agility. By trying to surpass themselves and others, they strain too far. So there is hardly one of them who has not fallen, some of them two or three times.

49   I was told that Flimnap very nearly broke his neck a year or two before my arrival. But by chance, one of the king's cushions lay on the ground. It weakened the force of his fall.

50   There is another entertainment which is seen only by the emperor, the empress, and the first minister, and only on special occasions. The emperor lays three fine silk threads six inches long on the table. One is blue, another red, and the third green. These threads are offered as prizes. They go to people to whom the emperor wants to show special marks of his favor.

51   The ceremony is performed in His Majesty's great chamber of state. The candidates undergo a very different sort of trial of agility from the others I've described. I've seen nothing like it in any other country of the Old or the New World.

52   The emperor holds a stick in his hands, both ends lined up with the horizon. Then the candidates step

sometimes leap over the stick, sometimes creep under it backward and forward several times, according as the stick is advanced or depressed. Sometimes

53 the Emperor holds one end of the stick, and his first minister the other; sometimes the minister has it entirely to himself. Whoever performs his part with
54 most agility, and holds out the longest in leaping and creeping, is rewarded with the blue-colored silk; the red is given to the next, and the green to the third, which they all wear girt twice round about the middle; and you see few great persons about this court, who are not adorned with one of these girdles. . . .

55 I had sent so many memorials and petitions for my liberty, that his Majesty at length mentioned the matter first in the cabinet, and then in a full council; where it was opposed by none, except Skyresh Bolgolam, who was pleased, without any provocation,
56 to be my mortal enemy. But it was carried against him by the whole board, and confirmed by the Emperor. That minister was *Galbet*, or Admiral of the Realm; very much in his master's confidence, and a person well versed in affairs, but of a morose and
57 sour complexion. However, he was at length persuaded to comply; but prevailed that the articles and conditions upon which I should be set free, and to which I must swear, should be drawn up by himself. These articles were brought to me by Skyresh Bolgolam in person, attended by two undersecretaries, and several persons of distinction. After
58 they were read, I was demanded to swear to the performance of them; first in the manner of my own country, and afterwards in the method prescribed by their laws; which was to hold my right foot in my left hand, to place the middle finger of my right hand on the crown of my head, and my thumb on the tip of

forward one by one. Sometimes they leap over the stick, and sometimes they creep under it backward and forward several times. It depends on how the stick is raised or lowered.

53   Sometimes the emperor holds one end of the stick, and his first minister the other. Sometimes the minister has it entirely to himself.

54   Whoever shows the most agility and holds out the longest in leaping and creeping gets the blue-colored silk thread. The red is given to the next and the green to the third. They all wear these threads wrapped twice around their waists. You see few great persons around this court who aren't dressed in one of these threads. . . .

55   I had sent many memos and petitions for my liberty. At last, His Majesty mentioned the matter—first in the cabinet, then in a full council. No one opposed it except Skyresh Bolgolam. He enjoyed being my enemy for no good reason.

56   But he was outvoted by the board, and the emperor approved their decision. Skyresh Bolgolam was *Galbet*, or Admiral of the Realm. The king had great confidence in him, and he knew his business very well. But he had a gloomy and sour nature.

57   However, he was finally persuaded to agree. Articles and conditions would be written to free me, and I was expected to swear to them. However, Skyresh Bolgolam insisted that he write them himself. He brought me these articles in person. He was accompanied by two under-secretaries and several other important people.

58   After the articles were read, I was ordered to swear to carry them out. I did so first in the manner of my own country, and afterwards in the manner set forth by their laws. This was to put my right foot in my left hand, the middle finger of my right hand on top of my head, and my thumb on the tip of my right ear.

59 my right ear. But because the reader may perhaps be curious to have some idea of the style and manner of expression peculiar to that people, as well as to know the articles upon which I recovered my liberty, I have made a translation of the whole instrument, word for word, as near as I was able; which I here offer to the public.

60 GOLBASTO MOMAREN EVLAME GURDILO SHEFIN MULLY ULLY GUE, most mighty Emperor of Lilliput, delight and terror of the universe, whose dominions extend five thousand blustrugs (about twelve miles in circumference) to the extremities of the globe;

61 Monarch of all Monarchs; taller than the sons of men; whose feet press down to the center, and whose head strikes against the sun; at whose nod the princes of the earth shake their knees; pleasant as the spring, comfortable as the summer, fruitful as autumn, dreadful as winter. His most sublime

62 Majesty proposeth to the Man-Mountain, lately arrived at our celestial dominions, the following articles, which by a solemn oath he shall be obliged to perform.

63 First, the Man-Mountain shall not depart from our dominions, without our license under our great seal.

64 Secondly, He shall not presume to come into our metropolis, without our express order; at which time the inhabitants shall have two hours' warning, to keep within their doors.

65 Thirdly, The said Man-Mountain shall confine his walks to our principal high roads; and not offer to walk or lie down in a meadow, or field of corn.

66 Fourthly, As he walks the said roads, he shall take the utmost care not to trample upon the bodies of any of our loving subjects, their horses, or carriages, nor take any of our said subjects into his hands, without their own consent.

59   Perhaps the reader is curious to know the peculiar style and manner with which these people expressed themselves. Perhaps you also wish to read the articles that gave me my liberty. So I have made a word-for-word translation of the document, as best I could. Here I offer it to the public.

60   From GOLBASTO MOMAREN EVLAME GURDILO SHEFIN MULLY ULLY GUE, most mighty Emperor of Lilliput, delight and terror of the universe. His lands cover five thousand blustrugs [about twelve miles around] and reach the edges of the globe.

61   He is the Monarch of all Monarchs, taller than the sons of men. His feet press toward the center of the earth, and his head strikes against the sun. The princes of the earth shake their knees at his nod. He is as pleasant as spring, as comfortable as summer, as fruitful as autumn, as dreadful as winter.

62   The Man-Mountain recently arrived in our heavenly land. His most noble Majesty now proposes to him the following articles. He shall be obliged to carry them out by a solemn oath.

63   First: The Man-Mountain shall not leave our land without written permission, stamped with our great seal.

64   Second: He shall not decide to come into our city without our clear order. And then the citizens shall have two hours' warning, to keep within doors.

65   Third: The Man-Mountain shall only walk on our main highways. He will not walk or lie down in a meadow or a field of corn.

66   Fourth: When he walks the highways, he shall take great care not to trample on the bodies of our loving subjects, their horses, or carriages. Nor shall he take any of our subjects into his hands unless they agree to it.

67   Fifthly, If an express require extraordinary dispatch, the Man-Mountain shall be obliged to carry in his pocket the messenger and horse, a six days' journey once in every moon, and return the said messenger back (if so required) safe to our Imperial Presence.

68   Sixthly, He shall be our ally against our enemies in the island of Blefuscu, and do his utmost to destroy their fleet, which is now preparing to invade us.

69   Seventhly, That the said Man-Mountain shall, at his times of leisure, be aiding and assisting to our workmen, in helping to raise certain great stones, towards covering the wall of the principal park, and other our royal buildings.

70   Eighthly, That the said Man-Mountain shall, in two moons' time, deliver in an exact survey of the circumference of our dominions by a computation of his own paces round the coast.

71   Lastly, That upon his solemn oath to observe all the above articles, the said Man-Mountain shall have a daily allowance of meat and drink sufficient for the support of 1,728 of our subjects; with free access to our Royal Person, and other marks of our favor.

72   Given at our palace at Belfaborac the twelfth day of the ninety-first moon of our reign.

73   I swore and subscribed to these articles with great cheerfulness and content . . . whereupon my chains were immediately unlocked, and I was at full liberty: the Emperor himself in person did me the honor to be by at the whole ceremony. I made my acknowledgements by prostrating myself at his

74   Majesty's feet: but he commanded me to rise; and after many gracious expressions, which, to avoid the censure of vanity, I shall not repeat, he added, that he hoped I should prove a useful servant, and well deserve all the favors he had already conferred upon me, or might do for the future.

67   Fifth: When a letter must be sent with great speed, the Man-Mountain shall carry the messenger and horse in his pocket. He must make such a six-day journey once every month. Then he must return the messenger safely to our Majesty, if necessary.

68   Sixth: He shall be our ally against our enemies on the island of Blefuscu. He must do his best to destroy their fleet, which is now preparing to invade us.

69   Seventh: When he has time, the Man-Mountain shall help our workmen to move certain great stones. These will be used to complete the wall of the main park and some of our royal buildings.

70   Eighth: The Man-Mountain shall survey the length of the border of our country exactly. He shall do this within two months by counting his own foot-steps around the coast.

71   Last: If he swears solemnly to all these articles, the Man-Mountain will have a daily allowance of food and drink. This will be enough to support 1,728 of our subjects. He will also be allowed to visit our Majesty freely, and will be favored by us in other ways.

72   This has been declared at our palace at Belfaborac, the 12th day of the 91st month of our reign.

73   I swore to these articles and signed them cheer-fully and happily . . . and then my chains were unlocked, and I was fully at liberty. The Emperor himself honored me by attending the ceremony in person. I showed my gratitude by bowing at his Majesty's feet. But he commanded me to rise.

74   He said many kind things to me, but I won't repeat them, for fear of being accused of vanity. He said that he hoped I would prove a useful servant. And he added that I well deserved all the favors he had already done for me, or might do in the future.

75   The reader may please to observe, that in the last article for the recovery of my liberty, the Emperor stipulates to allow me a quantity of meat and drink, sufficient for the support of 1,728 Lilliputians. Some

76   time after, asking a friend at court how they came to fix on that determinate number, he told me, that his Majesty's mathematicians, having taken the height of my body by the help of a quadrant, and finding it to exceed theirs in the proportion of twelve to one,

77   they concluded from the similarity of their bodies, that mine must contain at least 1,728 of theirs, and consequently would require as much food as was necessary to support that number of Lilliputians. By

78   which, the reader may conceive an idea of the ingenuity of that people, as well as the prudent and exact economy of so great a prince. One morning, about a

79   fortnight after I had obtained my liberty, Reldresal, Principal Secretary (as they style him) of Private Affairs, came to my house, attended

80   only by one servant. He ordered his coach to wait at a distance, and desired I would give him an hour's audience; which I readily consented to, on account of his quality, and personal merits, as well as of the many good offices he had done me during my solicitations at court. I offered to lie down, that he might the more conveniently reach my ear; but he chose rather to let me hold him in my hand during our conversa-

81   tion. He began with compliments on my liberty, said he might pretend to some merit in it; but, however, added, that if it had not been for the present situation of things at court, perhaps I might not have obtained it so soon. For, said he, as flourishing a con-

82   dition as we appear to be in to foreigners, we labor under two mighty evils; a violent faction at home, and the danger of an invasion by a most potent enemy from abroad. As to the first, you are to

75   The reader might be curious about something in the last of the articles for regaining my liberty. There the Emperor allowed me enough food and drink to support 1,728 Lilliputians.

76   Some time later, I asked a friend at court why they decided on that exact number. He told me that his Majesty's mathematicians had measured my height with a quadrant.[2] They found that I was 12 times taller than they were.

77   Based on the similarity of their bodies, they figured that mine must contain at least 1,728 of theirs. And so I would need as much food as was needed to support that number of Lilliputians.

78   From this, the reader may get an idea of these people's cleverness. You may also learn something of the wise, exact budget of their great Emperor.

79   Something happened one morning about two weeks after I was set free. Reldresal, Principal Secretary of Private Affairs (as they called him), came to my house. No one was with him except one servant.

80   He ordered his coach to wait at a distance. Then he asked me for an hour's talk with him. I readily agreed because of his nobility and personal virtues. He had also helped me during my appeals at court. I offered to lie down, so he might more easily reach my ear. Instead, he chose to let me hold him in my hand during our conversation.

81   He began by congratulating me on my freedom. He said he thought he could take some credit for it. However, he added that the present situation at court also had something to do with it. Otherwise, I might not have been freed so soon.

82   "To foreigners like you," he said, "we seem to be very prosperous. But we suffer from two great evils. We have violent disagreements at home, and the danger of an invasion by a very strong enemy abroad.

2 **quadrant:** an instrument used to measure height

83   understand, that for above seventy moons past, there have been two struggling parties in the empire, under the names of *Tramecksan*, and *Slamecksan*, from the high and low heels on their shoes, by which they distinguish themselves.

84   It is alleged indeed, that the high heels are most agreeable to our ancient constitution: but however this be, his Majesty hath determined to make use of only low heels in the administration of the government and all offices in the gift of the crown; as you cannot but observe; and particularly, that his Majesty's imperial heels are lower at least by a *drurr* than any of his court; (*drurr* is a measure about the

85   fourteenth part of an inch). The animosities between these two parties run so high, that they will neither eat nor drink, nor talk with each other. We compute the *Tramecksan*, or High-Heels, to exceed us in number, but the power is wholly on our side. We

86   apprehend his Imperial Highness, the heir to the crown, to have some tendency towards the High-Heels; at least we can plainly discover one of his heels higher than the other, which gives him a hobble

87   in his gait. Now, in the midst of these intestine disquiets, we are threatened with an invasion from the island of Blefuscu, which is the other great empire of the universe, almost as large and powerful as this of his Majesty. For as to what we have heard you

88   affirm, that there are other kingdoms and states in the world, inhabited by human creatures as large as yourself, our philosophers are in much doubt; and would rather conjecture that you dropped from the moon, or one of the stars; because it is certain, that

89   an hundred mortals of your bulk would, in a short time, destroy all the fruits and cattle of his Majesty's dominions. Besides, our histories of six thousand

83   "Let me explain the first evil, so you can understand. For more than seventy months, there have been two struggling parties in the empire. They are called *Tramecksan* and *Slamecksan* after the high and low heels on their shoes. This is how they are told apart.

84   "It is often said that high heels fit best into our ancient traditions. But even so, his Majesty has decided to use only low heels in running his government, and in all offices under his authority. You have surely noticed this. Moreover, his Majesty's royal heels are at least a *drurr* [about a 14th of an inch] lower than any of his court.

85   "Anger runs very high between these two parties. They will not eat, drink, or talk with one another. We figure the number of *Tramecksan*, or High-Heels, to be greater than ours. But the power is wholly on our side.

86   "We believe that the king's son, the heir to the throne, is somewhat inclined toward the High-Heels. At least we plainly see that one of his heels is higher than the other. This makes him hobble as he walks.

87   "And while we are quarreling within our own country, we are threatened with invasion from the island of Blefuscu. This is the other great empire of the universe, almost as large and powerful as this of His Majesty.

88   "Now, we have heard you say that there are other kingdoms and states in the world. You also say that these are inhabited by human creatures as large as you. But our philosophers much doubt this. They would rather suppose that you dropped from the moon or one of the stars.

89   "Just consider what 100 mortals of your bulk would do. In a short time, you would destroy all the fruits and cattle of His Majesty's realm. Besides, our histories of

moons make no mention of any other regions, than
the two great empires of Lilliput and Blefuscu.
90 Which two mighty powers have, as I was going to
tell you, been engaged in a most obstinate war for
six and thirty moons past. It began upon the following occasion.

91   It is allowed on all hands, that the primitive way
of breaking eggs before we eat them, was upon the
larger end: but his present Majesty's grandfather,
while he was a boy, going to eat an egg, and breaking
it according to the ancient practice, happened to cut
92 one of his fingers. Whereupon the Emperor his father
published an edict, commanding all his subjects,
upon great penalties, to break the smaller end of
their eggs. The people so highly resented this law,
that our histories tell us there have been six rebellions raised on that account; wherein one emperor
93 lost his life, and another his crown. These civil com-
motions were constantly fomented by the monarchs
of Blefuscu; and when they were quelled, the exiles
always fled for refuge to that empire. It is computed,
94 that eleven thousand persons have, at several
times, suffered death, rather than submit to break
their eggs at the smaller end. Many hundred large
volumes have been published upon this controversy:
95 but the books of the Big-Endians have been long forbidden, and the whole party rendered incapable by
law of holding employments. During the course of

96 these troubles, the emperors of Blefuscu did frequently expostulate by their ambassadors, accusing
us of making a schism in religion, by offending
against a fundamental doctrine of our great prophet
Lustrog, in the fifty-fourth chapter of the *Brundecral*
(which is their Alcoran). This, however, is thought to

6,000 months don't mention any other regions, only the two great empires of Lilliput and Blefuscu.

90   "And as I was about to tell you, these two mighty powers have been fighting a stubborn war for 36 months. It began in the following way.

91   "Everyone agrees that the oldest way of opening eggs before eating them is to break them on the larger end. But our present king's grandfather was about to eat an egg while he was a boy. And in breaking it in the old way, he happened to cut a finger.

92   "Then the king, his father, made a decree. He commanded all his subjects to break the smaller end of their eggs, or be punished severely. The people greatly disliked this law. History tells us of six rebellions against it. One emperor lost his life, and another his crown.

93   "These civil troubles were constantly stirred up by the kings of Blefuscu. Whenever things quieted down, the exiles always fled for refuge to that empire.

94   "We calculate that 11,000 persons have been killed from time to time over this issue. They have preferred to die rather than agree to break their eggs at the smaller end.

95   "Hundreds of large books have been published about egg-breaking. But the books of the Big-Endians have long been banned here. The whole party has been forbidden by law to hold jobs.

96   "Throughout these troubles, the emperors of Blefuscu frequently sent us ambassadors to raise objections. They accused us of causing a split in religion. They also said we violated a basic law of our great prophet Lustrog, in chapter 54 of the *Brundecral* [which is their Koran].

97   be a mere strain upon the text: for the words are these; *That all true believers shall break their eggs at the convenient end:* and which is the convenient end, seems, in my humble opinion, to be left to every man's conscience, or at least in the power of the chief

98   magistrate to determine. Now the Big-Endian exiles have found so much credit in the Emperor of Blefuscu's court, and so much private assistance and encouragement from their party here at home, that a bloody war hath been carried on between the two empires for six and thirty moons with various suc-

99   cess; during which time we have lost forty capital ships, and a much greater number of smaller vessels, together with thirty thousand of our best seamen and soldiers; and the damage received by the enemy is reckoned to be somewhat greater than ours. However, they have now equipped a numerous fleet, and are just preparing to make a descent upon us;

100   and his Imperial Majesty, placing great confidence in your valor and strength, hath commanded me to lay this account of his affairs before you.

101   I desired the Secretary to present my humble duty to the Emperor, and to let him know, that I thought it would not become me, who was a foreigner, to interfere with parties; but I was ready, with the hazard of my life, to defend his person and state against all invaders.

97 "But this seems to strain the meaning of the text. For these are the words: 'All true believers shall break their eggs at the convenient end.' In my humble opinion, the convenient end should be left to every man's conscience—or at least to be decided by the head of government.

98 "Now, the Big-Endian exiles have found much favor in the Emperor of Blefuscu's court. They have also gotten private help and encouragement from their party here at home. So a bloody war has been fought between the two empires for 36 months, with varying success.

99 We have lost forty great ships and many smaller ones during this time. And 30,000 of our best seamen and soldiers have been slain. The damage suffered by the enemy is thought to be somewhat greater. However, they have now built a great fleet, and they are getting ready to attack us.

100 "His Imperial Majesty has great confidence in your strength and bravery. So he has ordered me to explain all this to you."

101 I asked the secretary to assure the emperor of my loyalty. I told him that I thought it would be wrong of me to interfere in party matters, since I was a foreigner. But I was ready to risk my life to defend the king and his country against all invaders.

INTRODUCTION TO

A Modest Proposal

Irony is a contrast between how things appear and how they really are. In *verbal irony*, a person says one thing but really means another. Jonathan Swift was perhaps the greatest master of verbal irony in the English language. And his pamphlet "A Modest Proposal" is his most famous use of irony.

In the early 1700s, Ireland was suffering from terrible poverty and overpopulation. Swift, who was dean of St. Patrick's Cathedral in Dublin, was horrified by the sight of entire families begging and starving in the streets. He was also disgusted by English indifference to the problems in Ireland. For example, his barbs at English landlords are sincere. Their lack of concern for the poor struck Swift as utterly inhuman. Indeed, they seemed content to profit off the sufferings of others.

So in 1729, Swift published a pamphlet on the subject. Its full title was "A Modest Proposal for Preventing the Children of Poor People in Ireland from Being a Burden to their Parents or Country, and for Making them Beneficial to the Public."

Swift could simply have written a factual pamphlet about the problems and injustices in Ireland. He could also have proposed serious solutions. But such a pamphlet would have been easy to ignore. So Swift chose a different tactic.

Instead of writing as himself—an outraged priest—he adopted a different *persona*, or writer's voice. He pretended to be a wealthy Dubliner. And like other wealthy Dubliners of the day, Swift's persona fancies himself to be humane and caring. But in fact, his "modest proposal" is monstrous and horrifying—the selling and eating of poor Irish babies.

Through most of "A Modest Proposal," Swift's voice is bitterly ironic. He knows as well as the reader that eating children would be an awful solution to his country's suffering. But his pamphlet raises a terrifying question: How much more awful is his "modest proposal" than the apathy of the wealthy?

In addition to its brilliant use of irony, "A Modest Proposal" is a fine example of what is now called *black humor*. In black humor, subjects that are usually thought too grim for laughter are treated humorously. Part of the purpose of a work like "A Modest Proposal" is to horrify us with the sound of our own laughter.

On Strike
by Sir Hubert
von Herkomer

A Modest Proposal

Jonathan Swift

**FOR PREVENTING THE CHILDREN OF POOR
PEOPLE IN IRELAND FROM BEING A BURDEN TO
THEIR PARENTS OR COUNTRY, AND FOR MAKING
THEM BENEFICIAL TO THE PUBLIC**

1   *I*t is a melancholy object to those, who walk through
this great town, or travel in the country, when they
see the streets, the roads, and cabin doors, crowded
with beggars of the female sex, followed by three,
four, or six children, all in rags, and importuning
every passenger for an alms. These mothers instead
2   of being able to work for their honest livelihood, are
forced to employ all their time in strolling, to beg
sustenance for their helpless infants, who, as they
grow up either turn thieves for want of work, or leave
their dear native country to fight for the Pretender in
Spain, or sell themselves to the Barbadoes.

3   I think it is agreed by all parties, that this prodigious number of children, in the arms, or on the backs,
or at the heels of their mothers, and frequently of their
fathers, is in the present deplorable state of the kingdom, a very great additional grievance; and therefore

A Modest Proposal

Jonathan Swift

1   *P*eople who walk through this great town¹ or travel in the country witness a sad sight. The streets, roads, and cabin doors are crowded with female beggars followed by three, four, or six children, all in rags. They beg every passerby for charity.

2   These mothers cannot work for an honest living. Instead, they are forced to use all their time walking and begging to support their helpless infants. As these babies grow up, they must become thieves for lack of work. Or else they must leave their dear, native country to fight for the Pretender in Spain, or sell themselves to the Barbados.²

3   I think everybody can agree on one thing. There are far too many children in the arms, on the backs, or at the heels of their mothers, and often of their fathers. In the present sad state of the kingdom, this situation is a great, added shame.

---

1 **great town:** Dublin, Ireland
2 **Pretender ... Barbados:** When "A Modest Proposal" was written, James Edward, the son of the deposed King James II, wanted to seize the throne of England from abroad. He was therefore called the "Pretender" to the throne. The Irish poor often desperately immigrated to the Barbados in the West Indies, where they became little better than slaves.

4   whoever could find out a fair, cheap, and easy method
    of making these children sound and useful members of
    the commonwealth would deserve so well of the public,
    as to have his statue set up for a preserver of the
    nation.

5   But my intention is very far from being confined
    to provide only for the children of professed beggars;
    it is of a much greater extent, and shall take in the
    whole number of infants at a certain age, who are
    born of parents in effect as little able to support them,
    as those who demand our charity in the streets.

6   As to my own part, having turned my thoughts,
    for many years, upon this important subject, and
    maturely weighed the several schemes of other pro-
    jectors, I have always found them grossly mistaken

7   in their computation. It is true a child, just dropped
    from its dam, may be supported by her milk, for a
    solar year with little other nourishment, at most not
    above the value of two shillings, which the mother
    may certainly get, or the value in scraps, by her law-

8   ful occupation of begging, and it is exactly at one
    year old that I propose to provide for them, in such a
    manner, as, instead of being a charge upon their par-
    ents, or the parish, or wanting food and raiment for
    the rest of their lives, they shall, on the contrary, con-
    tribute to the feeding and partly to the clothing of
    many thousands.

9   There is likewise another great advantage in my
    scheme, that it will prevent those voluntary abor-
    tions, and that horrid practice of women murdering
    their bastard children, alas! too frequent among us,
    sacrificing the poor innocent babes, I doubt, more to
    avoid the expense, than the shame, which would
    move tears and pity in the most savage and inhuman
    breast.

4   Surely someone can find a fair, cheap, and easy method of making sound and useful members of society of these children. Whoever does so will deserve much from the public, and might have his statue set up as a savior of the nation.

5   But I mean to do much more than provide for children of admitted beggars. I intend to go much further. There are many other poor infants of a certain age. They are born to parents who can't support them any better than parents who demand charity in the streets. I want to deal with these children too.

6   For my part, I've thought long and hard for many years about this important subject. I've seriously considered several schemes of other planners. But I have always found that they simply didn't add up.

7   It is true that a newborn child can be supported by its mother's milk for a year with little other nourishment. At most, such a child needs two shillings[3] for food. A mother can lawfully get this much in money or scraps by begging.

8   It is exactly at one year old that I have a plan for them. They need not be a burden to their parents or the parish, lacking food and clothing for the rest of their lives. Instead, they shall contribute to feeding and partly to clothing many thousands.

9   There is another great advantage to my scheme. It will prevent voluntary abortions and the horrid practice of women murdering their illegitimate children. Alas, poor, innocent babes are too frequently sacrificed among us. I suspect that mothers do this more to avoid expense than shame. It is enough to move tears and pity in the most savage and inhuman breast.

---

3 **shillings:** A shilling was a coin worth twelve English pence. There were 240 pence in an English pound.

10   The number of souls in Ireland being usually reckoned one million and a half, of these I calculate there may be about two hundred thousand couples whose wives are breeders, from which number I subtract thirty thousand couples, who are able to maintain their own children, although I apprehend

11   there cannot be so many under the present distresses of the kingdom, but this being granted, there will remain an hundred and seventy thousand breeders. I again subtract fifty thousand for those women who miscarry, or whose children die by accident, or disease within the year. There only remain an hundred and twenty thousand children of poor parents annu-

12   ally born: The question therefore is, how this number shall be reared, and provided for, which, as I have already said, under the present situation of affairs, is utterly impossible by all the methods hitherto proposed, for we can neither employ them in handicraft, or agriculture; we neither build houses (I mean in

13   the country) nor cultivate land: They can very seldom pick up a livelihood by stealing until they arrive at six years old, except where they are of towardly parts, although, I confess they learn the rudiments much earlier, during which time, they can however be properly looked upon only as probationers, as I have

14   been informed by a principal gentleman in the county of Cavan, who protested to me, that he never knew above one or two instances under the age of six, even in a part of the kingdom so renowned for the quickest proficiency in that art.

15   I am assured by our merchants, that a boy or girl, before twelve years old, is no saleable commodity, and even when they come to this age, they will not yield above three pounds, or three pounds and half a crown at most on the exchange, which cannot turn to account either to the parents or the kingdom, the charge of nutriment and rags having been at least four times that value.

10   The number of people in Ireland is usually figured at one million and a half. Of these, I calculate
that there may be about 200,000 couples whose wives
are breeders. From this number, I subtract 30,000
couples who are able to support their own children.

11   I doubt that there are really 30,000 under the
present troubles in the kingdom. But even so, let
there remain 170,000 breeders. I then subtract
50,000 for women who miscarry, or whose children
die by accident or disease within the first year. There
remain only 120,000 children born to poor parents
each year.

12   So the question is, how shall this number be
raised and provided for? As I have already said, this
is utterly impossible by all the methods so far suggested. We can't employ them in construction or
agriculture, for we neither build houses (I mean in
the country) nor cultivate land.

13   They can seldom make a living by stealing until
they are six years old, unless they are very advanced
for their age—although I admit that they do learn
the basics much earlier. But during this time, they
can only be regarded as apprentices.

14   This has been explained to me by a notable gentleman in Cavan county, a place well known for able
thieves. He said he has not heard of more than one or
two good thieves under the age of six.

15   Merchants have told me that a boy or girl under
12 years old is simply not salable. And even when
they reach that age, they won't bring more than
three pounds—or three pounds and half a crown[4]—in
any market. This won't bring a profit either to parents or the kingdom. The cost of food and rags is at
least four times that much.

4   **crown:** a coin worth five shillings

16   I shall now therefore humbly propose my own thoughts, which I hope will not be liable to the least objection.

17   I have been assured by a very knowing American of my acquaintance in London, that a young healthy child well nursed is at a year old a most delicious, nourishing, and wholesome food, whether stewed, roasted, baked, or boiled, and I make no doubt that it will equally serve in a fricassee, or ragout.

18   I do therefore humbly offer it to public consideration, that of the hundred and twenty thousand children, already computed, twenty thousand may be reserved for breed, whereof only one-fourth part to be males, which is more than we allow to sheep, black

19   cattle, or swine, and my reason is that these children are seldom the fruits of marriage, a circumstance not much regarded by our savages; therefore one male will be sufficient to serve four females. That the

20   remaining hundred thousand may at a year old be offered in sale to the persons of quality, and fortune, through the kingdom, always advising the mother to let them suck plentifully in the last month, so as to render them plump, and fat for a good table. A child

21   will make two dishes at an entertainment for friends, and when the family dines alone, the fore or hind quarter will make a reasonable dish, and seasoned with a little pepper or salt will be very good boiled on the fourth day, especially in winter.

22   I have reckoned upon a medium, that a child just born will weigh twelve pounds, and in a solar year if tolerably nursed increaseth to twenty-eight pounds.

23   I grant this food will be somewhat dear, and therefore very proper for landlords, who, as they have already devoured most of the parents, seem to have the best title to the children.

16   So now I humbly propose my own thoughts. I hope they will not meet the least objection.

17   I have a very knowing American acquaintance who lives in London. He assures me that a young, well-nursed, healthy child is, at a year old, a most delicious, nourishing, and wholesome food. A child can be stewed, roasted, baked, or boiled. And I do not doubt that it will serve just as well chopped up in gravy or in a thick stew.

18   So I humbly suggest the following for public discussion. Of the 120,000 children already figured, we should save 20,000 for breeding. Of these, only one-fourth need be male, which is more than we allow for sheep, black cattle, or swine.

19   My reason is that these children are seldom the fruits of marriage. This institution is not much respected by our savages. So one male will be enough to serve four females.

20   The remaining 100,000, at a year old, can be sold to well-off people throughout the kingdom. The mother will always be advised to let them suck plentifully in the last month. This will leave them plump and fat for a good table.

21   A child will make two dishes at an entertainment for friends. And when a family dines alone, the fore or hind quarter will make a reasonable dish. Seasoned with a little pepper or salt, it will be very good boiled four days later, especially in winter.

22   On the average, I figure that a newborn child will weigh 12 pounds. If well-nursed, it will grow to 28 pounds in a year.

23   I admit this food will be somewhat expensive. So it is very proper for landlords, who have already eaten up the earnings of most of the parents. They seem to have the best right to eat the children too.

24   Infant's flesh will be in season throughout the year, but more plentiful in March, and a little before and after, for we are told by a grave author, an eminent French physician, that fish being a prolific diet, there are more children born in Roman Catholic countries about nine months after Lent, than at any

25   other season, therefore reckoning a year after Lent, the markets will be more glutted than usual, because the number of popish infants, is at least three to one in this kingdom, and therefore it will have one other collateral advantage by lessening the number of papists among us.

26   I have already computed the charge of nursing a beggar's child (in which list I reckon all cottagers, laborers, and four-fifths of the farmers) to be about two shillings per annum, rags included, and I believe no gentleman would repine to give ten shillings for the carcass of a good fat child, which, as I have said

27   will make four dishes of excellent nutritive meat, when he hath only some particular friend, or his own family to dine with him. Thus the squire will learn to be a good landlord, and grow popular among his tenants, the mother will have eight shillings net profit, and be fit for work until she produceth another child.

28   Those who are more thrifty (as I must confess the times require) may flay the carcass; the skin of which, artificially dressed, will make admirable gloves for ladies, and summer boots for fine gentlemen.

29   As to our city of Dublin, shambles may be appointed for this purpose, in the most convenient

24   Infants' flesh will be in season throughout the year. But it is more plentiful in March, and a little before and after. This has been explained by a serious author, a well-known French physician. In Roman Catholic countries, where fish is the main diet, more children are born nine months after Lent than in any other season.[5]

25   So a year after Lent, the markets will be more glutted than usual. This is because the number of Catholic infants is at least three times greater in this kingdom than that of Protestants. So my plan will have the extra advantage of decreasing the number of Catholics among us.

26   I have already figured the cost of nursing a beggar's child to be about two shillings a year, rags included. (I come up with the same figure for the children of most farmers, cottagers,[6] and laborers.) I believe no gentleman would refuse to pay ten shillings for the carcass of a good, fat child.

27   As I have said, this will make four dishes of excellent, nutritious meat, as long as one is only dining with one's family or some special friend. So a gentleman will learn to be a good landlord and grow popular among his tenants. And the mother will make a profit of eight shillings, then be fit to work until she produces another child.

28   I confess that the times demand a certain thrift, and thrifty folk may choose to skin the carcass. The skin, carefully tanned, will make fine gloves for ladies and summer boots for gentlemen.

29   Here in certain parts of Dublin, slaughterhouses may be put to this use. We can be sure that there will

5 **This has been explained . . . any other season:** The physician/author François Rabelais (c. 1494–1553) made this suggestion in his great comic novel *Gargantua and Pantagruel*. Lent is a period of 40 weekdays before Easter; it is traditionally observed with fasting and repentance.

6 **cottagers:** tenant farmers; farmers who work land owned by someone else

parts of it, and butchers we may be assured will not be wanting, although I rather recommend buying the children alive, and dressing them hot from the knife, as we do roasting pigs.

30   A very worthy person, a true lover of his country, and whose virtues I highly esteem, was lately pleased, in discoursing on this matter, to offer a
31   refinement upon my scheme. He said, that many gentlemen of this kingdom, having of late destroyed their deer, he conceived that the want of venison might be well supplied by the bodies of young lads and maidens, not exceeding fourteen years of age, nor under twelve, so great a number of both sexes in
32   every country being now ready to starve, for want of work and service: and these to be disposed of by their parents if alive, or otherwise by their nearest

33   relations. But with due deference to so excellent a friend, and so deserving a patriot, I cannot be altogether in his sentiments, for as to the males, my American acquaintance assured me from frequent experience, that their flesh was generally tough and lean, like that of our schoolboys, by continual exercise, and their taste disagreeable, and to fatten them
34   would not answer the charge. Then as to the females, it would, I think with humble submission, be a loss to the public, because they soon would become breeders
35   themselves: And besides it is not improbable that some scrupulous people might be apt to censure such a practice (although indeed very unjustly) as a little bordering upon cruelty, which, I confess, hath always been with me the strongest objection against any project, how well soever intended.
36   But in order to justify my friend, he confessed that this expedient was put into his head by the

be no lack of butchers. But I really recommend buying the children alive. Then they can be prepared hot from the knife, as we do in roasting pigs.

30   I have talked of this matter with a very worthy person, a true lover of his country whose virtues I greatly respect. He added a suggestion to my scheme.

31   He pointed out that many gentlemen in this kingdom have killed off their deer lately. So he thought the bodies of boys or girls might make up for the lack of venison. They should not be more than 14 years old, nor under 12.

32   In all countries, there are a great number of boys and girls now ready to starve because they cannot find jobs. Their parents, if they are alive, could sell them. Otherwise, they could be sold by their nearest relatives.

33   But with due respect to so fine a friend and so good a patriot, I cannot altogether agree. Based on frequent experience, my American friend has told me that the flesh of males is tough and lean. Like our schoolboys, they get too much exercise, so their taste is disagreeable. To fatten them would not make any difference.

34   As for the females, I must humbly argue that eating them would be a loss to the public. Soon, they could become breeders themselves.

35   Besides, it is possible that some strict people might criticize such a practice (however unjustly) as being almost cruel. I must confess that I have always found this the strongest objection against any project, however well-intended.

36   But to be fair to my friend, he confessed that he had gotten this idea from the famous Psalmanazar, a

famous Sallmanaazor, a native of the island Formosa, who came from thence to London, above twenty years
37 ago, and in conversation told my friend, that in his country when any young person happened to be put to death, the executioner sold the carcass to persons of quality, as a prime dainty, and that, in his time,
38 the body of a plump girl of fifteen, who was crucified for an attempt to poison the emperor, was sold to his imperial majesty's prime minister of state, and other great mandarins of the court, in joints from the gibbet, at four hundred crowns. Neither indeed can I
39 deny, that if the same use were made of several plump young girls in this town, who, without one single groat to their fortunes, cannot stir abroad without a chair, and appear at the playhouse, and assemblies in foreign fineries, which they never will pay for; the kingdom would not be the worse.

40   Some persons of a desponding spirit are in great concern about that vast number of poor people, who are aged, diseased, or maimed, and I have been desired to employ my thoughts what course may be taken, to ease the nation of so grievous an encum-
41 brance. But I am not in the least pain upon that matter, because it is very well known, that they are every day dying, and rotting, by cold, and famine, and filth, and vermin, as fast as can be reasonably
42 expected. And as to the younger laborers they are now in almost as hopeful a condition. They cannot get work, and consequently pine away for want of nourishment, to a degree, that if at any time they are accidentally hired to common labor, they have not strength to perform it, and thus the country and themselves are in a fair way of being soon delivered from the evils to come.

native of the island Formosa.[7] He came to London from there more than 20 years ago.

37   He told my friend what was done in his country when any young person happened to be put to death. The executioner would sell the carcass to wealthy people as a fine treat.

38   Psalmanazar knew of a 15-year-old girl who was crucified for trying to poison the emperor. Her plump body was sold to the emperor's prime minister of state and other great court officials. Cut in pieces right off the gallows, it sold for 400 crowns.

39   And I cannot deny that the same use might be made of several plump young girls in this town. Though they don't have any money, they cannot go outside without being carried by servants in a chair. And they always appear at the playhouse and at dinners in fine, foreign clothes, which they never pay for. The kingdom would be better off if they were eaten.

40   Some people are very depressed about the great number of poor people who are old, sick, or crippled. I have been asked to consider what course might be taken to ease the nation of such a serious problem.

41   But I am not the least bit worried about the matter. It is very well known that they are dying and rotting every day from cold, hunger, filth, and lice. They cannot be expected to die any faster.

42   And as for younger laborers, their situation is almost as hopeful. They cannot get work, and so they fade away for lack of food. And if, by accident, they are hired for common labor, they do not have the strength for it. So the country and the young men are both better off, freed from future evils.

7   **Psalmanazar ... Formosa:** George Psalmanazar (c. 1679–1763) was a Frenchman who claimed to be a native of Formosa (now Taiwan). He wrote a book entitled *An Historical and Geographical Description of Formosa.* In fact, he had never been there.

43   I have too long digressed, and therefore shall return to my subject. I think the advantages by the proposal which I have made are obvious and many as well as of the highest importance.

44   For first, as I have already observed, it would greatly lessen the number of papists, with whom we are yearly overrun, being the principal breeders of the nation, as well as our most dangerous enemies,

45   and who stay at home on purpose with a design to deliver the kingdom to the Pretender, hoping to take their advantage by the absence of so many good Protestants, who have chosen rather to leave their country, than stay at home, and pay tithes against their conscience, to an idolatrous Episcopal curate.

46   Secondly, the poorer tenants will have something valuable of their own, which by law may be made liable to distress, and help to pay their landlord's rent, their corn and cattle being already seized, and money a thing unknown.

47   Thirdly, whereas the maintenance of an hundred thousand children, from two years old, and upwards, cannot be computed at less than ten shillings apiece per annum, the nation's stock will be thereby increased fifty thousand pounds per annum, besides

48   the profit of a new dish, introduced to the tables of all gentlemen of fortune in the kingdom, who have any refinement in taste, and the money will circulate among ourselves, the goods being entirely of our own growth and manufacture.

49   Fourthly, the constant breeders, besides the gain of eight shillings sterling per annum, by the sale of their children, will be rid of the charge of maintaining them after the first year.

43   I have strayed from the subject too long, and will now get back to it. I think the advantages of my proposal are many, obvious, and extremely important.

44   First: As I have already said, it would lessen the number of Catholics, who overrun us yearly. They are the main breeders of the nation as well as our most dangerous enemies.

45   They stay at home for the purpose of turning the kingdom over to the Pretender. They hope to take advantage of the absence of so many good Protestants, who have chosen to leave the country. It is against the conscience of these Protestants to stay home and pay tithes to an irreligious bishop.[8]

46   Second: The plan will give poorer tenants something valuable of their own, which may be taken from them by law. The payment they get for their children may help to pay their landlords. Their corn and cattle have already been seized, and they have no money.

47   Third: The care for 100,000 children, two years of age and older, cannot be less than 10 shillings apiece each year. So the nation's overall wealth will increase 50,000 pounds per year.

48   Besides, a new dish will be profitable. It will be popular on the tables of rich, refined gentlemen throughout the kingdom. And the money will circulate among ourselves, since the goods are grown right here in our own country.

49   Fourth: By selling their children, repeated breeders will earn eight shillings per year. They will also be rid of the burden of caring for their children after the first year.

8   **They hope . . . irreligious bishop:** Here Swift attacks Protestant reformers who thought the established Anglican Church was too similar to the Catholic Church. An Anglican priest himself, Swift thought these reformers to be anything but "good" Protestants. A tithe is a fee required for church membership, usually a tenth of a person's income.

50   Fifthly, this food would likewise bring great custom to taverns, where the vintners will certainly be so prudent as to procure the best receipts for dressing it to perfection, and consequently have their houses frequented by all the fine gentlemen, who justly value themselves upon their knowledge in good eating, and a skillful cook, who understands how to oblige his guests will contrive to make it as expensive as they please.

51   Sixthly, this would be a great inducement to marriage, which all wise nations have either encouraged by rewards, or enforced by laws and penalties. It

52   would increase the care and tenderness of mothers toward their children, when they were sure of a settlement for life to the poor babes, provided in some sort by the public to their annual profit instead of

53   expense, we should soon see an honest emulation among the married women, which of them could bring the fattest child to the market, men would become as fond of their wives, during the time of their pregnancy, as they are now of their mares in foal, their cows in calf, or sows when they are ready to farrow, nor offer to beat or kick them (as is too frequent a practice) for fear of a miscarriage.

54   Many other advantages might be enumerated. For instance, the addition of some thousand carcasses in our exportation of barreled beef. The propagation of swine's flesh, and improvement in the art of making

55   good bacon, so much wanted among us by the great destruction of pigs, too frequent at our tables, which are no way comparable in taste, or magnificence to a well-grown, fat yearling child, which roasted whole will make a considerable figure at a Lord Mayor's feast, or any other public entertainment. But this, and many others I omit being studious of brevity.

50   Fifth: This food would bring great profits to taverns. Wine sellers will certainly be wise enough to get the best recipes for serving children to perfection. As a result, their taverns will be visited by fine gentlemen who rightly think they know how to eat well. And skillful cooks, who know how to please their guests, will take care to make children as expensive as they please.

51   Sixth: This would make marriage very appealing. All wise nations have encouraged marriage by offering rewards or enforcing laws and penalties.

52   The care and tenderness of mothers toward their children would increase. Mothers would feel sure that their poor babies will be supported for life. And in a way, this would be done by the public, providing mothers with profit instead of expense.

53   We would soon see healthy competition among married women, who would try to bring the fattest children to market. And men would become as fond of their pregnant wives as they now are of their pregnant mares, cows, or sows. Nor would they beat or kick their wives (as they do too often) for fear of a miscarriage.

54   I might list many other advantages. For instance, we would have about a thousand more carcasses of barreled beef to export. We could do the same with pork, and also improve the art of making good bacon.

55   Right now, we destroy far too many pigs to serve them on our tables. And they don't nearly match the taste or quality of a fat, well-grown, year-old child. Roasted whole, a child would make a fine dish at a Lord Mayor's feast, or any other public entertainment. But I won't get into this or many other issues in order to be brief.

56   Supposing that one thousand families in this city, would be constant customers for infants' flesh, besides others who might have it at merry meetings, particularly weddings and christenings, I compute that Dublin would take off annually about twenty thousand carcasses, and the rest of the kingdom (where probably they will be sold somewhat cheaper) the remaining eighty thousand.

57   I can think of no one objection, that will possibly be raised against this proposal, unless it should be urged that the number of people will be thereby much lessened in the kingdom. This I freely own, and it was indeed one principal design in offering it to

58 the world. I desire the reader will observe, that I calculate my remedy for this one individual kingdom of Ireland, and for no other that ever was, is, or, I think, ever can be upon earth. Therefore let no man talk to

59 me of other expedients: *Of taxing our absentees at five shillings a pound; of using neither clothes, nor household furniture, except what is of our own growth and manufacture; of utterly rejecting the materials and instruments that promote foreign luxury; of curing the expensiveness of pride, vanity, idleness, and gaming in our women; of introducing a vein of parsimony, prudence, and temperance; of learning to love our country, wherein we differ even from Laplanders, and the inhabitants of Topinamboo; of quitting our animosities, and factions, nor act any longer like the Jews, who were murdering one another at the very moment their city was taken; of being a little cautious not to sell our country and consciences for nothing; of teaching landlords to have at least one degree of*

56   Suppose that 1,000 families in this city would be regular buyers of infants' flesh. Others might have it at merry gatherings, especially weddings and christenings. I figure that Dublin would go through 20,000 carcasses annually. And the rest of the kingdom (where carcasses will probably be sold somewhat cheaper) would take the remaining 80,000.

57   I cannot think of any objection that can possibly be raised to this proposal. True, some people may worry that the number of people will decrease in the kingdom. I completely agree. Indeed, this was one of my main reasons for offering my scheme to the world.

58   I ask the reader to understand that I've devised this remedy for this one, individual kingdom of Ireland. I intend it for no other kingdom that ever was, is, or (I think) can ever be upon earth.

59   So let no man talk to me of these other measures:

- *Of taxing English landowners who do not live in Ireland at five shillings a pound;*
- *of not using clothes or household furniture unless they are made here in Ireland;*
- *of not buying any goods that will enrich foreign countries;*
- *of curing our women of their expensive pride, vanity, idleness, and gambling;*
- *of learning to be thrifty, wise, and temperate;*
- *of learning to love our country, even as Laplanders and Brazilian savages do theirs;*
- *of putting aside political quarrels, and not acting any longer like the Jews, who murdered one another at the moment their city was taken;*[9]

9 **of putting aside . . . city was taken:** The Romans destroyed Jerusalem in 70 A.D., taking advantage of quarrels among Jewish citizens.

mercy toward their tenants. Lastly of putting a spirit of honesty, industry, and skill into our shopkeepers, who, if a resolution could now be taken to buy only our native goods, would immediately unite to cheat and exact upon us in the price, the measure, and the goodness, nor could ever yet be brought to make one fair proposal of just dealing, though often and earnestly invited to it.

60   Therefore I repeat, let no man talk to me of these and the like expedients, till he hath at least a glimpse of hope, that there will ever be some hearty and sincere attempt to put them in practice.

61   But as to myself, having been wearied out for many years with offering vain, idle, visionary thoughts, and at length utterly despairing of success, I fortunately fell upon this proposal, which as it is wholly new, so it hath something solid and real, of no expense and little trouble, full in our own power, and whereby we can incur no danger in disobliging

62   England. For this kind of commodity will not bear exportation, the flesh being of too tender a consistence, to admit a long continuance in salt, although perhaps I could name a country, which would be glad to eat up our whole nation without it.

63   After all I am not so violently bent upon my own opinion, as to reject any offer, proposed by wise men, which shall be found equally innocent, cheap, easy, and effectual. But before something of that kind shall be advanced in contradiction to my scheme, and offering a better, I desire the author, or authors will be pleased maturely to consider two points. First, as

- *of taking a little care not to sell our country and consciences for nothing;*
- *of teaching landlords to have at least a little mercy toward their tenants;*
- *And last, of forcing our shopkeepers to be more honest, industrious, and skillful. If we all now decided to buy only our native goods, shopkeepers would immediately plot to cheat and overcharge us in matters of price, quantity, and quality. They have never yet made any effort to do business justly, even though they have been often and earnestly encouraged to do so.*

60 So I repeat—let no man talk to me of these measures, or others like them. First, let him give me just a glimpse of hope that anyone will ever make a hearty and sincere attempt to put them into practice.

61 As for myself, I grew weary after many years of offering vain, idle, fanciful ideas. And when I finally gave up on success, I luckily came up with this proposal. It is completely new, solid, and real, and will require no expense and little trouble. It is also something we can do completely on our own, so we run no risk of offending England.

62 For goods like these cannot be exported. The flesh is too tender to be preserved by salt for long. However, I do think that England would gladly eat up our whole nation without salt.

63 I am not too stubbornly set in my own opinion. So I will not reject any wise proposal which proves equally innocent, cheap, easy, and effective. But before anyone presents a rival and better scheme, I ask the author or authors to carefully consider two points.

64 things now stand, how they will be able to find food and raiment for a hundred thousand useless mouths

65 and backs. And secondly, there being a round million of creatures in human figure, throughout this kingdom, whose whole subsistence put into a common stock would leave them in debt two millions of pounds sterling, adding those who are beggars by profession to the bulk of farmers, cottagers, and laborers, with their wives and children, who are beg-

66 gars in effect; I desire those politicians, who dislike my overture, and may perhaps be so bold to attempt an answer, that they will first ask the parents of these mortals, whether they would not at this day think it a great happiness to have been sold for food at a year old, in the manner I prescribe, and thereby

67 have avoided such a perpetual scene of misfortunes, as they have since gone through, by the oppression of landlords, the impossibility of paying rent without money or trade, the want of common sustenance, with neither house nor clothes to cover them from inclemencies of weather, and the most inevitable prospect of entailing the like, or great miseries, upon their breed forever.

68 I profess in the sincerity of my heart that I have not the least personal interest in endeavoring to promote this necessary work, having no other motive than the public good of my country, by advancing our trade, providing for infants, relieving the poor, and giving some pleasure to the rich. I have no children,

69 by which I can propose to get a single penny; the youngest being nine years old, and my wife past childbearing.

64   First, as things stand now, how will they be able to find food and clothes for 100,000 useless mouths and backs?

65   Second, there are a million human beings living in poverty throughout this kingdom. This number includes not only professional beggars, but also most farmers, cottagers, laborers, and their wives and children, all of whom might as well be beggars. If you were to try to put all their possessions together, you would end up with a debt of two million pounds.

66   I make the following request to politicians who dislike my proposal and feel bold enough to say so. Let them ask the parents of these children how they feel about this matter. Don't they think they would have been happier if they had been sold for food at a year old, in the manner I've described?

67   Then they would have avoided lives of endless misfortune. They have been mistreated by landlords and have not had money or goods to pay rent. They have not had enough to live on, with neither house nor clothes to cover them in bad weather. And now they face the certainty of passing their sufferings along to their descendants forever.

68   I promise that I am sincere in my heart about this proposal. I haven't the slightest personal interest in pushing for this necessary work. I am only thinking of the public good of my country, by increasing our trade, providing for infants, relieving the poor, and giving some pleasure to the rich.

69   I have no children by whom I could get a single penny. My youngest is nine years old, and my wife is too old to bear children.

The Life of Samuel Johnson

Samuel Johnson once said that "no man but a block-head ever wrote except for money." Johnson did not always follow his own rule, and his writing did not make him rich. But it did make him one of the most famous Englishmen of his time. And thanks partly to James Boswell's *The Life of Samuel Johnson*, his fame continues today.

Johnson overcame great difficulties to achieve success. He was a sickly child, and illness troubled him throughout his life. His early poverty also made it hard for him to get an education. But he grew up to be tall, heavy, and strong, and became possibly the most learned man in England.

Johnson was born in 1709 in Lichfield, England. He spent his early years working as a schoolmaster and a bookseller. In 1737, he moved to London and became a writer.

One of his greatest achievements was his *Dictionary of the English Language*, published in 1755. It was the most ambitious English dictionary up to that time, and included many quotes from great English writers.

"Patriotism is the last refuge of a scoundrel," he once said. "Depend upon it, sir," he remarked on another occasion, "when a man knows he is to be hanged in a fortnight, it concentrates his mind wonderfully."

He devoted himself to every branch of study, from literature to politics. He wrote literary criticism and edited an edition of Shakespeare's works. His political writings were also very influential. No defender of American independence, he wrote, "How is it that we hear the loudest yelps for liberty from the drivers of Negroes?"

Samuel Johnson and James Boswell from a caricature by Thomas Rowlandson.

In 1765 and 1775, he received honorary degrees, and was known afterwards as *Dr*. Samuel Johnson. And in 1762, he was granted a lifetime pension of 300 pounds a year. By the time he died in 1784, he was greatly revered throughout England.

Today, Johnson is as at least as well-known as the subject of Boswell's *The Life of Samuel Johnson, LL.D.* as he is for his own writings. Indeed, the *Life* is certainly the most famous biography ever written in English.

As you read the following excerpts, note Johnson's sympathy for the poet Christopher Smart (1722–1771). Smart was sometimes confined to mental institutions because of his religious visions.

Unlike most Londoners, Johnson was sensitive to both Smart's piety and his mental problems. Johnson himself suffered bouts of severe depression. Moreover, his own religious beliefs led him to worry that he might suffer eternal damnation. Johnson's troubled inner life makes his achievements all the more remarkable.

from The Life of Samuel Johnson

James Boswell

Boswell Meets Johnson
1763

1 *T*his is to me a memorable year; for in it I had the happiness to obtain the acquaintance of that extraordinary man whose memoirs I am now writing; an acquaintance which I shall ever esteem as one of the most fortunate circumstances in my life. Though then
2 but two-and-twenty, I had for several years read his works with delight and instruction, and had the highest reverence for their author, which had grown up in my fancy into a kind of mysterious veneration, by figuring to myself a state of solemn elevated abstraction, in which I supposed him to live in the immense metropolis of London. . . .
3 Mr. Thomas Davies the actor, who then kept a bookseller's shop in Russel Street, Covent Garden, told me that Johnson was very much his friend, and came frequently to his house, where he more than once invited me to meet him; but by some unlucky accident or other he was prevented from coming to us.
4 At last, on Monday the 16th day of May, when I was sitting in Mr. Davies's back parlor, after having drunk tea with him and Mrs. Davies, Johnson unexpectedly came into the shop; and Mr. Davies having

from The Life of Samuel Johnson

James Boswell

Boswell Meets Johnson
1763

1   *T*his was a memorable year to me. For I was then lucky enough to become friends with that extraordinary man whose memoirs I am now writing. I shall always regard this friendship as one of the most fortunate things that ever happened to me.

2   I was then only 22 years old. But for several years, I had read and learned from his works with great enjoyment. In my mind, my high respect for him had grown into a kind of mysterious hero-worship. I imagined his life in the huge city of London to be solemn and otherworldly. . . .

3   Mr. Thomas Davies, the actor, then owned a book-seller's shop in Russel Street, Covent Garden. He told me that Johnson was his very close friend and often came to his house. More than once, Mr. Davies invited me there to meet him. But by some unlucky accident or other, Johnson was never able to join us.

4   At last, on Monday, May 16, I was sitting in Mr. Davies' back parlor. I had just drunk tea with him and Mrs. Davies when Johnson unexpectedly came to the shop.

5 perceived him through the glass door in the room in which we were sitting, advancing towards us—he announced his aweful approach to me, somewhat in the manner of an actor in the part of Horatio, when he addresses Hamlet on the appearance of his father's ghost, "Look, my Lord, it comes," I found that I had a

6 very perfect idea of Johnson's figure, from the portrait of him painted by Sir Joshua Reynolds soon after he had published his *Dictionary*, in the attitude of sitting in his easy chair in deep meditation, which was the first picture his friend did for him, which Sir Joshua very kindly presented to me, and from which an engraving has been made for this work. Mr. Davies

7 mentioned my name, and respectfully introduced me to him. I was much agitated; and recollecting his prejudice against the Scotch, of which I had heard much, I said to Davies, "Don't tell where I come

8 from." "From Scotland," cried Davies roguishly. "Mr. Johnson," said I, "I do indeed come from Scotland, but

9 I cannot help it." I am willing to flatter myself that I

10 meant this as light pleasantry to sooth and conciliate him, and not as an humiliating abasement at the expense of my country. But however that might be, this speech was somewhat unlucky; for with that

11 quickness of wit for which he was so remarkable, he seized the expression "come from Scotland," which I used in the sense of being of that country; and, as if I had said that I had come away from it, or left,

12 retorted, "That, Sir, I find, is what a very great many of your countrymen cannot help." This stroke stunned

13 me a good deal; and when we had sat down, I felt myself not a little embarrassed, and apprehensive of what might come next. He then addressed himself to

5   As Johnson approached, Mr. Davies saw him through the glass door of the room in which we sat. Mr. Davies announced his awe-inspiring approach to me. He sounded something like an actor playing Horatio, when he tells Hamlet that his father's ghost is coming: "Look, my Lord, it comes."[1]

6   I found that I already had a good idea of Johnson's appearance. For I had seen a portrait of him painted by Sir Joshua Reynolds[2] soon after Johnson had published his *Dictionary*. He was shown sitting in his easy chair, deep in thought. This was the first picture that Sir Joshua did of him, and the painter very kindly gave it to me. An engraving of it has been made for this book.

7   Mr. Davies politely introduced me to him, telling him my name. I was very nervous. I also remembered his prejudice against Scotsmen, of which I had heard much. So I had said to Davies, "Don't tell him where I come from."

8   "He's from Scotland," Davies told Johnson mischievously.

9   "Mr. Johnson," I said, "I do, indeed, come from Scotland, but I cannot help it."

10   I would like to think that I meant this only humorously, to soothe him and make peace with him. I did not mean it as a humiliating insult to my country. But even so, this remark was somewhat unlucky.

11   With his remarkably quick wit, he picked up on my words, "come from Scotland." I had meant it in the sense of being *of* that country. But he took it as if I had come away from it, or left it.

12   "That, sir," he snapped back, "is something a very great many of your countrymen cannot help."

13   This blow stunned me a good deal. When we sat down, I felt more than a little embarrassed, and worried about what might happen next.

1 **"Look, my Lord, it comes":** Shakespeare's Hamlet, Act I, Scene iv, line 42

2 **Sir Joshua Reynolds:** portrait painter (1723–1792)

14   Davies: "What do you think of Garrick? He has refused me an order for the play for Miss Williams, because he knows the house will be full, and that an order would be worth three shillings." Eager to take

15   any opening to get into conversation with him, I ventured to say, "O, Sir, I cannot think Mr. Garrick would

16   grudge such a trifle to you." "Sir," said he, with a stern look, "I have known David Garrick longer than you have done: and I know no right you have to talk

17   to me on the subject." Perhaps I deserved this check; for it was rather presumptuous in me, an entire stranger, to express any doubt of the justice of his animadversion upon his old acquaintance and pupil.

18   I now felt myself much mortified, and began to think that the hope which I had long indulged of obtaining his acquaintance was blasted. And, in truth, had not my ardor been uncommonly strong, and my resolution uncommonly persevering, so rough a reception might have deterred me forever from making any further attempts. Fortunately, however, I remained

19   upon the field not wholly discomfited; and was soon rewarded by hearing some of his conversation, of which I preserved the following short minute, without marking the questions and observations by which it was produced.

20   "People," he remarked, "may be taken in once, who imagine that an author is greater in private life than other men. Uncommon parts require uncommon opportunities for their exertion."

21   "In barbarous society, superiority of parts is of real consequence. Great strength or great wisdom is of much value to an individual. But in more polished times there are people to do everything for money; and then there are a number of other superiorities,

14   He then spoke to Davies, saying, "What do you think of Garrick?[3] He has refused me a ticket to the play for Miss Williams. He knows the house will be full, and that a ticket would be worth three shillings."

15   I felt eager to get into the conversation. So I dared to say, "Oh, sir, I cannot believe Mr. Garrick would refuse you such a small favor."

16   "Sir," he replied with a stern look, "I have known David Garrick longer than you have. I don't believe you have any right to talk to me about him."

17   Perhaps I deserved this scolding. It was rather rude of me to talk that way to a total stranger. What business did I have to question the justness of his criticism of his friend and pupil?

18   I now felt quite flustered. I began to think that my long-held hope of getting to know him was dashed. And truthfully, so rough a greeting might have stopped me from even trying. But my desire was strong, and my firmness uncommonly steady. So I stayed on the battlefield, not wholly defeated.

19   Soon, I was rewarded by hearing some of his talk. I wrote down the following remarks as I heard them. I have left out the questions and comments to which he was replying.

20   "People may be taken in," he remarked, "if they believe that an author is greater in private life than other men. Uncommon talents require uncommon opportunities to show themselves."

21   "In a savage society, great talents are really use-ful. Great strength or great wisdom are very valuable to a person. But in more polite times, there are peo-ple to do everything for money. And there are also a

---

3 **Garrick:** David Garrick (1717–1779) was a famous actor and theater manager. He was educated by Johnson.

such as those of birth and fortune, and rank, that dissipate men's attention, and leave no extraordinary share of respect for personal and intellectual superiority. This is wisely ordered by Providence, to preserve some equality among mankind."

22   "Sir, this book (*The Elements of Criticism*, which he had taken up) is a pretty essay, and deserves to be held in some estimation, though much of it is chimerical."

23   Speaking of one who with more than ordinary boldness attacked public measures and the royal family, he said, "I think he is safe from the law, but he is an abusive scoundrel; and instead of applying to my Lord Chief Justice to punish him, I would send half a dozen footmen and have him well ducked."

24   "The notion of liberty amuses the people of England, and helps to keep off the *taedium vitae*. When a butcher tells you that his heart bleeds for his country, he has, in fact, no uneasy feeling."

25   "Sheridan will not succeed at Bath with his oratory. Ridicule has gone down before him, and, I doubt, Derrick is his enemy."

Boswell and Johnson in a tavern.

number of social divisions, such as birth, money, and rank. These draw men's attention, so they have little respect for personal and intellectual talents. God has wisely arranged things this way to maintain some equality among mankind."

22   He said this upon picking up a copy of *The Elements of Criticism*:[4] "Sir, this book is pretty good, and deserves some respect. But much of it is made-up."

23   We talked about someone[5] who had shown unusual boldness in attacking public laws and the royal family. Johnson said, "I think he is safe from the law, but he is a vicious scoundrel. I wouldn't bother asking my Lord Chief Justice to punish him. Instead, I would send six servants to duck[6] him well."

24   "The idea of liberty amuses English people and helps keep off boredom. When a butcher tells you that his heart bleeds for his country, he is not really worried."

25   "Sheridan will fail at Bath with his lectures. Ridicule has gotten there ahead of him, and I fear that Derrick is his enemy."[7]

4   *The Elements of Criticism*: a book by the Scottish lawyer and philosopher Henry Home (1696–1782)

5   **someone**: The journalist and politician John Wilkes (1725–1797) was repeatedly expelled from Parliament for his radical views.

6   **duck**: In ducking, an offender was punished by being tied to a chair and forced underwater.

7   **"Sheridan . . . his enemy"**: Thomas Sheridan (1719–1788) was an Irish-born actor, author, and expert on the English language. In 1763, he gave lectures at the Oratory in Bath, England, where Samuel Derrick (1724–1769) was Master of Ceremonies.

26   "Derrick may do very well, as long as he can out-run his character; but the moment his character gets up with him, it is all over."

27   It is, however, but just to record, that some years afterwards, when I reminded him of this sarcasm, he said, "Well, but Derrick has now got a character that he need not run away from."

28   I was highly pleased with the extraordinary vigor of his conversation, and regretted that I was drawn away from it by an engagement at another place. I had, for a part of the evening, been left alone with him, and had ventured to make an observation now and then, which he received very civilly; so that I was satisfied that though there was a roughness in his manner, there was no ill nature in his disposition.

29   Davies followed me to the door, and when I complained to him a little of the hard blows which the great man had given me he kindly took upon him to console me by saying, "Don't be uneasy. I can see he likes you very well."

Boswell's First Visit to Johnson

30   A few days afterward I called on Davies, and asked him if he thought I might take the liberty of waiting on Mr. Johnson at his Chambers in the Temple. He said I certainly might, and that Mr. Johnson would take it as a compliment. So upon

31 Tuesday the 24th of May, . . . I boldly repaired to Johnson. His Chambers were on the first floor of No. 1, Inner-Temple-lane, and I entered them with an impression given me by the Reverend Dr. Blair, of Edinburgh, who had been introduced to him not long before, and described his having "found the Giant in his den," an expression, which, when I came to be

26   "Derrick may do very well, as long as he can out-
run his character. But as soon as his character
catches up with him, he's finished."

27   In all fairness, I should note something he said
years later when I reminded him of this sarcastic
remark. He said, "Well, Derrick now has a character
he doesn't need to run away from."

28   I was very pleased with the great vigor of his conversation. I was sorry to have to leave for an
appointment elsewhere. For part of the evening, I
was left alone with him, and I dared make a com-
ment now and then. He listened very politely. So
even though his manner was rough, I thought he was
not ill-natured.

29   Davies followed me to the door. I complained to
him a little of the beating the great man had given
me. But he comforted me by saying, "Don't worry. I
can see he likes you very well."

Boswell's First Visit to Johnson

30   A few days later, I called on Davies. I asked him if
he thought I should feel free to visit Mr. Johnson at
his rooms in the Temple.[8] He said I certainly should,
and that Mr. Johnson would take it as a compliment.
So on Tuesday, May 24, . . . I boldly went to Johnson.

31   His rooms were on the first floor of No. 1, Inner-
Temple-lane. As I entered, I remembered something
the Reverend Dr. Blair of Edinburgh had told me. He
had been introduced to Johnson not long before. He
described his visit to Johnson as like "finding the
giant in his den."

8   **Temple:** a row of buildings in Fleet Street, London,
frequented by lawyers

32   pretty well acquainted with Johnson, I repeated to him, and he was diverted at this picturesque account of himself. . . .

33   He received me very courteously; but, it must be confessed, that his apartment, and furniture, and morning dress, were sufficiently uncouth. His brown suit of clothes looked very rusty; he had on a little old shriveled unpowdered wig, which was too small for his head; his shirtneck and knees of his breeches were loose; his black worsted stockings ill drawn up; and he had a pair of unbuckled shoes by way of slip-

34   pers. But all these slovenly particularities were forgotten the moment that he began to talk. Some gentlemen, whom I do not recollect, were sitting with him; and when they went away, I also rose; but he

35   said to me, "Nay, don't go." "Sir (said I), I am afraid

36   that I intrude upon you. It is benevolent to allow me to sit and hear you." He seemed pleased with this

37   compliment, which I sincerely paid him, and answered, "Sir, I am obliged to any man who visits

38   me." I have preserved the following short minute of what passed this day:

39   "Madness frequently discovers itself merely by unnecessary deviation from the usual modes of the world. My poor friend Smart showed the disturbance of his mind, by falling upon his knees, and saying his prayers in the street, or in any other unusual place.

40   Now although, rationally speaking, it is greater madness not to pray at all, than to pray as Smart did, I am afraid there are so many who do not pray, that their understanding is not called in question."

41   Concerning this unfortunate poet, Christopher Smart, who was confined in a madhouse, he had, at another time, the following conversation with

32   When I got to know Johnson better, I repeated these words to him. He was amused by this colorful description of himself. . . .

33   He greeted me very politely. But I must admit that his room, furniture, and morning clothes were quite messy. His brown suit looked very rusty. He wore a little, old, shriveled, unpowdered wig which was too small for his head. His collar and the knees of his breeches were loose. His black wool stockings were not pulled up. And he was wearing a pair of unbuckled shoes instead of slippers.

34   But I forgot all these untidy details the moment he began to talk. Some gentlemen, whose names I don't remember, were sitting with him. When they went away, I also got up to go.

35   But he said, "No, don't go."

36   "Sir," I said, "I am afraid I am imposing on you. It is kind to allow me to sit and listen to you."

37   He seemed pleased with this compliment, which was quite sincere. "Sir," he replied, "I am grateful to any man who visits me."

38   I have kept the following short notes of what he said that day:

39   "Madness often shows itself by unnecessary changes from the usual ways of doing things. My poor friend Smart showed that his mind was disturbed by falling upon his knees and saying his prayers in the street, or in any other unusual place.

40   "Now, speaking reasonably, it shows more madness not to pray at all than to pray as Smart did. But I am afraid there are too many people who do not pray. And they could not be expected to understand his behavior."

41   Johnson had other things to say about the unlucky poet Christopher Smart. At another time, he had the following conversation with Dr. Burney:

42   Dr. Burney: BURNEY. "How does poor Smart do, Sir; is

43   he likely to recover?" JOHNSON. "It seems as if his
mind had ceased to struggle with the disease; for he

44   grows fat upon it." BURNEY. "Perhaps, Sir, that may
45   be from want of exercise." JOHNSON. No, sir; he has
partly as much exercise as he used to have, for he
digs in the garden. Indeed, before his confinement, he
used for exercise to walk to the alehouse; but he was

46   *carried* back again. I did not think he ought to be
shut up. His infirmities were not noxious to society.
He insisted on people praying with him; and I'd as
lief pray with Kit Smart as anyone else. Another
charge was, that he did not love clean linen; and I

47   have no passion for it." Johnson continued. "Mankind
have a great aversion to intellectual labor; but even
supposing knowledge to be easily attainable, more
people would be content to be ignorant than would
take even a little trouble to acquire it. . . ."

Boswell Quizzes Johnson

48   I know not how so whimsical a thought came into
my mind, but I asked, "If, Sir, you were shut up in a
castle, and a newborn child with you, what would you

49   do?" JOHNSON. "Why, Sir, I should not much like my

50   company." BOSWELL. "But would you take the trouble
of rearing it?" He seemed, as may well be supposed,
51   unwilling to pursue the subject: but upon my persevering in my question, replied, "Why yes, Sir, I would;
but I must have all conveniences. If I had no garden,

42 BURNEY. "How is poor Smart doing, sir? Is he likely to recover?"

43 JOHNSON. "It seems that his mind has stopped struggling with the disease. For he is growing fat with it."

44 BURNEY. "Perhaps, sir, that is from lack of exercise."

45 JOHNSON. "No, sir. He gets about as much exercise as he used to, for he digs in the garden. Indeed, before he was hospitalized, he used to walk to the alehouse for exercise. But he was *carried* back again.

46 "I did not think he should be shut up. His illness was not harmful to society. He insisted that people pray with him, and I'd be just as glad to pray with Kit Smart as anyone else. He was also accused of not loving clean linen. Well, I'm not passionate about it, either."

47 Johnson continued, "People have a great dislike of intellectual labor. But it wouldn't matter if knowledge were easily gained. More people would be happy to be ignorant than to take even a little trouble to get it. . . ."

Boswell Quizzes Johnson

48 I don't know what put such a trifling thought in my mind, but I asked, "Sir, what if you were shut up in a castle with a newborn child? What would you do?"

49 JOHNSON. "Well, sir, I would not much like my company."

50 BOSWELL. "But would you take the trouble to raise it?"

51 As you might expect, he seemed unwilling to pursue the subject. But I kept after him with my question, and he replied, "Why, yes, sir. I would, but I would want many conveniences. If I had no garden, I

I would make a shed on the roof, and take it there for fresh air. I should feed it, and wash it much, and with warm water to please it, not with cold water to

52 give it pain." Boswell. "But, Sir, does not heat relax?"
53 Johnson. "Sir, you are not to imagine the water is to be very hot. I would not *coddle* the child. No, Sir, the
54 hardy method of treating children does no good. I'll take you five children from London, who shall cuff five Highland children. Sir, a man bred in London will carry a burden, or run, or wrestle, as well as a man brought up in the hardiest manner in the country."

55 Boswell. "Good living, I suppose, makes the Londoners strong." Johnson. "Why, Sir, I don't
56 know that it does. Our chairmen from Ireland, who are as strong men as any, have been brought up upon potatoes. Quantity makes up for quality."

57 Boswell. "Would you teach this child that I have

58 furnished you with, anything?" Johnson. "No, I
59 should not be apt to teach it." Boswell. "Would not

60 you have a pleasure in teaching it?" Johnson. "No, Sir, I should not have a pleasure in teaching it."
61 Boswell. "Have you not a pleasure in teaching men? *There* I have you. You have the same pleasure in teaching men, that I should have

62 in teaching children." Johnson. "Why, something about that. . . ."

would build a shed on the roof, and take the child
there for fresh air. I would feed it. And I would wash
it well with warm water to please it, not with cold
water to give it pain."

52   BOSWELL. "But sir, wouldn't heat weaken it?"

53   JOHNSON. "Sir, don't imagine that the water would
be very hot. I would not *coddle*[9] the child.

54   "No, sir, the rugged method of raising children doesn't work. Give me five London
children, and they'll beat up five Highland[10]
children. Sir, a man raised in London can carry
a load, run, or wrestle as well as a man brought
up in the most rugged manner in the country."

55   BOSWELL. "I suppose it's good living that makes
Londoners strong."

56   JOHNSON. "Well, sir, I don't know that it does. Our
chair carriers from Ireland are as strong as
any men. But they have been brought up on
potatoes. Quantity makes up for quality."

57   BOSWELL. "Would you teach anything to the child
we've been talking about?"

58   JOHNSON. "No, I wouldn't want to teach it."

59   BOSWELL. "Wouldn't you take pleasure in teaching
it?"

60   JOHNSON. "No, sir, I would *not* take pleasure in
teaching it."

61   BOSWELL. "But don't you take pleasure in teaching
men? *There* I have you. You take the same
pleasure in teaching men that I would take in
teaching children."

62   JOHNSON. "Well, maybe you're on to something. . . ."

9 **coddle:** In addition to meaning to comfort or pamper,
coddle can also mean to cook in hot water.

10 **Highland:** a region in northern Scotland

Johnson's Eccentricities

63   . . . Talking to himself was, indeed, one of his singularities ever since I knew him. I was certain that he was frequently uttering pious ejaculations; for fragments of the Lord's Prayer have been distinctly
64   overhead. His friend Mr. Thomas Davies, of whom Churchill says, "That Davies hath a very pretty wife," when Dr. Johnson muttered "lead us not into temptation," used with waggish and gallant humor to whisper [to] Mrs. Davies, "You, my dear, are the cause of this."

65   He had another particularity, of which none of his friends ever ventured to ask an explanation. It appeared to me some superstitious habit, which he had contracted early, and from which he had never
66   called upon his reason to disentangle him. This was his anxious care to go out or in at a door or passage by a certain number of steps from a certain point, or at least so as that either his right or his left foot (I am not certain which) should constantly make the first actual movement when he came close to the
67   door or passage. Thus I conjecture: For I have, upon innumerable occasions, observed him suddenly stop, and then seem to count his steps with a deep earnestness; and when he had neglected or gone wrong in this sort of magical movement, I have seen
68   him go back again, put himself in a proper posture to begin the ceremony, and, having gone through it, break from his abstraction, walk briskly on, and join his companion. A strange instance of something of
69   this nature, even when on horseback, happened when he was in the Isle of Skye. Sir Joshua Reynolds has observed him to go a good way about rather than cross a particular alley in Leicesterfields; but this Sir

Johnson's Eccentricities

63   . . . Ever since I've known him, Johnson has had an odd way of talking to himself. I'm sure that he often utters religious exclamations, for I've heard him say bits and pieces of the Lord's Prayer.

64   Churchill[11] once said of his friend Mr. Thomas Davies, "Davies has a very pretty wife." Once, Johnson muttered, "Lead us not into temptation." Boldly and wittily, Mr. Davies whispered to Mrs. Davies, "You have caused this, my dear."

65   He did another odd thing that none of his friends ever dared ask him to explain. I believe it was some superstitious habit which he picked up early, so he was never able to reason himself out of it.

66   Whenever he went in or out of a door or passage, he always took anxious care to take a certain number of steps from a certain point. Or at least he made sure that either his right or left foot (I'm not sure which) would be the first to actually move when he came near the door or passage.

67   This is my best guess. For on many occasions, I have watched him suddenly stop and seem to count his steps very seriously. And if he had forgotten or made an error in this sort of magical movement, I have seen him go back.

68   He would then put himself in the proper stance to start the ritual all over again. Once he had done so, he would snap out of his spell. Then he would walk briskly along and join his companion.

69   He did something strange like this even on horseback in the Isle of Skye.[12] And Sir Joshua Reynolds has seen him go a long way around rather than cross a certain alley in Leicesterfields.[13] But Sir Joshua

---

11 **Churchill:** Charles Churchill (1731–1764), an English poet, satirist, and clergyman

12 **Isle of Skye:** a large island off the west coast of Scotland

13 **Leicesterfields:** a square in London

Joshua imputed to his having had some disagreeable recollection associated with it.

70   That the most minute singularities which belonged to him, and made very observable parts of his appearance and manner, may not be omitted, it is requisite to mention, that while talking or even musing as he sat in his chair, he commonly held his head to one side toward his right shoulder, and shook it in a tremulous manner, moving his body backward and forward, and rubbing his left knee in the same direc-

71   tion, with the palm of his hand. In the intervals of articulating he made various sounds with his mouth, sometimes as if ruminating, or what is called chewing the cud, sometimes giving a half whistle, sometimes making his tongue play backward from the roof of his mouth, as if clucking like a hen, and sometimes protruding it against his upper gums in front, as if pronouncing quickly under his breath, *too, too, too*: all this accompanied sometimes with a thoughtful look, but more frequently with a smile.

72   Generally when he had concluded a period, in the course of a dispute, by which time he was a good deal exhausted by violence and vociferation, he used to blow out his breath like a whale. This I supposed was a relief to his lungs; and seemed in him to be a contemptuous mode of expression, as if he had made the arguments of his opponent fly like chaff before the wind.

73   I am fully aware how very obvious an occasion I here give for the sneering jocularity of such as have no relish of an exact likeness; which to render complete, he who draws it must not disdain the slightest strokes. But if witlings should be inclined to attack this account, let them have the candor to quote what I have offered in my defense. . . .

thought this was because of some unpleasant memory he had of that alley.

70 I don't want to leave out even the smallest oddities that added to his appearance and manner. So I must add that he commonly tilted his head toward his right shoulder while talking or thinking. Then he shook it in a trembling way, moving his body back and forth. And he would rub his left knee with his palm in the same direction.

71 During pauses in speaking, he made various sounds with his mouth, sometimes like a cow chewing its cud. Or he would make a half whistle, or click his tongue backward off the roof of his mouth as if clucking like a hen. Sometimes he would place it against his upper front gums, as if saying quickly under his breath, *too, too, too*. He sometimes did all this with a thoughtful look, but more often with a smile.

72 Sometimes, after he had finished making a point in a quarrel, he would be quite tired out from fury and noisiness. Then he would blow out his breath like a whale. I suppose this relieved his lungs. It also seemed to express his scorn, as if he had made his opponent's thoughts fly like chaff[14] in the wind.

73 I well know that I am giving people who do not enjoy an exact likeness an obvious chance to sneer and make fun of me. But to make a portrait complete, the artist must not neglect the smallest strokes. If would-be wits wish to attack what I write, let them be honest enough to quote what I have said in my defense. . . .

14 **chaff:** seed coverings of wheat

Elegy Written in a Country Churchyard

Thomas Gray

*T*he curfew tolls the knell of parting day,
The lowing herd wind slowly o'er the lea,
The plowman homeward plods his weary way,
And leaves the world to darkness, and to me.

5   Now fades the glimmering landscape on the sight,
And all the air a solemn stillness holds;
Save where the beetle wheels his droning flight,
And drowsy tinklings lull the distant folds.

Save that from yonder ivy-mantled tower
10   The moping owl does to the moon complain
Of such, as wand'ring near her secret bower,
Molest her ancient solitary reign.

Beneath those rugged elms, that yew tree's shade,
Where heaves the turf in many a mold'ring heap,
15   Each in his narrow cell forever laid,
The rude forefathers of the hamlet sleep.

The breezy call of incense-breathing morn,
The swallow twitt'ring from the straw-built shed,
The cock's shrill clarion, or the echoing horn,
20   No more shall rouse them from their lowly bed.

Elegy[1] Written in a Country Churchyard

Thomas Gray

*T*he curfew bell tolls for the end of day.
The mooing cows roam slowly over the meadow,
and the plowman plods wearily homeward,
leaving the world to darkness—and to me.

5   The flickering landscape fades from sight,
and there is a solemn stillness in the air—
except where a humming beetle flies in circles,
and lazy tinkling sounds calm the distant sheep.

From that ivy-covered tower yonder,
10   a sad owl cries. She complains to the moon
of people wandering near her secret home,
bothering her long, lonely reign.

Beneath the shade of the rugged elms and the yew tree,
the soil is turned in many decaying heaps.
15   The ignorant forefathers of the village lie there forever,
each in his narrow little room.

Nothing will wake them from their lowly beds—
not the call of morning with its sweet, breezy breath;
not the swallow twittering in its nest of straw;
20   not the rooster's shrill trumpet, nor the echoing
      hunting horn.

---

1 **Elegy:** a poem or song expressing sorrow or mourning

For them no more the blazing hearth shall burn,
Or busy housewife ply her evening
    care:
No children run to lisp their sire's return,
Or climb his knees the envied kiss to share.

25   Oft did the harvest to their sickle yield,
Their furrow oft the stubborn glebe has broke;
How jocund did they drive their team afield!
How bowed the woods beneath their sturdy stroke!

Let not Ambition mock their useful toil,
30   Their homely joys and destiny obscure;
Nor Grandeur hear with a disdainful smile,
The short and simple annals of the poor.

The boast of heraldry, the pomp of power,
And all that beauty, all that wealth e'er gave,
35   Awaits alike th' inevitable hour.
The paths of glory lead but to the grave.

Nor you, ye proud, impute to these the fault,
If Mem'ry o'er their tomb no trophies
    raise,
Where through the long-drawn aisle and fretted vault
40   The pealing anthem swells the note of praise.

Can storied urn or animated bust
Back to its mansion call the fleeting breath?
Can Honor's voice provoke the silent dust,
Or Flatt'ry soothe the dull cold ear of Death?

45   Perhaps in this neglected spot is laid
Some heart once pregnant with celestial fire,
Hands that the rod of empire might have swayed,
Or waked to ecstasy the living lyre.

For them, the blazing hearth shall burn no more,
nor will the busy housewife care for them in the
    evening.
No children will run lisping of their father's return,
or climb on his knees to share the envied kiss.

25   The harvest often fell to their sickles,
and their furrows often broke the stubborn soil.
How happily they drove their teams in the field!
How the woods fell beneath their strong axes!

Let not ambitious folk mock their useful work,
30   their simple joys and unknown fates.
Let not grander folk smile scornfully upon hearing
the short and simple records of the poor.

The boast of heraldry,[2] the splendor of power,
and all that comes from beauty and wealth
35   come to the same, certain end.
The paths of glory lead only to the grave.

And proud folk, don't blame them
if no trophies are raised in their memory over their
    tombs.
For them, no choirs will sing anthems of praise
40   in long church aisles with magnificent ceilings.

Can a carved urn or a lifelike bust
put the fleeting breath back into a human shape?
Can the voice of honor call forth the silent dust?
Can flattery soothe the dull, cold ear of death?

45   Perhaps in this forgotten spot lies
some heart once filled with the fire of the stars.
Perhaps his hands might have held an emperor's staff,
or he might have wakened with delight to a lyre's song.

2 **heraldry:** coats of arms

But Knowledge to their eyes her ample page
50 Rich with the spoils of time did ne'er unroll;
Chill Penury repressed their noble rage,
And froze the genial current of the soul.

Full many a gem of purest ray serene,
The dark unfathomed caves of ocean bear:
55 Full many a flower is born to blush unseen,
And waste its sweetness on the desert air.

Some village Hampden that with dauntless breast
The little tyrant of his fields withstood;
Some mute inglorious Milton here may rest,
60 Some Cromwell guiltless of his country's blood.

Th' applause of list'ning senates
    to command,
The threats of pain and ruin to despise,
To scatter plenty o'er a smiling
    land,
And read their hist'ry in a nation's eyes

65 Their lot forbade: nor circumscribed alone
Their growing virtues, but their crimes confined;
Forbade to wade through slaughter to
    a throne,
And shut the gates of mercy on mankind,

The struggling pangs of conscious truth to hide,
70 To quench the blushes of ingenuous shame,
Or heap the shrine of Luxury
    and Pride
With incense, kindled at the Muse's flame.

But knowledge never unrolled to their eyes
50 her plentiful page, filled with time's riches.
Cold poverty curbed their noble feelings
and froze the warm wishes of their souls.

The bottomless caves of the ocean hold
many bright, clear gems.
55 Many flowers are born never to have their colors seen,
their sweetness wasted on the desert air.

Here may rest some village Hampden, who bravely
stood against some little tyrant of his fields;
or perhaps some mute, unknown Milton;
60 or else some Cromwell, guiltless of shedding his
    country's blood.[3]

Their luck did not allow them to be praised by
    listening leaders,
or to ignore threats of pain and ruin.
They were never able to scatter plenty over a grateful
    land
and read their own story in a nation's eyes.

65 But their virtues were not all that were kept in check.
Their crimes were limited too.
They were forbidden to wade through slaughter to
    gain a throne,
or to shut the gates of mercy on mankind.

Nor did they struggle to hide their pangs of conscience
70 as blushes of innocence vanished from their faces.
Nor did they burn incense at the shrine of luxury
    and pride,
flattered by the words of poets.

3 **Here may ... country's blood:** John Hampden
   (1594–1643) fought against Charles I in the English Civil
   Wars. Hampden's cousin, Oliver Cromwell (1599–1658)
   ruled England for a few years after the execution of
   Charles I.

Far from the madding crowd's ignoble strife,
Their sober wishes never learned to stray;
75 Along the cool sequestered vale of life
They kept the noiseless tenor of their way.

Yet ev'n these bones from insult to protect
Some frail memorial still erected nigh,
With uncouth rhymes and shapeless sculpture decked,
80 Implores the passing tribute of a sigh.

Their name, their years, spelt by th' unlettered muse,
The place of fame and elegy supply:
And many a holy text around she strews,
That teach the rustic moralist to die.

85 For who to dumb Forgetfulness a prey,
This pleasing anxious being e'er resigned,
Left the warm precincts of the cheerful day,
Nor cast one longing ling'ring look behind?

On some fond breast the parting soul relies,
90 Some pious drops the closing eye requires;
Ev'n from the tomb the voice of Nature cries,
Ev'n in our ashes live their wonted fires.

For thee, who mindful of th' unhonored dead
Dost in these lines their artless tale relate;
95 If chance, by lonely Contemplation led,
Some kindred spirit shall inquire thy fate,

Haply some hoary-headed swain may say,
"Oft have we seen him at the peep of dawn
Brushing with hasty steps the dews away
100 To meet the sun upon the upland lawn.

Far from the frenzied crowd's filthy troubles,
they never learned to stray from their earnest wishes.
75   All through the cool, secluded valley of life,
they kept to their quiet way.

Yet even these bones are protected from insult
by some nearby, fragile tombstone.
Its crude rhymes and shapeless sculpture
80   beg of a passerby the honor of a sigh.

Their names and years are carved by some ignorant
engraver in place of fame or an elegy.
Many holy texts are written there
to teach the wise farmer to die.

85   We are all at the mercy of dumb forgetfulness.
Who ever gave up this pleasing but troubled life,
leaving the warm neighborhood of cheerful day,
without casting one longing, lingering look behind?

The parting soul depends on some loving breast,
90   and craves mourners' tears upon closing his eyes.
Nature's voice cries even from the tomb,
and the fires of life keep burning in our ashes.

And what of me, now thinking of the unhonored dead
and telling their simple tale in these lines?
95   By chance, some kindred spirit may be led here
by lonely meditation and ask of my fate.

Then perhaps some white-haired farmer will say this:
"We often saw him at the break of dawn,
brushing the dew away with hasty steps,
100   eager to meet the sun in the meadows up the hill.

"There at the foot of yonder nodding beech
That wreathes its old fantastic roots so high,
His listless length at noontide would he stretch,
And pore upon the brook that babbles by.

105 "Hard by yon wood, now smiling as
        in scorn,
Mutt'ring his wayward fancies he would rove,
Now drooping, woeful wan, like
        one forlorn,
Or crazed with care, or crossed in hopeless love.

"One morn I missed him on the customed hill,
110 Along the heath, and near his fav'rite tree;
Another came; nor yet beside
        the rill,
Nor up the lawn, nor at the wood was he.

"The next with dirges due in sad array
Slow through the churchway path we saw him borne.
115 Approach and read (for thou canst read) the lay,
Graved on the stone beneath yon aged thorn."

The Epitaph

Here rests his head upon the lap of Earth
A youth to Fortune and to Fame unknown:
Fair Science frowned not on his humble birth,
120 *And Melancholy marked him for her own.*

Large was his bounty, and his soul sincere,
Heaven did a recompense as largely send:
He gave to Mis'ry all he had, a tear:
He gained from Heaven ('twas all he wished) a friend.

"Over yonder is a swaying beech tree
with a fantastic wreath of roots.
He used to stretch among them lazily at noon,
gazing into the brook that babbles by.

105 "Close to those woods, sometimes smiling as if
          scornfully,
he would wander, muttering his stray imaginings.
Sometimes he would droop, deathly pale, like some-
          one grieving,
or crazed with worry, or helplessly in love.

"One morning, I missed seeing him as usual on the hill,
110 in the fields, and near his favorite tree.
Another morning came. But still he was not by
          the brook,
nor in the meadow or the woods.

"The next morning, we saw him carried slowly
along the path to the church while dirges played.
115 Come near and read (for you can read) the song
engraved on the stone beneath this aged hawthorn
          bush."

The Epitaph[4]

Here the head of a youth unknown to fame and
fortune rests his head upon the earth's lap.
He went to school, despite his humble birth,
120 *and sadness chose him for her own.*

His generosity was great, and his soul sincere,
and Heaven repaid him well and fully.
He gave to misery all he had—a tear,
and he gained from Heaven the only thing he
wanted—a friend.

4 **Epitaph:** inscription on a tomb or gravestone

125
No farther seek his merits to disclose,
Or draw his frailties from their dread abode,
(There they alike in trembling Hope repose)
The bosom of his Father and his God.

125   *Do not ask to hear more about his merits*
or seek his faults in their awful home.
Both his merits and his faults wait trembling with
      hope
in the bosom of his Father and his God.

E L E G Y

Written in a Country Church Yard.

 HE Curfew tolls the knell of parting day,
The lowing herd wind flowly o'er the lea,
The plowman homeward plods his weary way,
And leaves the world to darkneſs and to me.

Illustration to Gray's "Elegy," 1753 edition